SURVIVING THE

OREGON TRAIL

1852

SURVIVING THE

OREGON TRAIL

1852

As Told by
Mary Ann and Willis Boatman
and Augmented with Accounts
by other Overland Travelers

by

WELDON WILLIS RAU

Washington State University Press
Pullman, Washington

Washington State University Press
PO Box 645910
Pullman, Washington 99164-5910
Phone: 800-354-7360
Fax: 509-335-8568
E-mail: wsupress@wsu.edu
Web site: www.wsu.edu/wsupress

Library of Congress Cataloging-in-Publication Data

Rau, Weldon W.
    Surviving the Oregon Trail, 1852 / by Weldon Willis Rau.
        p. cm.
    Text based primarily on the diaries of Mary Ann and Willis Boatman aug-
mented with accounts by other overland travelers.
    Includes bibliographical references and index.
    ISBN 0-87422-237-0 (alk. paper) — ISBN 0-87422-238-9 (pbk. : alk. paper)
        1. Oregon National Historic Trail—History. 2. Overland journeys to the
Pacific. 3. Frontier and pioneer life—West (U.S.) 4. West (U.S.)—Description
and travel. 5. West (U.S.)—History—1848–1860. 6. Pioneers—West (U.S.)—
Biography. 7. Boatman, Mary Ann—Diaries. 8. Boatman, Willis—Diaries. 9.
West (U.S.)—Biography. I. Boatman, Mary Ann. II. Boatman, Willis. III. Title.

F597.R28 2001
917.804'2—dc21   00-068658

Cover art: "Approaching Chimney Rock," by William Henry Jackson. *Scotts Bluff
National Monument*

Table of Contents

To my wife Jane, our son Greg, and his wife Vreni

Preface

SINCE CHILDHOOD I have enjoyed knowing that my great grandparents, Willis and Mary Ann Boatman, were among the many thousands of mid-nineteenth century travelers who ventured west on the Oregon Trail. Furthermore, over the years it was intriguing to me to know that both ancestors left written materials regarding the 1852 journey from Illinois and their lives as pioneers in the Northwest. It was not until my retirement years, however, that I found the time or inclination to thoroughly examine these family documents. Fascinated with their vivid descriptions of the many facets of the journey and of daily life along the way, my interest was piqued to learn more about this major endeavor that so many emigrants felt compelled to undertake.

Some fifteen years have passed since my wife and I began library research on the subject and embarked on the first of numerous Oregon Trail field trips. My original intent was simply to make the Boatman journals available. However, after studying their accounts as well as those of other 1852 journalists and diarists, it became apparent that a combination of these materials would provide a more comprehensive view of the overland experience. Furthermore, as the reader will observe, the Boatmans were not always careful in respect to identifying when or where events and experiences occurred. By comparing all of the records, however, it has been possible to determine, or at least speculate about, the time and place of certain incidents in the Boatman story.

Only through the recorded words of those who actually made the trek west are we best able to sense the emigrants' emotions, visualize their observations, and understand their interpretation of events and situations. Therefore, it has been this author's intent to let the story be told by the ordinary people who endured extraordinary hardships on the long and tiresome journey. I have added commentary largely for the purpose of connecting together the numerous stories and accounts.

Also, as a professional geologist, I felt obligated to interject brief interpretations of the unique geological settings that the emigrants passed through, which had a significant, if not profound, effect on the travelers. They encountered unfamiliar obstacles—steep and rocky terrain, deserts, alkali flats, excessive dust, and restrictive river channels—as well as such wonders as hot springs and oddly shaped buttes and bluffs. Hopefully, an awareness and better understanding of the relationship between geology and emigrant travel will add to the interest of the story.

During the course of my research in libraries and while retracing the Oregon Trail, numerous individuals cheerfully gave assistance. To all, I gratefully acknowledge your efforts. Special thanks are due to the staff of the Washington State Library System, especially to Connie Manson and Lee Walkling of the Washington Division of Geology and Earth Resources. Among those who assisted me in the field, I wish to thank Don Thomas, Dick Klein, Dave Welch, and Vic Bolon. Bob and Karen Rennells as well as Randy Brown were most helpful as field guides in parts of Wyoming. Appreciation also is due for the direction and assistance provided by Glenn Birch of Cokeville, Wyoming; Jim Evans (regretfully, now deceased) of Baker City, Oregon; and Judge Clyde Hall of the Shoshone-Bannock Tribe at Fort Hall, Idaho. I am indebted to the following property owners who not only granted permission to enter their land, but also gave assistance and direction: the Bearl Stewart family in the Blue Mountains, Oregon; Mr. Fager of the Grande Ronde Valley, Oregon; and Mr. and Mrs. Lyle Woodbury of Declo, Idaho.

Numerous others individuals willingly supplied background data, guidance, or their personal knowledge. Among them are Cliff Crawford of the Skamania County Historical Society in Washington; Helen Sundell, Charles W. Martin, and Will Bagley of the Oregon-California Trails Association (OCTA); Hazel Hood of the Ezra Meeker Historical Society, Washington; Margaret Shields of the Lewis County Historical Society in western Washington; Frank Green of the Washington State Historical Society; Tom Reeves of the Idaho Historical Society; the staff of the Oregon Historical Society; Kirt Othberg and John Welham of the Idaho Geological Survey; the Wyoming Geological Survey staff; the Iowa Geological Survey staff; and Mary Oman of the Bureau of Land Management, Oregon.

I likewise wish to thank those who either supplied or assisted in obtaining illustrations for the manuscript. Among them are Greg MacGregor of OCTA; Vern Lenzen of the Western Heritage Museum in Omaha, Nebraska; Cecil Housel of the Oregon Historical Society; Katherine Wyath and Chad Wall of the Nebraska Historical Society; Dean M. Knudsen of Scotts Bluff National Monument; and Elaine Miller of the Washington State Historical Society.

Special thanks are extended to Rose Ann Tompkins of OCTA for her excellent work in preparing the Oregon Trail maps, and to Katherine Reed of the Washington Department of Natural Resources for her helpful editorial advice.

Local experts reviewed various segments of the manuscript. Bob Berry of Omaha critiqued much of the Nebraska section; OCTA members Bob and Karen Rennells of La Barge and Randy Brown of Douglas reviewed parts of the Wyoming chapters; and Dave Welch of Steilacoom, Washington, critiqued sections on Oregon and Washington. Their helpful suggestions contributed significantly to the accuracy of the manuscript. I wish to extend my particular gratitude to Susan Badger Doyle of OCTA for her professional review and detailed edit of the entire manuscript. Her meticulous effort was an invaluable contribution.

Getting a manuscript published can be as challenging as writing it. In this regard, I am deeply grateful to Glen Lindeman, Editor of the Washington State University Press, and his staff for their genuine interest and support throughout the publishing process. It has been a pleasant experience. Only because of Glen's sincere interest in the story, helpful suggestions, and guidance, together with the professional assistance of the WSU Press staff, has this book become a reality.

Last, but far from least, I extend my sincere thanks and appreciation to my wife Jane, who through all the years has willingly assisted and given her full support to this endeavor. There were times, especially in the field, when she cheerfully endured less than comfortable situations. As a partner, she has served a most important role in the development of this project.

I believe that man will not only endure: he will prevail.
—William Faulkner (1897–1962)

Introduction

THIS NARRATIVE DEALS primarily with the experience of venturing west during the peak year of emigrant travel, 1852. Only because diarists and journalists faithfully recorded daily events do we have documentation of the long and difficult mid-nineteenth century journey across the continent. Through the efforts of these people of vision and determination, it is possible to learn about their daily routine, their impressions of what they saw, and the emotions they felt regarding the events that took place along the way.

Although material from many diaries and journals is incorporated here, the accounts of Mary Ann and Willis Boatman, a young, newlywed couple from Illinois, are featured. Mary Ann's narrative, presented here in full, serves as the principal source for the first, long months of the journey, whereas Willis wrote largely about the latter part of the trip and experiences as pioneers in the Northwest. Mary Ann's hand-written manuscript, contained in four notebooks, is in the possession of the author.[1] As indicated in her text, it was written fifty-three years after the 1852 journey. An unknown person made typescripts of her manuscript in the 1930s, copies of which are known to have been placed at the University of Washington, the Washington State Historical Society, and among family members.

Willis prepared two hand-written versions of his story, both of which are also in the possession of the author.[2] It is unknown when he prepared these manuscripts. Typescripts also were prepared of each. In 1937, one version appeared in *Told by the Pioneers*, vol. 1, a Public Works Administration publication. Materials from both versions of Willis's story have been incorporated here.

Although none of the Boatman manuscripts are diaries, it is known that Mary Ann kept an account during the trek.[3] Because her surviving story, written more than a half-century after the journey, contains exceptional detail, it is believed she wrote her narrative in 1905 with her original account in hand. Unfortunately, the original was destroyed, probably because it contained material of a personal nature.

The latter part of her story lacks the details, particularly of time and place, that she vividly recorded in the first part. Obviously tiring during the trek, her record keeping may not have been as complete during the latter days of the journey, a pattern to which many a journalist succumbed. Enthusiasm, no doubt, had dwindled and more effort was required in meeting the needs of survival.

Although Mary Ann did not, for unknown reasons, quite finish the account in 1905, Willis related interesting details regarding the latter part of the long and grueling journey. He also recalled some significant and exciting historical events of which they were a part following their arrival in the Puget Sound country. The two stories, together with other short accounts told by their children and several newspaper reports, are here combined. Editing of all material has been limited and only for the purpose of clarity.

As noted, neither Mary Ann nor Willis discussed the complete trek, leaving sections of the journey unmentioned or only broadly generalized. In order that the reader better perceives the entire experience, additional material is incorporated here from other select diaries and journals, largely for the year 1852. Therefore, in an attempt to present a complete and comprehensive account of traveling west to Oregon in 1852, the Boatmans' observations are augmented by those of other travelers.

The westward movement—first largely consisting of Oregon-bound settlers, then joined by Mormons to Salt Lake, then gold seekers to California, and then pioneers to other western regions—began essentially in 1841. This great westward migration by way of wagon roads along the Platte River and westward from there mainly continued for some twenty-five years. It reached a peak in the early 1850s and dwindled considerably in the late 1860s, particularly with completion of the transcontinental railroad to California in 1869. According to the noted Oregon Trail historian Merrill J. Mattes, an estimated 500,000 people traveled along the Platte River in the 1840s to 1860s. Mattes further states that possibly as many as 70,000 used this route in 1852.[4]

The Boatmans participated in the largest westward migration of any year along the central wagon route. Even though the majority of the

Mary Ann Boatman, age 32, in a portrait taken in Washington Territory, 1865. *W.W. Rau family collection*

emigrants went to the California gold fields, Mattes estimates that some 10,000 proceeded to Oregon Territory that year. In his classic, *The Plains Across*, John D. Unruh Jr. suggests that the figure may be as high as 20,000.[5]

It is often pondered why so many Americans decided to sell their farms or businesses and trek thousands of miles over arid deserts and rugged mountains to reach a supposed utopia. By the middle of the nineteenth century, frontier America had reached the Missouri River. Many persons were discontent with hard times on nonproductive farms. Some were experiencing financial difficulties and wished to improve their economic situation. Others were fleeing the restraints of society, or even evading capture from the law. Indian missionary work drew some, and others were running from a bad romance. Furthermore, illness was prevalent in the Mississippi Valley.

But, in spite of these and many other reasons, the restlessness of young men probably was foremost in convincing so many that, although far away, Oregon must be the answer to achieving prosperity, health, and happiness. Little did they know, or care to know, of the sickness, hazards, and just plain arduous conditions that lay ahead for those who succumbed to this dream known as "Oregon Fever."

Of course, those who would profit from this infectious fever, the promoters and entrepreneurs, the suppliers of equipment and provisions, as well as the writers of guidebooks, and others, all encouraged the westward movement with glorified descriptions of travel and life in the West. Such persuasive propaganda further stimulated the enthusiasm of many pioneers.

The U.S. government also presented interesting incentives to encourage Americans to move west. During the early part of the nineteenth century, much had appeared in the American press glamorizing the Oregon Country in an attempt to encourage people to emigrate to and eventually outnumber the British in that land. The United States wanted to establish a population dominance in Oregon in order to strengthen its legitimate claims to the country. From 1818, the British and Americans, mainly fur traders, officially had jointly occupied the Pacific Northwest. By 1840, American settlers were beginning to significantly outnumber the British in the region.

Because the federal government had paid little attention to the governmental affairs of Americans in the Oregon Country, however, settlers there had to establish their own governing body. In 1843, they created a Provisional Government for settling disputes and making general governmental decisions. Finally, in 1846, a boundary on the 49th parallel was agreed upon as a division between American and British possessions, and in 1848 the United States established Oregon Territory. The Provisional Government came to an end.[6]

With the boundary established, the U.S. government still continued to encourage emigration by offering free, or very inexpensive, land. This was another important factor in convincing many a dreamy but ambitious young man to take the giant leap westward. In 1850, Congress passed the Donation Land Act, specifically designed for Oregon Territory. The measure encouraged Americans already there to stay, and further enticed others to emigrate to this new American possession. It provided the opportunity for free land to be acquired by those who had settled in the territory prior to 1850—the law granted 320 acres to single men and 640 acres to married men over the age of eighteen.

The act was extended between 1850 and 1855, and included Washington Territory, formed in 1853. During this period, 160 acres were granted to single men and 320 acres to married men over twenty-one years of age. In 1854, Americans were further enticed to Oregon and Washington when the Preemption Act of 1841 was extended to these territories. It granted any head of family, who did not already own 320 acres, the right to buy 160 acres for $1.25 per acre.[7]

Therefore, by 1852 incentives were sufficiently convincing for many young men to join the overland trek to what was perceived in their minds as a land of Eden. Many died en route. Some estimate that as many as ten percent of those who began the trip were buried along the way.[8] Of those that survived, many came to the end of the trail penniless and physically exhausted. But, in spite of all their hardships, most of these hardy people did eventually realize their vision of success and happiness.

Americans of the times were themselves largely the product of a pioneering ancestry. During the eighteenth century and early part of the nineteenth century, families had made their way westward, generation after generation. They continued from such Atlantic states as New York, Pennsylvania, or Virginia, to Ohio, Kentucky, or Tennessee, then on to Indiana and Illinois, and finally Missouri or Iowa in a restless search for fertile farm land. The ancestors of Willis and Mary Ann Boatman were no exception.

Willis's grandparents, John and Anny Willis, moved from Virginia to Kentucky in 1802. In 1828, when Willis was two years old, his parents moved to Indiana. There Willis spent most of his youth on a farm. In 1850, after his father died, the family moved to Decatur, Illinois, where his mother passed away the following year. Willis, with his brother John, then ventured to Sangamon County, Illinois.[9]

Mary Ann's ancestors, originally from England, arrived in Virginia in 1640. Later generations moved to Kentucky, and then eventually to a farmstead located a few miles south of Springfield, Sangamon County, Illinois. It was here that Mary Ann met Willis.[10]

With a strong pioneering background and from a mid-nineteenth century central Illinois setting, this young married couple were about to begin the most significant westward move since their English ancestors had crossed the Atlantic Ocean many years before.

Notes

1. Mary Ann Boatman, hand-written, unpublished manuscript describing a journey on the Oregon Trail, 1852 (family document no. 1).
2. Willis Boatman, "Story of My Life," hand-written manuscript (family document no. 2). A version is printed in *Told by the Pioneers,* vol. 1, U.S. Public Works Administration, Washington Pioneer Project, 1937, 184–90.
3. Marjorie Alice (Boatman) Rau, a granddaughter of Willis and Mary Ann Boatman, personal communication with the author.
4. Merrill J. Mattes, *Platte River Road Narratives* (Urbana and Chicago, Illinois: University of Illinois Press, 1988), 5.
5. Mattes, 5; and John D. Unruh Jr., *The Plains Across: The Overland Emigrants and the Trans-Mississippi West, 1840–60,* paperback edition (Urbana, Chicago, and London: University of Illinois Press, 1982), 50.
6. Gregory M. Franzwa, *The Oregon Trail Revisited,* third edition (Gerald, Missouri: Patrice Press, 1983), 7–10.
7. *Washington Centennial Farms: Yesterday and Today* (Olympia, Washington: Washington State Department of Agriculture, 1989), 13–16.
8. Aubrey L. Haines, *Historic Sites along the Oregon Trail,* third edition (St. Louis, Missouri: Patrice Press, 1987), 4; Unruh, 58–61; and Ezra Meeker, *Personal Experiences on the Oregon Trail: The Tragedy of Leschi,* fifth reprint (Seattle, Washington: Meeker, 1912), 27.
9. Willis Boatman's grandparents on his father's mother's side, John and Ann Willis, moved from Pittsylvania County, Virginia, to Madison County, Kentucky, in 1802. Willis's grandparents on his father's side, Jessee and Anny Boatman, were living in Kentucky when Willis's parents, Jacob Boatman (a son of Jessee and Anny), and Elezure Willis (a daughter of John and Anny Willis), met and were married in 1824. Little is known about Jacob and Elezure other than that they farmed and had a family of four girls—Polly, who died when about two years of age, Elizabeth, Letty Ann, and Sarah—and two boys, John and Willis. In 1828, when Willis was about two years old, the family moved from Kentucky to Sullivan County, Indiana. In 1837, his father Jacob died, but his mother with the help of her children continued to maintain the farm where Willis spent most of his youth. In 1850, his mother Elezure sold the farm

and moved to Decatur, Illinois. When she died in the following year, Willis and his bother John, with very little possessions or wealth between them, ventured to Sangamon County, Illinois. Willis Boatman, hand-written biography (family document no. 3).

10. William and Hannah Ball, Mary Ann's great great grandparents, arrived from England in 1640 and settled in Virginia, where they built the family mansion known as "Millenbeck." Their son, Mary Ann's great grandfather John Ball, and wife Nancy (Adams) Ball moved to Kentucky, where they owned a large farm. Mary Ann's grandfather, William Richardson, married John Ball's daughter, Jane Ball. They lived in Louisville, Kentucky, where William was a wealthy tobacco merchant who owned two steamboats on the Kentucky River. In 1822, he (William Richardson) sold all of his holdings and moved to Sangamon County, Illinois. Mary Ann's mother, Mary Ann Snow, with her adopted parents, moved from Madison County, Kentucky, to Illinois in 1825, where she met Louis Richardson, son of William and Jane (Ball) Richardson. Louis Richardson and Mary Ann Snow were married in 1826 and settled on Lick Creek, south of Springfield, Sangamon County, Illinois.

Louis and Mary Ann (Snow) Richardson had thirteen children. Mary Ann (Richardson) Boatman was the fourth child and her older bother, of whom she writes, was the second. Very little is known about Mary Ann's mother, Mary Ann (Snow) Richardson, other than that she most likely was a strong woman to have raised such a large family. Furthermore, she must have been a good and perhaps compassionate mother as her daughter, Mary Ann, wrote fondly of her.

Mary Ann Boatman's father, Louis Richardson, was ordained in 1859 as a Baptist minister and, although he served as a minister of the Sugar Creek church for a short time, he preached mostly without compensation. While he has been described as brusque, outspoken, and abrupt, he was regarded as a man with high moral character and was respected in the community.

In 1838, the Louis and Mary Ann Richardson family moved from Lick Creek to Sugar Creek in the same county, sixteen miles south of Springfield, Illinois. Mary Ann Boatman (family document no. 1); and a description of Louis B. Richardson, source unknown (family document no. 4).

An oil painting by George Simons depicting Council Bluffs, Iowa (Kanesville), in the early 1850s. This was a major jumping-off place for emigrants crossing the Missouri River. *Durham Western Heritage Museum, Omaha, Nebraska*

Chapter One

Leaving Home

I went to work together with my brother John Boatman and William Richardson, my wife's brother, getting ready to start for the great Willamette Valley. We bought a wagon, three yoke of oxen, and one yoke of cows.—Willis Boatman

WILLIS BOATMAN AND MARY ANN RICHARDSON were married on October 14, 1851, in Sangamon County, Illinois. He was twenty-four and she eighteen. Willis and his brother John Boatman had arrived in the county earlier that year from Decatur, Illinois. They had brought few possessions with them and therefore Willis had little in the way of resources with which to begin married life. That fall, in keeping with his past agrarian experience, Willis rented a farm and planted a crop of wheat with the intention of settling down. Meanwhile, his brother John had decided to join a family planning to move to Oregon. Thus, during the winter, Willis heard much about the far off land of Oregon.

Although intrigued with the idea of starting a new life in a distant country, young Willis managed to stave off his wanderlust until the family that John had planned to accompany changed their minds about going west, leaving John without a partner. After much discussion with John and Mary Ann's older brother, William Richardson, the three young men made the momentous decision to form their own little group and, in the coming spring, start out for the Willamette Valley in Oregon Territory. Mary Ann, having some trepidation about such a long trip, had little choice but to accept their decision.

Leaving home was a subject duly discussed in most accounts of the journey west. Many would never again see those family members and friends left behind. The occasion was usually a somber one with emotions running high and tears being shed. A description of a typical scene was related in Catherine Scott Colburn's recollections. Thirty-eight years after the 1852 journey west from her home in Tazewell County in northern Illinois, she wrote,

> silently weeping women and sobbing children, and . . . an aged grand-father standing at his gate as the wagons filed past, one trembling hand shading his eyes, the other grasping a red handkerchief. . . . "Good-by, good-by.!" say . . . the children with flushed tear-stained faces, grouped at the openings in the wagon cover. The old grandsire's response was choked with emotion and drowned in the creaking of the wagons.[1]

In Sangamon County, Illinois, sixteen miles south of Springfield, Mary Ann began her story of their westward journey in a similar vein, relating her thoughts and emotions on the day of departure.

> I will try, in a way, and a poor one at that, to give a few outlines of our journey across the plains and the last day at my . . . home that I loved so dear.
>
> It was the morning of the 29th day of March in the year of 1852 . . . that . . . had been set for our start on the long and uncon-sidered journey to [a] land of prosperity and gold, the greed of all mankind, more precious than all else on earth. The sun shone with as much luster and beauty as though no sorrow could ever enter our long journey.
>
> That day was my brother William's 22nd birthday. He was . . . alive with the thought that the time had come for our departure as were my husband and his brother John Boatman. We were to be as one family, all equal owners in team and provisions. . . . For me there was no joy as I had always loved my home and parents so dear and had known nothing of the hardships of a long journey, but, I was easily assured that it was the best thing for us all. My father and mother being of a favorable spirit, thought it the proper thing for us to do, saying if we liked the country, they would soon follow us.
>
> . . . The hour had come and the oxen yoked and hitched to the big wagon, drove up in front of [the] gate, [the] gate that I had opened and passed through from childhood to woman[hood]. . . . I tried to think it was for the best and leave the impression in my mother's mind that I would be a woman in my departure and not a child. So we all went to work loading our worldly belongings in the ox-mobile, bedding, clothing, cooking utensils, provisions enough to last six months, medicine, in fact everything for the comfort of a

long journey . . . [except] preparation for death, but it came when it was least expected.

About 10 o'clock everything [was] loaded into the big ox wagon. Then came the hardest task of all for me, . . . to say goodbye. But the time had come, . . . a loving embrace, . . . a farewell kiss, a "God bless you all." Yes, I stepped out of that dear old house that had been my home all of my life . . . never to enter it again, nor to see my loving mother again. In a year and two months she would be called to abide in a home beyond, where no sorrow, pain, or death are known, to meet her loved ones that had gone on before. Yes, as I said, the time had come. I walked out over the path that I had trod all my short life where I had sported and played with my brothers and sisters and schoolmates. Everything looked so dear to me on that morning. Dear father opened the old gate for me, then [helped] me . . . climb into the big wagon. Then came the words "gee, whoa, get up Deke and Dime, Buck and Brite." Those were the oxen's names. . . . the whip cracked and we were off.

A successful journey depended largely on having the proper equipment. The wagon, of course, was the major item needed for the trip. They varied greatly in design, displaying the innovative nature of the American frontiersman. The Conestoga wagon, manufactured in Pennsylvania, was regarded as the Cadillac of wagons as it was light in weight and sturdily built with high wheels. However, most travelers used wagons that were some variation of those employed around the farm, having been modified to haul sufficient supplies for the six-month trip, and serve as living quarters with sleeping arrangements and general shelter from the elements. This usually was accomplished by the addition of a second or false bottom in the wagon with the supplies placed beneath. The false bottom served as a floor for the living area. It was recommended that the wheels be wide and constructed of wood that would suffer minimal shrinkage in a dry climate. The running gear was removable and the wagon box constructed so that it could be made water tight and used as a boat when fording streams.[2]

Many wagons were brightly painted and it was not uncommon to see slogans decorating wagon covers. In this regard, Enoch W. Conyers, a single young man who left Quincy, Illinois, on April 30, 1852, in company with Mr. and Mrs. William Burns and family, recorded the following on May 25:

It is quite amusing to note the different mottoes on the wagon covers, such as "From Danville, Ill., and bound for Oregon," "Bound for California or bust." One wagon just passing, their team consisting of four yoke of two-year-old calves, with the motto, "Root, little hog or die," scrawled on both sides of the wagon cover, and on another wagon cover is written, "Bound for Origen."[3]

The uniqueness of these "mottoes" allowed fellow travelers to more easily identify each other along the trail.[4]

Martha H. Ellis, who also traveled on the Oregon Trail in 1852, departed from Albia, Iowa, and later recalled some details of their wagon.

It had heavy wheels, broad and deep beds, which were divided into two floors, the lower used for provisions and things not needed for every day, and the upper used for clothing in daily use, and was general lounging place during the day and family bedrooms at night. It had a high, arched, canvas-covered roof. In the right-hand corner in the front was our water can and cup. Attached to the wagon bed at the back was the cupboard for victuals, dishes and cooking utensils, and what is lacking in height it made up in width and depth. It generally took four yoke of oxen to draw these heavily loaded wagons.[5]

M.E. Bonney was eight years old at the time of the 1852 journey to Oregon in company with her parents, Mr. and Mrs. Timothy Bonney, and three other children. Many years later, she recalled the arrangements inside the family wagon.

Our wagon, fitted to meet all needs, served as a day coach, diner, baggage car, all in one. The long wagon box had a chest across each end, the one in the rear being used for pots, pans, dishes, etc.; the one in front for food for daily needs. the bulk of the supplies (flour, sugar, beans, hardtack, etc) was stored in the wagon, for enough of such perishable food had to be provided for the entire trip.

The bows over which the canvas was stretched were high enough for a short person to stand erect under them. Many articles of clothing were hung from these bows.[6]

Oxen usually drew the wagons, although horses and mules sometimes were used. Oxen, although slower, were better able to withstand the rigors of a long journey and could better forage off the land than horses or mules. Furthermore, Indians were not as likely to steal oxen as they would horses. Because of the important service that oxen like Deke and Dime, Buck and Brite performed, their masters usually treated them with utmost respect, caring for their maladies in the best manner available. These animals were vital to the success of the journey. Besides oxen, most families had loose livestock including horses, possibly sheep, and cattle, some of which were milk cows. All became a part of the procession. Sometimes cows were yoked in to either relieve or assist the oxen.[7]

Much advice was available to travelers in the form of guidebooks, newspaper accounts, and other publications regarding what and what not to take on the long journey, but emigrants did not always take heed. Many started out with the family furniture, heavy stoves, and other burdensome equipment, much of which eventually was discarded along the way to lighten the load for the overworked oxen.

In addition to a wagon, other equipment usually taken included an ax, shovel, handsaw, auger, a hundred feet or so of rope, firearms (handgun, rifle, shotgun), an eight or ten gallon keg for water, a churn, and, if the emigrant intended to farm in Oregon, a plow and crosscut saw were advised. For cooking, some recommended a sheet iron stove, but because stoves were heavy, many cooked by an open fire using a tin reflector for baking. A dutch oven and iron skillet were essentials. Metal utensils were preferred so that breakage would not be a problem. These included tin plates, cups, bowls, a coffeepot, and iron knives, forks, and spoons.

Basic provisions included a six months supply of sea biscuits or hard tack, bacon, beans, rice, dried fruit, tea, coffee, sugar, flour, cornmeal, vinegar, salt, pepper, lard, saleratus (bicarbonate of soda), and molasses. Most families were supplied with milk and butter from their own cows.[8] Ezra Meeker included eggs that he packed in cornmeal, dried pumpkins, beef jerky, and brandy for "medicinal purposes."[9] In addition to spirits, the medicine kit usually included such items as quinine for malaria, hartshorn for snakebite, citric acid for scurvy, opium, laudanum, morphine, calomel, and tincture of camphor.[10]

After one day's travel, the Boatmans met the first of their traveling companions. Mary Ann's story continues.

> **We drove twelve miles where we camped for the night. There we joined the company [the Deacon Thomas Turner party] that we were to travel with.[11]**
>
> **Although only 12 miles from home and members of the same church, they were strangers to us young folks. My parents were**

acquainted with the old Deacon and his wife. After unyoking the oxen and feeding them, . . . setting the tent for the first time, [and] supper over, we spent the evening . . . making the acquaintances of our new friends and neighbors. . . . [By bedtime] we all began to feel kindly . . . toward [each] other. The men folk held a meeting and put it to a vote who would serve as captain of the company. The choice fell on the old Deacon Turner. He was a good pious gentleman, . . . well worthy of the honor bestowed him. All being excited with the thought of starting on such a journey, and too, of leaving home and friends, . . . it was midnight before all was quiet.

At four o'clock in the morning [March 30] all was on the stir and by 10 o'clock the captain called "Come, all aboard for Oregon," for there was no Washington in those days.[12]

Now dear readers, don't imagine a [group] of men and women clad in the best of fine broadcloth and cashmere . . . waiting in a first class depot looking and waiting to see and hear the old iron horse come snorting and steaming in, hauling a long train of cushioned seats and sleepers and dining car attached. No, [it was] far different. [Mary Ann, writing in 1905, is relating to the finest of travel conditions for those times.] [There were] 18 of us at the start all told; ten men, five women, and three children.

The men included Willis and John Boatman, William Richardson, the Deacon Thomas Turner, Thomas Turner Jr. and his wife's father, and probably four hired men, making a total of ten men. However, of the five women Mary Ann mentioned, only three are known—Mary Ann, Mrs. Thomas Turner, and the wife of Thomas Turner Jr. Perhaps the remaining women were wives of hired hands. Apparently, all three children belonged to the younger Turners.

> We all wore homespun and home woven clothes. . . . For the head covering, when the weather was cold, . . . we [used] a hood made of some woolen material to protect the head from cold, and for hot sun and warm weather, a sun bonnet with wooden splints to hold it out. It would have been useless to have anything like hats that could be destroyed by hard use as they had to last the entire trip. The men were clad in much the same manner.

Jane D. Kellogg and her husband John left Elkhart, Indiana, on March 17, 1852, in a party of six men, three women, and three children. She wrote about the women's clothing:

> We wore bloomers all the way, the better to enable us to walk through the sagebrush. They were made with short skirts and pants reaching to

the shoe tops. Everyone wore them. On our whole journey we used cold water, had a washboard, and the washing was very clean; did our washing in the evening, and when dry, folded the cloths and put heavy weights on them, or wore them just as they dried. We were not particular about our looks.[13]

Ezra Meeker vividly related his observations of the clothing worn by travelers in 1852.

We had a community of women wearing bloomers without invidious comment, or, in fact, any comment at all. Some of them were barefoot or wore moccasins, partly from choice and in some cases from necessity. The same could be said of the men, as shoe leather began to grind out from the sand and heat. . . . Patches became visible upon the clothing of preachers as well as laymen. . . . The grandmother's cap was soon displaced by a handkerchief or perhaps a bit of cloth. Grandfather's high crowned hat disappeared as if by magic. . . . They wore what they had left or could get, . . . Rich dresses were worn by some ladies because they had no others; the gentlemen drew upon their wardrobes until scarcely a fine unsoiled suit was left.[14]

Mary Ann continues:

[When] the word from the captain came [to] start . . . we were saved the painful task of bidding any one goodbye, as all were strangers to us. Not wishing to see our new made friends part with children and neighbors, we started in advance of the train.

Our train consisted of five covered wagons, four drawn by cattle as we had both oxen and cows in our teams. One was drawn with horses, . . . the one the old Deacon had for himself and family to ride in. After the farewell greeting and tear shedding had somewhat subsided, the train proceeded on. No stop was made until late in the afternoon. Then the camp was made for the night. . . . Again we all came together as one family. . . . It was decided that, . . . after the evening meal was over and all preparations made for the night, that all of the people that wished to would come together at the Deacon's camp fire before retiring and he would read a chapter from the Bible and sing some sacred hymns and offer a prayer for us wandering Israelites in the wilderness of sin. For a while this arrangement went well for the old Deacon not only possessed [a] kind and loving disposition, but was well acquainted with passages of scripture . . . [upon which] his church was founded. . . . He claimed to have the power of healing by repeating . . . words . . . [from] the Bible to himself in a whisper and rubbing the patient. . . . If it was a toothache, the face was the part rubbed; if rheumatism in any of the limbs, that was the part rubbed. He was a deacon in the Baptist church, . . . the same faith . . . [as] my parents, my brother William, and myself. . . . I can only speak for myself, I was in favor of the religious worship. . . . He express[ed] a desire that we should observe the Sabbath Day by laying by and devoting it to religious rest. . . . the men were all in favor. . . . When it was put to vote every man voted in favor of resting one day out of seven to lay still and rest man and beast. . . . It was the custom in those days for women to keep silent, . . . especially in men's affairs, such things as voting on church work and such like. They were expected to obey the teachings of the Apostle Paul, keep silent and ask your husband at home. . . . I don't know what the Apostle Paul thought we women would do if our husbands should happen to be like us, not know himself. I presume in that case we would go without knowing!

Many travelers started out with the best of intentions to follow a routine of "laying by" on Sunday. However, it soon became apparent to many that a rigid schedule was impractical. Time for rest and religious worship would have to be taken when and where it was convenient to do so. On some occasions, Sunday fell on days when they were trekking though difficult country. It was to their advantage to press on to a more desirable campground. Thus, stopovers for a day or two of rest, washing, baking, or worship were usually reserved for the more comfortable and safer places along the trail, regardless of what day of the week it was. Furthermore, those who found themselves lagging behind for whatever reason simply could not afford to stop over as frequently as they would like. It was essential that their journey be completed before winter set in.

To resume, all went well. Everybody kept well. [We] had no difficulty in finding good camping grounds, plenty of wood and water [and] could find all the corn to buy that our teams could eat. Everybody well and happy traveling through Illinois, Missouri, and Iowa, or at least portions of the three states.

The above statement is Mary Ann's only reference to the route they took from central Illinois to Kanesville, now Council Bluffs, Iowa, where they crossed the Missouri River to journey into Nebraska, then part of a politically unorganized territory. Therefore, their path through Illinois, Missouri, and Iowa is unknown. An examination of the journals and diaries of other early travelers reveals that there were numerous routes westward to Kanesville, depending on where the journey originated. Since the Boatmans left from central Illinois, a few miles south of Springfield, they likely traveled directly west to the Mississippi River. They may have crossed the river at or near Quincy, Illinois, as others did. After entering Missouri, many continued westward across northern Missouri before turning north into Iowa. From there, they could have continued in a northerly direction, possibly following close by the Missouri River, to Kanesville.

> Yes, all went well with the exception of once in a while some one would [get] stuck in the mud or give his team an extra lash and a loud "get up." We all liked very much to sit around the old Deacon's campfire and listen to his evening conversation as it was always instructive and full of kindness. . . . Another old gentleman in the crowd . . . sometimes occupied the time . . . [relating] his experiences of the early days in Illinois.
>
> I don't think I have properly described the families that we . . . traveled with. The old Deacon I have so often mentioned. . . . his name was Turner. His family and his son's family [and our's] made three families all told.
>
> . . . the time passed very pleasantly. Some days were very unpleasant, as it being spring time there were often a day or two that the rain would kept a constant drizzle, some snow often with it at night. On those occasions we managed to get near a woods, so . . . [we would] have plenty of fuel. So . . . oftime we were late . . . getting settled down at night . . . so our visits around the captain's camp fire became more infrequent and the evening devotions became neglected by all. But a good feeling and respect for one another continued. . . . the Sabbath Day was always observed as a day of rest for man and beast.
>
> All went well until we reached the Mormon settlement in the outskirts of Missouri.

The Missouri River settlement that the party reached was known at the time as Kanesville. Although Mormons are credited for establishing the town, it had been a frontier community since 1837 when a blockhouse was erected there by a company of dragoons under Captain D.B. Moore to protect the Pottawattomie Indians from their tribal enemies. It was located in what is now downtown Council Bluffs, Iowa. The following year, the facility was converted to a Jesuit mission, but by 1841 the mission was terminated because the Indians it served supposedly became "incorrigible drunkards." The Indians bought liquor from disreputable whites, using money paid to them by the U.S. government for the use of land.[15]

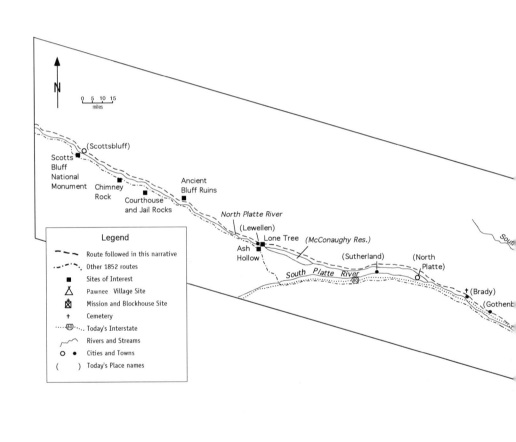

N

0 5 10 15
miles

(Scottsbluff)

Scotts
Bluff
National
Monument

Chimney
Rock

Courthouse
and Jail Rocks

Ancient
Bluff Ruins

North Platte River

(Lewellen)

Lone Tree

(McConaughy Res.)

Ash
Hollow

(Sutherland)

(North
Platte)

South Platte River

Sout

† (Brady)

(Gothenb

Legend

- – – – Route followed in this narrative
- –·–·– Other 1852 routes
- ■ Sites of Interest
- △ Pawnee Village Site
- ⊠ Mission and Blockhouse Site
- † Cemetery
- ····(80)···· Today's Interstate
- ‿‿ Rivers and Streams
- ○ ● Cities and Towns
- ( ) Today's Place names

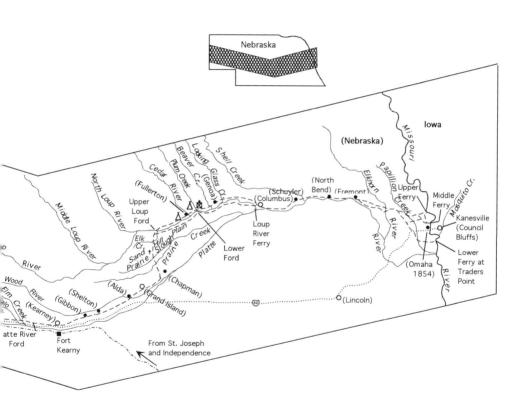

Mormons began arriving in the area in 1846. In that same year, they crossed the river and established "Winter Quarters," which eventually became the town of Florence, now a northern part of Omaha, Nebraska. In 1847, some 2,000 Mormons left this campground for Utah. In the spring of 1848, a remaining 4,000 Mormons crossed back to the east side of the river to a place then called Miller's Hollow. The name Miller's Hollow soon was changed to Kanesville in honor of Thomas Leiper Kane, a gentile friend of the Mormons. After the last of the Mormons left in 1853, the name of the community was officially changed from Kanesville to Council Bluffs. Originally in 1804, Lewis and Clark applied the term "Council Bluff" to an Indian meeting ground about twenty miles north on the Nebraska side of the river. Later, the entire area on both sides of the Missouri from the mouth of the Platte to the counseling site became known as Council Bluffs.[16]

The Council Bluffs area had long been a jumping off place for trappers, traders, missionaries, and emigrants prior to the arrival of the Mormons, who followed existing trails westward from there to the north side of the Platte River (the Mormon Trail). Many more non-Mormons eventually followed these trails than Mormons did. Between the 1840s and 1860s, over 500,000 emigrants passed along the north and south sides of Platte River Valley. Of these, a total of 185,000 (one-third), including the Boatmans, followed the Mormon Trail along the north side of the Platte. Of those, 35,000 (roughly one-fifth) were Mormons.[17]

Kanesville is mentioned in numerous diaries and letters. Among them, Dr. Thomas White arriving from Indiana in 1852 and bound for Oregon, who later described the town in a letter to S.P. Williams, dated April 19, 1853. "Kanesville as you know is about 2 miles or so from the Missouri River, the waters of which are as dirty as a mud puddle. This town of Kanesville, is stuck in among the gulches, that run out into the Bluffs, about 8 miles up the River from Council Bluffs."[18]

The Reads—Martha and Clifton and their three children, Lucy, Lydia, and Clifton Jr. from Marengo, Illinois—arrived at Kanesville on May 19, 1852. Martha recorded the following observations for that day.

> Traveled 6 miles to Kingsville [Kanesville], stopt awhile. Found quite a town but all log buildings fronted with siding. Inhabitants mostly Mormons, a pretty hard set. Traveled on 4 miles to the river, campt there, found bad muddy water. Weather clear and quite warm.[19]

Charles Stevens, a tailor by trade in company with his wife Ann and seven children on their way to Oregon, wrote the following about Kanesville in a May 21, 1852, letter to his brother Levi.

> We came here on thursday the 19th [of May]. . . . This place is one of those places [where] you had better think. It is the place that the Mormons started, and is filled with them now, yet I should think that the largest part of them are going to Salt Lake, this spring. There is only now and then a farm in all thies parts that has an inch of ground turned up for a new crop, and about one third of the Houses in town are for sale, the place is in a ravine, or at the lower end of one, with a high, very high roling country. The bottom of the Missouri, I should think were from two to four miles wide, and the bluffs on the east side are verry high, and in the distance look like the craggy peaks of New England mountains, yet I have not seen a stone in any of them.
>
> In the day time the town perfectly filled with teams, fitting out making companies, loading up, and preparing to cross the river. I have been told that the ferries were four weeks behind, we had our passage engaged for this morning but it has rained all day and all we have done is load up.[20]

Of course, the reason Stevens had "not seen a stone in any of" the high bluffs is because the bluffs here are composed entirely of thick deposits of wind blown sand and silt called loess.[21] From the wide expanse of barren deposits left by glaciers and melt waters following the last Ice Age, prevailing winds removed and redeposited these fine sediments, forming today's deep, rich soils of Iowa and Nebraska.

Also today, the city of Council Bluffs encompasses a much larger area than did Kanesville in 1852. It has grown to include not only the original gulch in which Kanesville was first established, but also the surrounding hills and bluffs, as well as the adjacent flood plain on the east side of the Missouri. It was on the flat lowland that the early travelers, Mormons and non-Mormons alike, camped while waiting to cross the Missouri River.

Notes

1. Catherine Scott Colburn, "The Long Wearisome Journey," *Morning Oregonian* (Portland, Oregon), June 17, 1890, 16.
2. Gregory M. Franzwa, *The Oregon Trail Revisited*, third edition (Gerald, Missouri: Patrice Press, 1983), 25–31; and William N. Byers, "The Odyssey of William N. Byers," edited by Merrill J. Mattes, in *Overland Journal*, vol. 2, no. 2 (1984), 24; published by the Oregon-California Trails Association, Independence, Missouri.

3. Enoch W. Conyers, "The Diary of E.W. Conyers, a Pioneer of 1852," in *Transactions of the Thirty-third Annual Reunion of the Oregon Pioneer Association* (Portland, Oregon, 1905), 423, 434.
4. John D. Unruh Jr., *The Plains Across: The Overland Emigrants and the Trans-Mississippi West, 1840–60*, paperback edition (Urbana, Chicago and London: University of Illinois Press, 1982), 329.
5. Martha H. Ellis, "Martha H. Ellis," in *A Small World of Our Own*, by R.A. Bennett (Walla Walla, Washington: Pioneer Press Books, 1985), 168.
6. M.E. (Bonney) Shorey, "A Pioneer Story," in *History of Pierce County*, vol. 2, by W.P. Bonney (Chicago, Illinois: Pioneer Historical Publishing, 1927), 1225–26.
7. Byers, 24; Franzwa, 31; and Unruh, 75.
8. Byers 24; Colburn, 16; and Jane D. Kellogg, "Memories of Jane D. Kellogg," in *Transactions of the Forty-first Annual Reunion of the Oregon Pioneer Association* (Portland, Oregon, 1913), 87–88.
9. Ezra Meeker, *Personal Experiences on the Oregon Trail: The Tragedy of Leschi*, fifth reprint (Seattle, Washington: Meeker, 1912), 7.
10. Merrill J. Mattes, *The Great Platte River Road: The Covered Wagon Mainline Via Fort Kearny to Fort Laramie*, Nebraska State Historical Society, vol. 25 (1969), 82.
11. According to Willis, they camped at Waverly, Illinois.
12. Washington did not become a territory until the following year, 1853.
13. Kellogg, 93.
14. Meeker, 20.
15. E. Laveille, S.J., *The Life of Father De Smet, S.J., 1801–1873,* reprint edition (Chicago, Illinois: Loyola University Press, 1981), 91–92, 220.
16. Robert Berry, written communication, 1999; and Mattes, *The Great Platte River Road*, 122–23.
17. Merrill J. Mattes, "The Northern Route of the Non-Mormons: Rediscovery of Nebraska's Forgotten Historic Trail," in *Overland Journal*, vol. 8, no. 2 (1990), 4–7; published by the Oregon-California Trails Association, Independence, Missouri.
18. Thomas White, "To Oregon in 1852, Letter of Dr. Thomas White," edited by Oscar O. Winther and Gayle Thornbrough (Indianapolis, Indiana: Indiana Historical Society, 1964), 9.
19. Martha S. Read, "A History of Our Journey," in *Covered Wagon Women: Diaries and letters from the Western Trails*, 1852, vol. 5, edited and compiled by Kenneth L. Holmes and David C. Duniway (Glendale, California: Arthur H. Clark, 1986), 217.
20. Charles Stevens, "Letters of Charles Stevens," edited by Ruth Rockwood, in *Oregon Historical Quarterly*, vol. 37, no. 2 (1936), 140–41.
21. Iowa Department of Natural Resources, Geological Survey Bureau, Trowbridge Hall, Iowa City, Iowa, personal communication, 1997.

Chapter Two

Across the Wide Missouri

Hundreds of wagons were ahead of us and we had to wait our turn as we did when I was a boy going to the mill. —Willis Boatman

WHILE THE BOATMANS WAITED to cross the Missouri River, their innocence and trust in their fellow man on the Oregon trek were first challenged. Although petty thievery was commonplace along the trail, organized banditry, particularly cattle rustling, was most prevalent around jumping-off places such as Kanesville. Many overlanders suffered stock losses in these areas, thefts that usually were committed by bands of white robbers, or at least gangs led by white men.[1] The Boatman family and their friends were among the many encountering foul play.

> We made camp about the middle of the afternoon as we wanted to find out the best place to ferry the river. So, the men folks went to Council Bluffs to find out when we could be ferried across the river, as hundreds of teams were . . . waiting to cross over. [Also they went to see about] the prospect of getting a larger supply of provisions for our six month's trip as we expected to be only six months on the road. . . . Some of the hired men were left in charge of the stock, old Mr. Turner and his wife kept watch over the camp, we girls, as we termed ourselves, went out to call on the neighbors and try to buy eggs and butter. As for milk we had that [because] we all had cows in the teams. But, our cows were not giving milk. [We] could get it [from] those that had it if we wanted to. But we did not think it best to use milk from cows driven all day in teams. So, we did not use milk at all.
>
> [When] we met our neighbors, as we termed them, they were very inquisitive to know what route we were going to take after

crossing the river and how long we calculated to remain in camp. . . .
[They said] a large train of their people would start for Salt Lake
City as soon as the grass got far enough advanced to furnish feed for
their cattle. At the same time [they] assured us that it would be better for us to remain camped where we were as our cattle could run at
large without having a guard all of the time. So, we silly girls thought
we had good news for all, never once mistrusting that they were
setting a trap to drive our cattle off. When [our] men got back to
camp they brought word that we could not cross the river for at least
a week. . . . Of course, we felt perfectly safe about the cattle that
night as they had told [our] men it would be good to let them run
unguarded in an open prairie surrounded with woods.

 . . . [That] night some of our new acquaintances, men of course,
called on us to inquire about [our] plans and how soon we expected
to move on. Our folks told them that they had decided to move on
so to be close to the ferry . . . if by chance their turn should [come],
all would be ready [even though] our neighbors were so kind in their
instructions about it being entirely safe to leave the stock unguarded.
[Nevertheless] they [our men] stationed a guard out until the teams
had all eaten to satisfaction and had laid down for the night. The
men that were on guard, thinking we were yet in civilization, came
to camp and went to bed. But, for all that, the men slept with one
ear open, so if there was any move[ment] among the cattle . . . they
might hear their bells. About three o'clock in the morning they hear
the cattle begin to stir. Suspicious of our neighbors, at once some of
the men in camp, my husband and brother [included,] were soon on
their trail. As the stock were quite a way in advance they continued
on the trail not daring to let the bells get out of [hearing range].
They at once became convinced that some person or persons were
driving them away. As soon as the sound of the bells became inau-
dible in camp every man started out except the old captain who had
ordered his horse saddled and sent in pursuit of them, having suspi-
cions aroused at the thought that the strange men that had visited at
the camp in the evening before, had something to do with it. Well
for a time all was confusion and excitement, as the men on horseback had returned with the word that the cattle had entered a thick
forest where it was impossible to pursue on horseback. But our faithful
boys, as I termed them for they were nothing else but boys in my
way of thinking today, kept . . . in pursuit of them and finally overtook them in a swamp five miles or more from camp.

 [Sometime before the men returned with the cattle], . . . one of
the visitors of the evening before came to our camp and made inquiry about the cattle, if the men in pursuit had found any trace of

them. . . . When informed by the old man [Deacon Turner] that they were in a thickly timbered swamp some five of six miles away, [he] made no hesitation in saying that the boys would never be able to get them out of the woods as there was a large swamp that if stock got out in it . . . the brush was so thick and the earth so soft that it would be impossible to get them out. But they did get them out after a hard half day's work. Maybe you don't think there was rejoicing in camp when the tired and hungry men all got home at camp. We all asked so many questions, [but] all they could tell us was that they come on to a little log house far out in the woods with a woman in it. When asked for the men folks she looked frightened and said she did not know where they were. When asked if she had seen any stray cattle, [she] murmured out in a frightened way and said a band had passed a short time before going toward the swamp which was a little way. As they hurried on they met a man [who] said he had not seen anything of the stock. So, [because he could hardly have not seen them] they came to the conclusion that he was the man, or one of them, that [had been] . . . driving them off. Well, after the hungry men got something to eat everybody went to work preparing for moving on.

That afternoon we traveled about five miles [and] camped near the Council Bluffs.[2] There we were delayed. [In] ten days, about the 20th of May, it came our turn to cross the Missouri River. At this place we finished laying in our provisions as this was the last place to obtain any supplies of any kind, for our six months journey across the wilderness.

Crossing the Missouri River in the Kanesville locality was, for many, a tedious and dangerous task. It would be the largest river encountered until they reached the Columbia. By 1852, there were three crossing sites in the Kanesville area: the upper ferry about ten or twelve miles upstream, the lower ferry at Traders Point some six miles downstream, and a middle ferry just upstream from the present Missouri River bridge leading into downtown Omaha.[3]

Many diarists recorded their experiences in crossing the river as well as observations of the general scene. Particularly apparent was the danger in making the actual crossing with a frequent occurrence of accidents, some of which proved fatal. Ezra Meeker, with his young wife Eliza Jane and infant son, crossed the Missouri at the lower ferry on May 17 and 18, 1852, apparently only a couple of days before the Boatmans did. Even though the Meekers and the Boatmans were to eventually become neighbors and business associates in Washington Territory, no known record indicates that they became acquainted on the trek west.[4]

After having spent but one winter in Iowa, the youthful and later renowned Ezra Meeker, together with his family, had left Eddyville, Iowa, early in April 1852. William Buck, a bachelor (whom Ezra called his partner), accompanied them. The following is Meeker's vivid description of the lower landing area upon their approach.

> As we neared the landing . . . we encountered a sight indeed long to be remembered. The "flatiron of white" [that they had observed from a distance] . . . proved to be wagons with their tongues pointed to the landing—a center train with other parallel trains extending back in the rear and gradually covering a wider space the farther back from the river one would go. Several hundred wagons were thus closely interlocked, completely blocking the approach to the landing by new arrivals. . . . All round about were camps of all kinds, from those without covers of any kind to others with comfortable tents, nearly all seemingly intent on merrymaking, while here and there were small groups engaged in devotional services. We soon ascertained these camps contained the outfits in great part of the wagons in line in the great white flatiron, some of whom had been there for two weeks with no apparent probability of securing an early crossing.[5]

Tales of accidents, regardless of which crossing was used, give testimony to the dangers the emigrants faced. Enoch W. Conyers recorded the following observation at one of the sites.

> There are but two small scows, that are now ferrying. Two wagons make a load for either scow, and they are propelled by two men using oars, and they charge $4 per wagon, and we swim our own cattle. . . . The current is very swift in the river and accidents are happening ever day to one or the other of these scows.[6]

Meeker noted one such accident that occurred at the lower ferry site just prior to his crossing.

> At the turbulent river front the turbid waters had already swallowed up three victims, one of whom I saw go under the drift of a small island as I stood near his shrieking wife the first day we were there. Two scows were engaged in crossing the wagons and teams. In this case the stock had rushed to one side of the boat, submerged the gunwale, and precipitated the whole contents into the dangerous river. One yoke of oxen, having reach[ed] the far shore, deliberately entered

the river with a heavy yoke on and swam to the Iowa side, and were finally saved by the helping hands of the assembled emigrants.[7]

On May 19, the day after the Meekers crossed, Conyers recorded yet another accident.

> Whilst waiting our turn . . . one of the ferry flats . . . sunk. One man was drowned and two others barely escaped with their lives. This evening we learned of an other accident which happened to this same ferry flat this afternoon a little after we crossed. At the time of the accident, there was but one wagon and several yoke of oxen aboard the flat. This team and wagon were owned by a young man and his sister—name unknown—and at the time of the accident they were both in the wagon, which, as usual with all emigrant wagons, had a cover on it. When the flat had reached near the center of the river the cattle became uneasy and began crowding to one side of the boat, so much so that the flat filled and the waggon and cattle all went overboard. The flat righted up, but was filled with water. The wagon went rolling and bobbing up and down as the current carried it down stream. . . . The emigrants on shore were frantic with excitement, women running up and down the shore screaming and wringing their hands, children crying, men hollowing . . . for the ferry-men to go and rescue those in the wagon. Finally the waggon brought up on a sandbar about fifty yards below. No one that witnessed the accident, believed it possible that either of the occupants would be found alive, but to the great surprise and joy of all, the young man through great exertion succeeded in extricating himself from under the contents of the wagon and crawled out on top of the wagon cover. He immediately turned his attention to the condition of his sister and soon brought her alive

A ferry crossing on the Missouri River as viewed from Kanesville, Iowa. This may well have been the middle ferry where the Boatmans are believed to have crossed. *Bostwick-Frohardt Collection, owned by KMTV and on permanent loan to the Durham Western Heritage Museum, Omaha, Nebraska*

to the surface. Some Indians were standing on the shore, witnessed the accident, and seeing the perilous condition of the young man and his sister, plunged into the stream, swam out to them and brought them both safely to shore.[8]

The Boatmans managed to cross over safely, although it took much effort. It is not known for certain which ferry they used. However, they almost certainly did not cross at the upper site in the Florence area some ten to twelve miles upstream from Kanesville. The distance to get there from anywhere in the immediate Kanesville vicinity was considerably longer than the five miles Mary Ann stated they traveled to reach the waiting area near the bluffs. Based on Mary Ann's description of the ferry itself in the following section, either the lower or middle site was used. However, her statement regarding where they went after making the crossing presents the best evidence that they took the middle ferry. She relates, **"we were then camped in a wild uncivilized country, 53 years ago . . . where the city of Omaha, Nebraska stands today"** ("today" being 1905 when she prepared her story). The middle crossing led almost directly into the present downtown area of Omaha.

Here is Mary Ann's description of the ferry:

> **Crossing rivers in those day was far different [than] . . . what it is today. It requires a great deal of manual labor to propel one of the ferry boats. The one that ferried thousands of emigrants across the river at Council Bluff was a scow which was pulled [along] a rope made fast on each side of the river. A pulley on a short rope [that rode on the long rope was] attached to the boat to keep it from going down stream. Where the water was shallow, they used spike poles and where it was deep they used oars. Two wagons were all that could be ferried at one time. Just think what a slow process, and hundreds of wagons waiting and hundreds coming every day. Well, we got over the river at last by swimming the cattle. In that work my brother William came near losing his life by drowning. Poor boy, he was only spared for a more painful death.**

Obviously, it was risky business crossing the Missouri River on flimsy ferries in 1852. The arrival of a steamboat, however, spared some emigrants from the dangers of boarding makeshift watercraft. In this regard, Meeker recalled the following after crossing:

> We crossed on the 17th and 18th of May and drove out a short way on the 19th, but not far enough to be out of hearing of a shrill steamboat

whistle that resounded over the prairie, announcing the arrival of a steamer.

I never knew the size of that steamer, or the name, but only know that a dozen or more wagons could be crossed at one time, and that a dozen or more trips could be made during the day, and as many at night, and that we were overtaken by this throng of a thousand wagons thrown upon the road, that gave us some trouble and much discomfort.[9]

Enoch Conyers identified the steamer as the *El Paso*.[10]

May 18—Tuesday—This morning a steamer was seen coming up the river, and a crowd of emigrants rushed to the landing to be in readiness to board her as soon as she touched the shore, with the intention, if possible, to induce the captain to ferry them across the Missouri. . . . He finally agreed to commence ferrying tomorrow morning at the rate of $10 per wagon and four yoke of cattle included, and $2 for every extra yoke. . . . The steamer's name is The *El Paso*. . .

May 19—Wednesday . . . At the sight of the steamer our joy was unbounded to know that we will now escape the danger of crossing the Missouri in one of those miserable little flatboats, for some accident happens to them nearly every trip they make.[11]

A second steamboat showed up in the Kanesville area shortly after the arrival of the *El Paso*. Caleb and Alice Richey, members of the Akin, Richey, and Ingram train, noted that they crossed on the *Robert Campbell*.[12] Furthermore, they acknowledged that the *El Paso* was in operation. James Akin Jr. stated in his diary that they crossed on May 18 and 19. He does not reveal how he got over, but presumably also on the *Robert Campbell*. James Akin Jr. was nineteen and the oldest of eight children of the James and Eliza Richey Akin family who had left Salem, Iowa, on April 15, 1852, headed for Oregon.

Among others who recorded boarding a steamboat in the Kanesville area was Polly Coon with her six-year-old daughter Cornelia Evelyn Coon. As members of the Crandell train from Wisconsin, they were on their way to Oregon to be reunited with Polly's husband, Thomas Lewis Coon, who had traveled west earlier.[13] On May 18, Polly wrote:

Arrived Kanesville procured our fitout and after being detained about 3 days came down to the Missouri and lay one night on its banks. The next morning took the steamboat ferry and crossed, driving 3 miles to a lake where we stayed 24 hour, packing and repairing and forming our train.[14]

Martha and Clifton Read with their three children, from Marengo, Illinois, also crossed the river at Council Bluffs in a steamer during the same week.

> Crossed the river about 2 miles below here, in a steam boat, had to pay $14. Find a hard set along here. One man drowned in trying to cross this river in a small boat and swim his cattle after.[15]

Mary Ann Boatman does not mention either vessel. Possibly, the Boatman-Turner party crossed just before the steamers arrived, or perhaps the greater expense of boarding a steamboat may have been a factor in their decision to utilize a flatboat.

On the westward trek, the Missouri River was the first major obstacle to overcome for those who had proceeded to the Kanesville area. Even though steamboats provided relief for many from the dangers of a flatboat crossing, one can well imagine from the cited incidents of just a few days that a number of accidents and even deaths occurred at these crossings in the spring of 1852.

Emigrants who crossed in mid May 1852 enjoyed favorable weather, as attested to by James Akin Jr., who faithfully recorded conditions during this period.[16] His party arrived in Kanesville on May 8 and, as already mentioned, crossed the Missouri on the 18th and 19th. His account, together with that of Martha Read, gives a nearly complete record of the weather in the area during a two-week period, from Sunday May 9 through Saturday May 22.[17] They recorded beautiful, pleasant, warm, or clear conditions, except for rain on the evenings of the 12th and 15th and wind on the 16th and 18th; it rained all day on the 21st and until the afternoon of the 22nd. Thus, most of those who made the crossing in mid May 1852 were favored with at least reasonably pleasant weather. However, it probably was miserable for those who crossed in the rain on May 21 or 22.

Having safely, although apparently precariously, crossed the Missouri River, the Boatmans now entered the frontier. They no longer enjoyed the secure feeling of being in the settled and politically governed portion of the nation. Although they were now in an unorganized territory within the United States, in their minds they had left their native country behind and were on their own, though they were among thousands embarking on the same destiny. Their apprehensions and fears, largely precipitated by exaggerated rumors of Indian trouble ahead, together with a natural concern of danger from wild animals and entering an unfamiliar environment, put them on guard.

Mary Ann vividly describes their preparations for the daily procedures to be followed during their journey beyond the Missouri River. She also reveals the thoughts and dreams she shared with her fellow travelers as they began the long and tedious trek across the wilderness. Lacking, however, are details of the exact locations for the events she describes. Assuming they used the middle crossing, their first day of travel would have been primarily along the ridges through present-day Omaha, described by Martha Read as "a very uneven section of country with now and then a small grove."[18] Today, modern development has somewhat modified the unevenness of the terrain, but Omaha's topography still retains rolling hills, with valleys carved down through the loess soil by small tributary streams leading to the Missouri River.

A day or so of traveling from the Missouri would have placed them near Big Papillion Creek, or as the emigrants called it, "Pappea" Creek. At this crossing, the Boatman party may have encountered Indians demanding a toll. Sarah Pratt, twenty years of age, single, and in company with her parents Sally and Silas Pratt, together with a sister and several brothers, arrived here on June 9. They were from Jackson County, Michigan, on their way to California by way of Salt Lake. That day Sarah recorded, "crossed Papea Creek on bridge, paid 50 cents toll to the Indians."[19]

The second day's travel would have brought the Boatmans to the Elkhorn River vicinity where they most likely encountered a crowd of emigrants waiting to cross on a ferry. On May 22, Conyers noted, "arrived at Elkhorn Creek at 12:30 P.M. and found about 150 teams ahead of us. But as luck would have it we got across . . . at 7:30 P.M."[20]

Among others, Martha Read on May 26 also recorded that a ferry was in operation here. "Came to Elkhorn River, crossed ourselves and wagons in a ferry boat and swam our cattle."[21]

John T. Kerns, a presumably single young man who left Rensselaer, Indiana, on March 15 for Oregon, crossed the Elkhorn River the same day as Conyers. Kerns wrote, "we came to Elkhorn River which we ferried, paying $2.00 per wagon . . . we had to swim our teams and loose cattle."[22]

An eleven-mile flood plain extended from the Elkhorn River crossing to the first contact with the Platte River in the vicinity of today's Fremont, Nebraska—another easy day's journey. John Kerns described this countryside on May 23 as "low and level, besides rich, producing a luxuriant Growth of grass."[23] Today, in the spring season travelers largely view cultivated fields of young corn here.

For the next fifty miles (about a three day's journey), the early travelers followed over flat terrain along the north side of the Platte River until reaching the Loup River, a major tributary to the Platte flowing from the northwest. On May 24 and 25, Kerns described this stretch generally as "all prairie except what timber is along the river. The country is very handsome."[24] Today, this prairie is completely cultivated with corn and other crops. In this stretch of road, emigrants crossed Shell Creek at a ford or bridge for which the Indians reportedly demanded a toll. Most travelers from the Kanesville area arrived at the Loup River on their fifth or sixth day of travel after leaving the Missouri.

Here are Mary Ann's observations of the first few days of travel beyond the Kanesville crossings.

> We [were then] camped in a wild uncivilized country, 53 year ago[25] . . . where the great city of Omaha, Nebraska stands today. . . . Oh, if those hills and bluffs could talk they could tell of joys and sorrow that could make the population laugh and cry by turns. . . . our faces . . . [were] turned westward; our last camping in civilization had passed. From now on we got to face the savage. We were now camped for the night. Word had been sent back from the emigrant[s] . . . ahead of us that they were having trouble with the Indians and for all to move in large trains as it was unsafe for small parties to start out. So a meeting was called and our party got in with a Mr. Scott [who] had something like twenty men in his train. The men all got together and formed a company of about 30 wagons [Willis says 31 wagons and approximately 120 people]. . . . as before, the old Deacon was elected captain.
>
> [The party included the] Turners, 2 families, Boatman and Richardson, four, [the] Scott family [and] ten men, Skile and Stiles families, McBurney and Ladd families, and the old blacksmith and two men with him. There were [other] names I cannot remember. . . . All [were] . . . armed with guns and plenty of ammunition at hand ready for any attack that might occur at any time.
>
> After supper was served throughout the various divisions of the camp, the evening of the 22nd of May [Saturday] was spent perfecting regulations for the long and dangerous trip and in the forming of acquaintances and the interchange of salutations and congratulations. Little groups now larger, now smaller, by the constant moving to and fro . . . members of the camp . . . chatted the evening up to a

seasonable bed time [and] all retired. Nothing . . . disturbed the quietness of the night. . . . the hush of sleep's wanted hour had stolen slowly over the entire encampment and nothing without indicate[d] remaining life, save the barking of some stray wolf or the outburst of some infant member of the villa camp. [All were] wearied and worn and overtaxed by the hurry of the previous day, and bustle and excitement.

Just as the sun was gladdening the clear east . . . throwing its golden light over the fair west, the cattle we[re] driven in from the grass growing plains to be yoked and hitched to the wagons for our first day's journey through a wild and unknown country inhabited only by savage Indians and wild beasts. No wonder is it that our leader thought it a proper thing to do that we should all observe the Sabbath day and unite in asking kind providence to guide us over such a perilous journey.

. . . on the 23rd of May [Sunday], all was in readiness, the commander called out [to] start. Into that hour was crowded memories of the home-land and friends now forever abandoned, for the prospect of a home in the far off west. There flowed and mingled the tears of regret and hope. There and then rose the earnest prayer for providential guidance. . . . at that hour [there] swelled out upon the soft clear air of as lovely [a] morning as ever, the gentle wind sent her . . . breeze to waft the sweet perfume, to gladden the hearts of man and beast.

May 23, 1852, was a Sunday. Therefore, it seems there is a discrepancy in Mary Ann saying their starting date was the 23rd, inasmuch as she specifically stated that they had agreed not to travel on the Sabbath. Perhaps, they started on Monday, May 24.

At 10 o'clock the march commenced. The sound came [to] start. At the word all was ready, our faces turned toward the west [and] our backs . . . toward our home and loved ones. Slowly the teams crawled on and on. . . . [Those] on foot were some times far in advance until late in the afternoon when a halt was called where water and fuel were obtainable. The wagons were formed in a circle to form a corral, to unhitch and unyoke the cattle . . . as they were in a strange country and among strange cattle, it made it difficult to handle them. . . . They [were] unhitched, unyoked, and given liberty to roam . . . over the green plain. . . . Everybody was engaged, some gathered sticks or turfs to make a fire, others brought water, set tents, [or] watched the cattle, [while] the women folks made preparations for the evening meal. Children romped, played hide and go seek, all happy as no sorrow had, as yet, entered their young hearts. Supper [was soon] ready throughout the entire village of tents. All being tired and hungry partook freely of the evening meal, it now being the first of our camping out on the lonely plains. [But] not [really] lonely either, for as far as the eye could see was one line of covered wagons and tents [with] smoke rising from camp fires. Just [then] the sun was gladdening the clear west and throwing its golden fare-wells upon the lonely plain that stretched into the wilderness, and clad the shoulders of the rocky range. [The] paradise-[like] plain and mountain country [was held] in its radiant embrace.

The loud call of the leader and captain pealed through the moving village, a circle was formed and the head of several families were in presence waiting the commander's orders. One man from every family was chosen to stand guard until midnight, then were to be released by another force of men, the arrangement satisfactory to all. The cattle . . . being driven for commencement in a new country, were turned forth upon the grass. Rich and abundant pastures . . . stretched from the place of their halt westward seemingly until it boarded against the foothills of the Indian territory in the distance . . . the guards and cattle have gone out a mile or more. The men . . . stand or sit with gun in hand, ready for any attack whatever that might be made by Indians or wild beasts that, by chance . . . be roving over the plains in search of what they might devour.

I turn now to the village of wagons and tents. . . . The evening had been an ideal one, its loveliness beyond describing with word or pen, had been chatted away [in] little groups clustered here and there around the pleasant camp fires. Now and then someone . . . would say, "Oh, I wish my sweetheart had come along too"; then again some young lady would say, "I wish I had stayed with my John Henry, he wanted me too." . . . Then a more sober man who had left his wife and babies at home would say, "I am glad that my family is at home where they can live safely without fear of Indians or wild beasts" . . . another would say, "Oh, my dear home, my kind parents and loving brothers and sisters, shall we ever meet again on this side of life, or shall we have to wait the resurrection morning?"[26] Another would exclaim, "What a jolly time we will have when we get to Or-egon and establish our donation claim of 160 acres of rich land. We'll just hitch old Buck and Brite to the plow and break up 25 or 30 acres of my land and sow it in wheat, build a cabin as timber is plentiful and then we be right at home."[27] Poor foolish people, never thinking . . . what a journey of 2,000 miles would be [like] to both man and beast through a desert of uninhabited country. Of course there were plows and wheat in Oregon, but where . . . would the money come [from] to pay for plows or wheat as most . . . emigrants

[had] all or most of their belongings invested in wagons, cattle, provisions, and other supplies for the long journey ahead. . . . All of this kind of conversation and a great deal more too numerous to mention, passed the evening away to a reasonable bed time as twilight was now closing in, shutting out the light of day.

The few remaining chunks of burning sticks had been heaped together, the smoke was sending its last curling clouds heavenward, the coals fast turning to ashes. [Suddenly the] sound of horses heavy trod was heard approaching the camp. For a short time all was excitement and alarm, as we had heard before leaving the Missouri river that Indians had made an attack on . . . emigrants that had gone before us. So all the men that were in camp rushed for their fire arms, while the women and children crouched behind tents and under wagons, saying, as they thought their last prayer, their hearts ready to burst with fear, and eyes wet with tears. [But, as soon as] the riders were in front of the camp our fears [were] all put to flight, as it was only a dozen or more friendly Indians who chanced to be passing by and stopped to beg something to eat. After having a short conversation with the men of the camp in broken English language and signs, pointing to the cooking utensils, then their mouths, . . . they soon gave all to understand that they were peaceable and only wanted something to appease the appetite. . . . Something for them to eat was hurried . . . handed to the leader who gave signs that he would go away, so they mounted the ponies and galloped away. . . . those who had sought safety under the wagons and behind tents came crawling out saying, "I knew all the time that they were friendly Indians and that there was no use getting the guns out and showing . . . cowardliness. Just think [we] women folks did not as much get a poker or butcher knife." "No," said some one near by dressed in male attire, "but you hid under the wagon." [On this] second night of our camp on the plains [May 24 or 25], we all had a good night rest, [except] the guards who came in at midnight.

The whole population of the moving village was astir bright and early. Breakfast throughout the entire camp eaten in haste as everybody was in a hurry to start and make good time while grass [was] plentiful and teams in good condition. So, the cooks had their kitchen work all done by the time the cattle were yoked and hitched to the wagons.

Notes

1. John D. Unruh Jr., *The Plains Across: The Overland Emigrants and the Trans-Mississippi West, 1840–60*, paperback edition (Urbana, Chicago, and London: University of Illinois Press, 1982), 152.

2. This would be the actual bluffs and not the town later known as Council Bluffs. The Boatmans likely camped on the flood plain along Mosquito Creek.

3. Merrill J. Mattes, *The Great Platte River Road: The Covered Wagon Mainline Via Fort Kearny to Fort Laramie*, Nebraska State Historical Society, vol. 25 (1969), 124.

4. Ezra Meeker, *Personal Experiences on the Oregon Trail: The Tragedy of Leschi*, fifth reprint (Seattle, Washington: Meeker, 1912), 24.

5. Ibid., 10.

6. Enoch W. Conyers, "The Diary of E.W. Conyers, a Pioneer of 1852," in *Transactions of the Thirty-third Annual Reunion of the Oregon Pioneer Association* (Portland, Oregon, 1905), 430.

7. Meeker, 10–11.

8. Conyers, 431–32.

9. Meeker, 24.

10. The *El Paso*, launched at St. Louis in 1850, was approximately 180 feet long and 28 feet wide. In 1852 it ascended the Platte River to Guernsey, Wyoming, the only steamboat ever to go there. In 1853 it ascended the Missouri River to the mouth of the Milk River—the first steamer to reach that place. It became snagged and was lost near Boonville, Missouri, on the Mississippi River, April 10, 1855. Frederick Way Jr., compiler, *Way's Packet Directory, 1848–1994: Passenger Steamboats of the Mississippi River System since the Advent of Photography in Mid-Continent America* (Athens, Ohio: Ohio University Press, 1983), 143.

11. Conyers, 431.

12. Caleb and Alice Richey, letter to Lafayette and Hanna Richey, Salem, Iowa, in Appendix D of *The Oregon Trail Diary of James Akin Jr. in 1852: The Unabridged Diary with Introduction and Contemporary Comments by Bert Webber* (Medford, Oregon: Webb Research Group, Pacific Northwest Books, 1989), 75. The *Robert Campbell*, a 268 ton vessel, was built at Hannibal Missouri in 1849. It was destroyed in a wharf fire at St. Louis, October 13, 1853. Way, 395.

13. Polly Coon, "Journal of a Journey over the Rocky Mountains," in *Covered Wagon Women: Diaries and Letters from the Western Trails*, 1852, vol. 5, edited and compiled by Kenneth L. Holmes and David C. Duniway (Glendale, California: Arthur H. Clark, 1986), 174–75.

14. Ibid., 186.

15. Martha S. Read, "A History of Our Journey," in *Covered Wagon Women: Diaries and Letters from the Western Trails*, 1852, vol. 5, edited and compiled by Kenneth L. Holmes and David C. Duniway (Glendale, California: Arthur H. Clark, 1986), 218.

16. James Akin Jr., *The Oregon Trail Diary of James Akin Jr. in 1852: The Unabridged Diary with Introduction and Contemporary Comments by Bert Webber* (Medford, Oregon: Webb Research Group, Pacific Northwest Books, 1989), 23–25.

17. Read, 217–18.

18. Ibid., 219.

19. Sarah Pratt, "The Daily Notes of Sarah Pratt, 1852," in *Covered Wagon Women: Diaries and Letters from the Western Trails*, 1852, vol. 5, edited by Kenneth L. Holmes and David C. Duniway (Glendale, California: Arthur H. Clark, 1986), 169–70 and 183.

20. Conyers, 433.

21. Read, 219.

22. John T. Kerns, "Journal of Crossing the Plains to Oregon in 1852," in *Transactions of the Forty-second Annual Reunion of the Oregon Pioneer Association* (Portland, Oregon, 1914), 158.

23. Ibid., 159.
24. Ibid.
25. This statement reveals that Mary Ann prepared her manuscript in 1905.
26. This may well have been Mary Ann's personal statement.
27. This appears to be from the conversation of Willis, his brother John, and brother-in-law William.

Willis Boatman, age 39, in a portrait taken in Washington Territory, 1865. *W.W. Rau family collection*

Chapter Three

Cholera

In a few days one of the Turner's children died and before we reached the Platte River another one was sick and died a day or two after. About the same time the father was taken sick and died on the Platte and was buried at Elm Creek.
—Willis Boatman

M ARY ANN BOATMAN CONTINUES her story by summing up a month of traveling across Iowa and into present-day Nebraska, prior to their first contact with dreaded cholera.

> All went well for a month, going through the regular routine of a camping and traveling life, laying by, as we termed it, on the Sabbath day to rest the teams and some times on a week day to wash up . . . cloths and bake bread, as we got tired of baking bread every evening and morning.

Meanwhile, Willis related an interesting incident that took place a few days west of the Missouri River as they approached the Loup River.

> We moved on nicely till we got near the loop fork,[1] where we met some parties returning to the settlement who told us that the Indians had attacked a train of emigrants and stolen their cattle, that they were a treacherous race of Indians and we had better pass there in strong companies. So we waited till another train came up [the Scott party?] and then moved on [to] the river where we saw but very few Indians. Notwithstanding, we doubled our guard both at camp and with the stock, but everything was quiet through the night and in the morning the guards that were with the cattle came in to get breakfast. Upon going out to get the stock they found that one of Scott's best cows was missing. All hand[s] turned out to hunt for her but she could not be found, so we concluded to give her up.

We started out again. My brother and several others armed and mounted themselves on good horses and concluded that they would take another look over a little farther where there was a small grove of timber. They struck out and sure enough, they found the cow down under a bank, guarded by an Indian, in a little thicket of willows.

This incident introduced the Boatman party to the only kind of problem that they and other emigrants were to experience with the native population in 1852. There were no murderous attacks, but rather mischievous pilfering occurred. Many Indians had no qualms about taking advantage of opportunities to take cattle, clothing, food, or anything else that the emigrants left unguarded. Travelers eventually learned not to fear malicious attacks from the Indians, but to be constantly on guard against attempts at thievery.

Mary Ann continues her story by describing a young girl that she befriended during this time.

One character in our train I think would be of great interest to some of my readers, especially to parents . . . [was] a little girl about ten years old [whose] first name was Addie. If my memory serves me right her name was Addie Walker. She was in company with her uncle William Buck and his wife and babe.[2] It seems she had gone to spend a fortnight with her uncle and aunt so she could . . . help . . . them get things ready. . . . Both families expected to meet at Council Bluff on an appointed day two weeks hence. As our tents were close together and we women folk, all strangers to one another, soon began to feel an interest in one another's affairs. I learned how little Addie had become separated from her parents and that her uncle and aunt were constantly [on the lookout for them.] On every arrival of a train of wagons they would . . . search to see if they had come. On several occasions [they] had gone to other ferries on the [Missouri] river in search of her parents, but only to return with disappointment. So, until it came their turn to ferry over the river . . . they camped with our company and joined our train of thirty wagons, hoping to come up with her folks if they had gone on and if behind they might overtake the train. Every evening, if a train was in sight some[one] of the family would go in search of them. Poor little girl, I can almost hear her pitiful sobs saying, "If I could find papa and mama and my twin sister. She and I looked so near alike it is hard to tell us one from the other." I went with her several times to look for her folks but never could find them. The thirty wagons that organized in [our] train on the west side of the [Missouri]

> river continued together until about the first of June. After that date
> I never saw little Addie Walker, but I will tell you something about
> her father and mother and sisters, after I get to Portland, Oregon.
> So, I will leave her now for six months then I will tell you about her
> folks.

Unfortunately, Mary Ann did not complete her account of the journey as far as Portland. Therefore, she never told the story of Addie Walker's parents and sisters. A conclusion of the Addie Walker story will remain an intriguing mystery unless someone eventually gleans the concluding details from records left by Addie's family in Oregon.

> There was nothing of much interest [in] our travels the first month,
> only some hard rain and wind storms on several occasions blew tents
> down and caused the cattle to . . . hunt a sheltered nook, but not so
> severe as to cause any disaster. Occasionally we would meet a train
> of Indians with their herds of horses, dogs, squaws, papooses, [and]
> pet wolves. So passed away the first month of our journey in the
> wilderness of disappointment and sorrow.

The statement, "of disappointment and sorrow," was Mary Ann's way of suggesting what was to come. Thus far, all had gone well in proceeding beyond the Missouri.

Upon arrival at the Loup River in the vicinity of today's Columbus, Nebraska, travelers were confronted with a decision—whether to cross the Loup River on a primitive ferry and follow along the south side of the stream for some distance before heading south to the Platte River, or to continue on the north side of the Loup River to one of several fording places. The ferry was regarded as unsafe by some. Furthermore, it cost $3 per wagon to cross and the cattle had to swim.

Inasmuch as neither Mary Ann nor Willis were particularly faithful about recording their whereabouts, it remains uncertain which route they took or where they crossed the Loup River when they reached there, probably in late May. Four other 1852 travelers, however, provide useful descriptions of this area. Most emigrants traveled through here during late May and early June, when the foremost event was the onslaught of cholera.

The Crandell train from Wisconsin, which was bound for Oregon, chose to cross on the ferry. Polly Coon noted that on May 27 they paid the $3 fee per wagon and swam the cattle. The following day, they witnessed the first scenes of sickness and death. Polly wrote, "today one man was buried—another dying & still another sick. The disease was Diareah which they had not medicine to check & the result was death."

On June 1, Polly recorded that they had crossed over to the Platte River and, having traveled twenty-five miles without water, were exhausted.

The next day, June 2, they continued a few miles before stopping for breakfast. Nearby they saw two new graves. "One of them was a man laid on the ground & the dirt heaped over him—the other was a woman who had died 2 days before."

That evening, shortly after making camp along the Platte, a violent storm struck, lasting most of the night. Polly wrote, "The wind blowing from nearly every point of the compass. . . . Some of the tents were blown down & those that were not required 2 or 3 men to hold them all night." Polly further noted on the next morning, June 3, they were "very much dejected" after the night's drenching. The Crandell train, therefore, halted to make repairs and dry out during the following two days.

On June 5, they crossed the Wood River and encountered much evidence of sickness, and the following day traveled well beyond Elm Creek. They passed at least a dozen graves "made within 3 or 4 days," and Polly made her first reference to the malady as "cholera."[3]

The California-bound McAuleys[4] from Henry County, Iowa, were among those who chose not to use the Loup River ferry and instead proceeded more than thirty miles up the north side toward the Lower Ford, located some three miles east of today's Fullerton, Nebraska, and just beyond a tributary known as Plum Creek.[5]

The McAuley party included 17-year-old Eliza Ann McAuley, the diarist, her 22-year-old brother who was the leader, a 28-year-old sister, Margaret, and two young friends, Merrick, 16, and Winthrop, 20. On April 7, 1852, the McAuleys had departed from Mt. Pleasant, Henry County, Iowa, leaving behind their mother Ester and married sister Catherine. The young McAuleys were on their way to meet their father, James McAuley, who had preceded them to California. Here, Eliza Ann McAuley describes their journey along the Loup River and for some distance beyond.[6]

Beginning on May 24, they traveled for two days on the north side of the river. On the 25th, they passed what Eliza described as "a Sioux village

in ruins [and] a stockade fort" near Plum Creek. This actually was a Pawnee village. A large portion of the Pawnee nation had been centered along
the Loup River where, at one time, they occupied at least three major
villages. The Sioux raided them and many Pawnee were killed, and in 1846
the Sioux burned the villages.[7] Eliza's mention of a "stockade fort" probably referred to a blockhouse built by the U.S. government to protect the
Pawnee Mission located about a mile from the Pawnee village on Plum
Creek.[8] The mission was established in 1834 by a Presbyterian, John
Dunbar, near Plum Creek's confluence with the Loup Fork. It was described by earlier travelers as consisting of two double log houses and six
smaller structures, with pig pens, fenced fields, and fruit trees. The Sioux
raid in 1846 forced Dunbar to abandon the mission and retire to Bellevue
on the Missouri River.[9]

On May 26, after having traveled some thirty-two miles from the
ferry, the McAuleys forded the Loup River at or near the Lower Ford. In
the afternoon of the next day, the party came to and camped in "sand
hills."

Continuing on and leaving the sand hills, they next negotiated a
marshy area where their "wagons would sink to the hub." This most likely
was Prairie Slough Creek, a few miles north of today's Chapman, Nebraska.
That evening the McAuleys camped near Wood River, which they crossed
the following day at a site located about two miles south of present-day
Alda, Nebraska.[10]

By May 31, they were within a few miles of Elm Creek. That evening
Eliza related that they "all gathered in Ezra's [Meeker] tent . . . and had a
merry time." The Meekers and the McAuleys, who all were from Iowa,
would often travel close together until July 17, at which time the Meekers
continued on ahead, leaving Ezra's partner, William Buck, and the McAuleys
behind to build a section of road in the Bear River country.

On June 1, Eliza McAuley recorded that, although they had heard
about much sickness on the Platte River's south side trail, they encountered the first fresh grave they had seen since leaving the Missouri River.
The following evening, June 2, a day or so beyond Elm Creek, Eliza's party
was badly battered when a terrific "storm broke in all its fury. . . . When I
awoke the bed was nearly floating, and two of the boys were trying to hold
the tent up." They finally gave up "and all took to the wagons, which were
anchored to stakes driven in the ground." The next morning, all of the
tents and one wagon were blown over. After a late start, Eliza recorded that
they saw a number of graves that day.[11]

Many diarists recorded the June 2 storm striking between the Loup and Platte rivers. Inasmuch as Mary Ann and Willis rarely gave precise dates as to when events occurred, this storm is useful in helping establish a time frame for a number of incidents in the Boatman story, as will be related shortly.

The Clifton Read family also chose to follow along the north side of the Loup River for over thirty miles before crossing, probably at or near the Lower Ford.[12] Prominent in Martha Read's remarks, and less evident in those of Eliza McAuley's, are references to numerous fresh graves along the way and reports of spreading cholera among the emigrants during this part of the journey. The Reads arrived at the Loup River on May 29, only five days behind the McAuleys. Apparently, during that short period of time the disease had fully broken out in the Loup-Platte area. The Reads had passed three fresh graves by the time they reached Looking Glass Creek.

On June 1, Martha noted that they had traveled twenty miles to the Cedar River and "saw the remains of two large Indian towns and the embankment where the Soos and Pawnees had a fight and the Soos drove the Pawnees out and burned their town."[13] A major Pawnee village some one-half mile in length and consisting of at least 175 houses once occupied an area near the mouth of the Cedar River.[14]

The Reads forded the Loup River on June 2 and headed toward the Platte. They saw four graves of persons from Illinois, and "passed another man that was taken with cholera today."[15]

The Reads also suffered through the June 2 storm, with its severe nighttime thundershowers. By the evening of June 4, they were near the Wood River and Martha noted three more graves and the deaths of two more people, all believed to be due to cholera. As they moved on, the situation grew worse. On June 7, they passed eleven graves and stopped that "morning to bury one women out of our company. She had Diarrhea." A bark coffin was constructed and a hymn sung, "so that she was buried very decent."

By June 9, they had passed Elm Creek and Martha recorded seeing twenty more graves and two dead persons yet to be buried.

The upper crossing of the Loup River, about fifty miles upstream from the ferry, was deemed the safest by some.[16] Although a rather shallow ford, it nevertheless had a quicksand bottom and teams had to move rapidly across. The Enoch W. Conyers group chose to take this route.[17] On May 28, they traveled along the north side of the Loup River, crossing Looking Glass Creek and Beaver Creek before arriving at Plum Creek. Here they found "the charred remains of a [Pawnee] mission house, burned by some Indians, perhaps three or four weeks before."

The following day, the Conyers party came to the Cedar River. After crossing, they continued some eighteen miles before arriving at the upper Loup ford at 7:30 in the evening. By 9:30 P.M., they had completed the crossing, although "obliged to keep our oxen in a fast walk to prevent the wagon from sinking in the quicksand." While at the ford, they observed an accident that, fortunately, proved not to be serious. Because of a sharp curve before leaving the water, "one wagon just ahead of us tipped over just at the edge of the water." Inside was a woman with a small baby. Bystanders rescued them immediately and "neither was hurt very badly."[18]

After resting on Sunday May 30, they set out the next day south to Prairie Creek. Conyers recorded that the road was "very heavy and sandy." This would have been the sand hills area mentioned by many travelers.

By June 2, the Conyers party had crossed the Wood River and was camped along the Platte River near Elm Creek. That evening, Conyers wrote, "it rained very hard," another reference to the June 2 storm. The following day, Conyers noted that at least three people in their party were sick. He thought it was due to water they took from a well dug the evening before. A day or so later and somewhere beyond Elm Creek, one of those taken ill died.[19]

From the above four accounts, especially that of Martha Read, it is apparent that by late May 1852, a dreadful cholera outbreak had made its appearance along the Loup and Platte trails. Of all the adversities encountered by emigrants on the long journey west, disease outweighed all other obstacles. Oregon Trail historian John D. Unruh Jr. estimates that nine out of ten deaths were due to disease.[20] Of all the maladies that befell emigrants, such as measles, smallpox, mumps, mountain fever, and other ailments, the most feared and frequently fatal was cholera. It had struck with great severity along the Platte River in the late 1840s and continued into the early 1850s, particularly in 1852.

The emigrants actually classified cholera as several ailments. If an afflicted person did not die, the illness often was referred to as diarrhea, cholera morbus, or as some other non-lethal version. But, if death ensued, it was termed Asiatic cholera. The first sign of the illness was diarrhea. Other symptoms included a sore throat, and stomach and leg cramps. Vomiting usually came last and was the most devastating, frequently proving fatal. Some of those afflicted lingered for days, but most were stricken suddenly and died quickly, sometimes within hours, and always after great pain. Remedies prescribed in those days included laudanum (a derivative of opium), together with stimulants such as pepper, camphor, ammonia, or peppermint.[21]

The disease is caused by the bacterium *Vibrio cholera* and can be spread only by human contamination, not by rodents or fleas.[22] It is believed that unsanitary ships from the Orient brought cholera to New Orleans. It then spread up the Missouri River Valley aboard steamboats, and then westward to the overland trails via the various jumping-off towns.[23] As can well be imagined, the presence of thousands of emigrants on both sides of the Platte River made for unsanitary camp sites and conditions. Much of the domestic water, particularly from shallow wells and other surface sources, soon became polluted with the disease-causing organism.

On the north side of the Platte, cholera was most prevalent from the Loup River west to Fort Laramie. Numerous accounts in addition to those referenced here record frequent deaths and fresh graves lining the trails, sometimes in rows of fifty or more. Occasionally entire families succumbed.[24] Sometimes, children seemingly had immunity to the disease and were left orphaned. Large trains broke up; those families with sick members often were compelled to stay behind, while the remainder of the train hurriedly pressed on in an attempt to escape. Many buried the dead inadequately, either in too shallow of graves or in burials unprotected from digging wolves and other animals. Many graves were left unmarked for fear, unnecessarily, of looting by Indians.[25]

Ezra Meeker presented the astounding estimate of there being six fresh graves to the mile over a 400-mile section of the trail from the Loup River to the Laramie River.[26] He further pointed out that this observation only was for the north side of the Platte. Meeker suggested that as many as 5,000 deaths may have occurred on the plains in 1852.

Mary Ann's story continues with a graphic description of these times. Although the Boatmans did not specifically indicate where and how they had crossed the Loup River, Mary Ann's reference to the "Sand Hill Plain" provides the clue as to where they were—in the hilly and sandy region between the Loup River fords and the Prairie Creek crossing.

Peace and good will, one toward the other, all obeying the regular orders of the captain, [but] as everything in this life has to have a change, so it came to our lot. We had come to a country which our guide book gave the name Sand Hill Plain. As near as I can describe . . . it was a comparatively level country with mounds varying in size from a good sized hay stack to that of a common haycock that every boy and girl who has been reared on a farm knows how to make. There were sloughs and small outlets from them that would mire a cow, brut, or horse down. Grass was good, water in abundance, [and] wood plentiful as willow brush grew on the outlet of the swampy land. Mosquitoes! Oh, they came in clouds so thick at night that one had to close their mouth to keep from having it filled with mosquitoes instead of grub. The men folk . . . on guard built fires to make smoke for the cattle to stand by, for all that, they stampeded and came running into camp. We thought for awhile that all the tents would be tramped to the ground and the ones occupying them would be tramped to death. And too, the wolves howling on every side. But as kind providence guided us that night, no casualty happened to our people or stock at that time. So we traveled on for two or three days in about the same routine of scenery and circumstances with the exception of two things. . . . one was that the Indians had all disappeared. For some days not one had put in his appearance. . . . the other was the air at night seemed to be laden with unwholesome odor. Not knowing the cause of either, supposed the Indians had gone to some more favorable locality for hunting and fishing. We camped one evening, if my memory serves me right, it was the 4th of June [this date may be in error; about May 31 is more likely[27]]. One of the old captain's sons had been sent on ahead to select a camping place for the night, as that had been customary from the . . . start for some one to go on to look out a suitable location for camp. This chore usually fell to the son of the old captain, a youth about 16 year of age. . . . he had a horse to ride and no team to drive as the hired men did that work. The camping place was perfect, wood, water, grass in abundance. About 4 o'clock we called a halt.

The day had been an ideal one. Nowhere on the globe could it have been better. The sun had warmed the atmosphere to a gentle heat while the low soft wind caught up the delicate perfume of the wild flowers of every hue, nodding their lovely feathered crests, seemingly beckoning us on. Looking in any direction you chose there was

the handy work of the Creator. One would almost come to the conclusion that sorrow had forever [been] banished from such a lovely
spot on God's green earth. But no—that enemy called death, who
has no set time to make his appearance, was hovering near with a
sickle in hand seeking whom he might devour.

[Coming to] . . . a halt . . . the wagons [were placed] in a circle
to form a corral, so that if any of the oxen should become unruly . . .
they may be corralled and yoked. . . . Everyone was . . . busy, some
unyoking the team and some gathering wood. The women folks got
out the cooking utensils, in preparation for the evening meal. In
almost one breath a dozen voices cried out, "Boys, there is a herd of
elk!"[28] A rush [was] made for the guns, but Mr. Elk did not wish to
have his steak fried and his bones boiled for a lot of hungry emigrants, so he soon carried his elkship far out of reach of the rifle
shot. The herd consisted of only three large ones, but that was sufficient to excite the whole population of our train, as we were all getting quite hungry for fresh meat. . . . We had not been able to get
anything except our supplies that we had on hand.

After a frugal meal was served throughout the various divisions
of our camp, the evening was spent in different ways. We girls, as we
were termed, roved around the plain gathering wild flowers and seeing what some little mounds could have been made for and . . . what
could have made them. [We came] near one six or eight feet high
with a hole near the top. Being anxious to make some new discovery,
we at once began to contrive some plan to reach the cavity in the
side. After considering the subject, it was decided that one of the
party should climb up and investigate the strange phenomenon. We
piled a few sod one on the other sufficiently high. I being the tallest
of the three, it was decided I should make the ascent. Being willing
to have the honor of a new discovery I accepted the proposition. I
mounted the pile of sod with the aid of the two girls [and] managed
to reach the cavity. Oh horror! Horrible was the sight and scent. The
mound was a natural one, the Indians had made an excavation in the
mound to bury their dead, if one could call it bury. From the looks
they had been shoved in just any way to get them in. I made the
decent much faster than the ascent. The mound was full of dead
Indian's bones and hair. I presume the wolves had scratched the earth
off of them. At any rate, I was satisfied [and] had no [interest in]
making any more discoveries.

Eliza Ann McAuley also mentions seeing Indian burials. On May 20,
her third day out from the Missouri River, she recorded:

Today we passed some Indian burial grounds, a large one with a small
one on each side. The large one had been dug into, so that we could

see the skeleton in a sitting posture. At two o'clock we came to the Elk Horn River.[29]

It would appear from Mary Ann's account that the Boatmans were farther along on the route than the McAuleys—probably beyond the Loup River—when Mary Ann and her friends made their gruesome discovery.

> We had strolled perhaps a half or three quarters of a mile from camp. When we returned the men, who had driven the stock to pasture, had all returned [except] those whose turn it was to stand guard. They too had passed several such looking mounds and on looking in had made similar discoveries. . . . One man, who had ridden on a mile or two ahead in search of the Walker family [little Addie's parents], returned saying he had passed quite a number of graves . . . [made] by the emigrants that had gone on before us. [Also], the train of emigrants that he had come to inquire about the Walker family, told of the suffering of the emigrants [ahead] as they were dying from that dreadful disease cholera; that [it] had been the cause of the disappearance of the Indians from that section of country. They were dying in such large numbers that they were not very particular how they disposed of the dead so [long as] the living got out. . . .
>
> The sun was sinking low in the western horizon. The camp fire smoldering to ashes. There was something out of customary habit at

A sketch of an emigrant ferry crossing on the Elkhorn River, ca. 1854. *Nebraska State Historical Society, RG3351-17*

the Captain's tent. He had not, at any time, omitted the evening devotions as he was very zealous. If circumstances would permit he would read a chapter from the Bible and he and his pious wife would sing a hymn, then offer up a prayer. One and all could join in if they wished to. If the evening was stormy or darkness prevailed . . . he would only have family prayers. Everyone could attend the evening service if they wished to, but [the] few [that did] at the start, quit. A few of the leading men who had been deacons or class leaders in their churches at home would come in ear shot, raise their hats, seemingly very devoted. But alas, it was only a short time until it was plainly visible that they had left all their religion, if they ever had any, at home locked up in the church book, that is judging from the way that they conducted themselves on the journey. At the time that they were most needed, they forgot all else but [them]selves.

As I have said, something was wrong [at Deacon Turner's tent]. On investigating the cause we soon learned that the old Captain was in great pain, although sitting on his chair and moaning aloud. His faithful wife and children [were] doing all that could be done for him in a place like that, his feet in hot water and hot clothes applied to the painful part. At first [his opinion] was that the trouble was an attack of cholera morbus, but in a few hours the case developed in[to] incurable cholera. Everything was done that was in human power. . . . Medicine came . . . from almost every tent. There was no lack [of] help.

. . . The night passed and the morning [presumably, June 1] broke [with a] golden light on the eastern horizon. The landscape [was] one aspect of beauty; each blade of grass covered with dew-drops, the sun transforming them into a seemingly . . . paradise bedecked with diamonds. The old Captain was unconscious. Those [in] attendance had given up all hope of life. The news spread like wildfire through camp that cholera had made its appearance. . . . At nine o'clock the reverend old gentleman expired. All that could be done to prolong his life had been done. Now came the last act that human hands could accomplish, to prepare and bury the body. What to be done; no coffin, no clergyman to perform funeral services. No one thought he could be laid to rest without some kind of a coffin. [It] must be made. As one of his wagons and ours had double floors or bottoms in them, it was decided to take the [one] out of his wagon and make a rough coffin. The wagon was unloaded and the bottom taken out. The men . . . handy with saw and hammer soon constructed a rough coffin. A grave was dug. The body dressed and placed in the box with as much solemnity as tho the funeral service had been conducted by some . . . clergymen of today.

Willis's description of this event is extremely brief:

Everything moved on nicely till our leader, Mr. Turner, was taken very sick one night and died the next day. We buried him on the sandy ridges between the Elkhorn and Platte rivers. We moved on with heavy hearts, reluctant to leave one whom all had learned to love and respect.

Willis could have been more precise by locating the Reverend's internment beyond the Loup River, rather than the Elkhorn River. There are no sand hills or ridges in the Elkhorn River vicinity. Furthermore, by June 1, the party should have been far beyond the Elkhorn. Since Mary Ann mentioned that they were in a "Sand Hill Plain," it seems likely that Deacon Turner was buried somewhere between the upper fords of the Loup River and the Prairie Creek crossing.[30]

In the afternoon all of the people of the train gathered around [the] grave to pay their last regards to one of its highly respected officers. As soon as the body was lowered and covered some of the families began to get ready to move on, and in less than an hour were on the move. Some moved on two or three miles and waited for those who lingered longer. Late in the afternoon the whole caravan moved on and at sunset came up with the other part of the train that had camped to wait for those that lingered behind. Among those that went on were the two families that I have made mention of so often—the Buck and Lain families that little Addie traveled with [Mary Ann hasn't mentioned the Lain family until now]. They did not stop with the train at all [but] went on. That was the last we ever saw of them. In a month after, I was walking, looking, and reading the names written on the head boards of the graves that lined the roadside at old camping places. At one of the grave yards, as we termed them, I saw Mr. William Buck['s] name written on a board at the head of a grave. We never saw nor heard of them any more. Whether they all died and left their bones to bleach on the plains, we never knew and never will.

At camp that evening all was sad.[31] By no ways was anybody at ease. My brother William was sick. My husband and his brother and myself worked with him all night; kept hot cloths rang out of hot water on the affected parts. At one time during the night we thought his time had come to leave us for ever. No, we thought we could not spare him. My kind husband so tenderly lifted him up in his arms while his dear brother and I rubbed his cold limbs with hot cloths. On toward morning [presumably, June 2] he spoke and said he felt much better. We, that is my husband, his brother and myself, thought it best to lay by for a day or two but all the rest of the company said

no. That it would be better to try and get out of the cholera stricken
district. So it was decided to go on. William said he thought it best
to move on as he felt so much better. At an early hour all was ready
to go. My brother was fix[ed] as comfortable as could be under the
circumstances, . . . the bed being placed as near the center of the
wagon as could be. I was detail[ed] nurse, sitting by his side, ready
to administer to any desired wish that he might make known; giving
him medicine every half hour. At camping time he was decidedly
better. All felt encouraged, hoping the fatality had passed. That night
camp was made on the bank of a small stream of water. If I remember correct the name was Little Sandy.[32] At any rate its banks were
sand and shoe mouth deep at the shallowest places. There was plenty
of wood and water. Fires [were] kindled, tents set, cattle unyoked
and brother better. Everybody felt encouraged. But alas, our cup of
sorrow was not full. A little son of John Turner [Jr.], a grandson of
the old gentleman that was buried two days before,[33] was stricken
in the night with the dreaded disease. To add more inconvenience to
those who had the care of the sick, a hard rain came down in sheets,
accompanied with wind that almost took on the force of a hurri-
cane. [It] blew all the tents down, extinguished all lights and fire,
uprooted small trees along the bank of the creek. [We] expected every moment to have the wagons lifted off the earth and carried, no
telling where. As the storm was of short duration, those occupying
their temporary houses soon succeeded in crawling out from beneath the ruins. With the aid of match[es] and tallow candle[s] lighted
and placed in tin lantern[s], soon the canvas houses [were] repaired
and [everybody was] soon resting their tired bodies in damp bed[s]
on cold and wet sand.

Several other diarists, as previously discussed, reported the storm on
the evening of the June 2—the only storm of this severity to occur in early
June. Assuming that this is the same storm that Mary Ann describes, it
appears that the Turner boy took sick on the evening of June 2. This confirmed date also makes it possible to place reasonably accurate dates on
events recorded by Mary Ann for several preceding and following days.[34]

The Turner family was doing all that loving parents could to alleviate their dear little boy's suffering, but to no avail. He grew rapidly
worse as the sun was pushing up her golden circle in the eastern
horizon, seemingly gladdening earth and sky with its emitting rays.
The guards came in. The storm had been so severe and the night so
dark that they did not attempt to try to come in at midnight for
reinstatement, saying the wind blew with such force that they were

compelled to lie flat on the ground and hold to tufts of grass to keep
from being blown away.

Now death had visited our moving village again; the sick boy
has paid the debt that all living must pay sooner or later. Oh, the
agonizing cry of that mother has never left my memory. But little
did she think that her sorrow would be replenished two fold greater
in a few days. The dear little one must be put away. There must be
some kind of a coffin made. What will it be of? Our boys had a
double bottom in their wagon [but] we thought it had better be
saved in case some grown person might need be buried. There was a
feed box attached to our wagon and one to the wagon of the Turner
family, so it was decided to take the two feed boxes and construct
a rude coffin. While preparations were being made to bury the
child . . . others who were not engaged in that work were busy getting ready to move on. About 10 o'clock [morning of June 3, or
possibly June 4; see Coon statement below] the poor little boy [was]
laid to rest in a lonely wilderness. Oh, it was so hard to leave him.
He had been so good and kind to his little sisters.

Polly Coon recorded on June 4, three miles east of the Wood River
crossing, "A boy died today in a camp near us of diareah."[35] Could this
have been the Turner child? If so, this would have placed the Boatman-
Turner-Scott train within three miles of the Wood River crossing on June
4. Polly further stated on June 5 that at the Wood River ford: "among the
camps on this creek there was much sickness & 5 had died since yesterday."[36]

Some of the people in the train . . . were becoming dissatisfied and
wanted to be on the go, sick or well. Of course it seemed almost
inhuman to haul a dying person in a heavy ox-wagon over rough
roads. After the little boy was laid to rest the heads of the different
families talked the matter over and decided to move on all together.
So the moveable village was soon in motion, traveling on until late,
then camping for the night, [following] about the same routine of
former camping times. Guards were chosen to look after the cattle
and some to guard the camp. It was becoming more evident that
some of the people were getting dissatisfied and wanted to hurry on,
which would have been a proper thing to do. But how could it be
done[?] Some [were] sick and others threatened with the dreaded
disease. And too, our party was getting small as some had gone on
and others sick. It was not considered safe to travel in small company as we were in a country infested with savage Indians. There
was a man by the name of Skile[s] who had hired Mr. [William]

Scott to transport his family from Springfield, Illinois to Portland, Oregon. His family consisted of himself, wife, baby, mother, and sister. Mr. Scott had furnished him with one wagon and one yoke of steers. He seemed the most determined to go on and leave the train than any other man in the company. All went as well as could be expected; no one felt at ease, [and] startled at every sound, not knowing what might happen to the men out with the stock, and too, the camp was liable to be attacked by Indians or some other enemy.

The night pass[ed] in quietude with the exception of, now and then, the howl and barking of wolves that infested the whole plain. On camping that evening we saw one large black wolf come trotting along near camp. There were a half dozen shots fired at him [but] he was to[o] smart to be caught napping and carried his hide and tallow out of rifle range.

All seemed in better spirits as brother was convalescing and all in camp appeared to be in good health. But to our surprise in the morning, an investigation proved with[out] a doubt that old lady Skiles was sick. But her son was determined to move on. So, as soon as possible all were on the go. But [the] poor old lady did not trouble them very long. When we called a halt for noon she had breathed her last breath. Now there was another body to put away and this necessitated another box to fill the place of a coffin. Then came the last resort, the upper floor of our wagon had to be taken out to make the box. Perhaps you do not understand about the upper floor of a wagon. There was a bottom in the wagon bed and one a foot and a half above it. Under this upper one was placed the provisions so they would not be disturbed while climbing in and out of the wagon and sleeping in it. It was taken out and a rough coffin made and the old lady buried as quickly as possible.

The order was to hitch up and move on a ways for a camping place for night. Mr. Skiles taking the lead, we traveled until almost dark when we came to a locality were water and wood could be obtained, expecting every moment to come up where Mr. Skiles and family were camped, but no. Next morning, started early expecting to come up with them, but never saw or heard from them from that [time] to this. [We] never knew what become of them. Mr. Scott thought when Skiles came to the forks of the Oregon and California road . . . he went to California, but no one knows. They may have been murdered by Indians or Mormons or all died among strangers. Mr. Scott never heard from his team. On some occasions whole families died of Cholera, [and] frequently you [would] see children left with[out] parents.

It was late before supper was over. Traveling so late made it inconvenient to cook by camp fire. We women folks hurried up as fast as we could [and] soon had a snack ready for the men. In a very short time the guards were off with the cattle. When the guards came in at midnight to change off guards, Mr. John Turner, father of the little boy who died a few days before, was sick and could not fill his place as guard [and] someone else went instead. He gradually grew worse every hour. His wife and mother, in fact everybody, was trying to do something to alleviate his suffering, but to no avail. At day break it was plainly notable to all that his time on earth was short. This was more than Mr. Scott and the rest of the company could stand, as none of their folks had been sick. [They] were determined that they should not contract the disease from any of our sick, so they all yoked up their teams and were soon on the road. That left the Turners and ourselves alone. We could not think of leaving Turner's folks and John Turner dying. We had started with them from Illinois and they were old acquaintance of my parents. W[h]y no, not for one moment would we think of doing such a thing as leaving them. About Ten o'clock John Turner bid his folks a last farewell, advising them to turn back and try to get home. His wife's father was with them [and] he was an old man. Our men folks and Turner's hired men nailed up a rough coffin and in the afternoon got Turner buried.

In a summary of the deaths in the Turner family, Willis reveals the location of their group at the time of the burial of John Turner Jr.

In a few days one of the Turner's children died and before we reached the Platte River another one was sick and died a day or two after. About the same time the father was taken sick and died on the Platte and was buried at Elm Creek.

Although Mary Ann only mentions the death of one Turner child, according to Willis a second child also died. However, in respect to the first son, if he became ill on the night of the June 2 storm, then, according to Mary Ann's account of the following days, the father, John Turner, died on about June 6 or 7.

They [the Turners] all talked the matter over and came to the conclusion [that] the best thing they could do would be to retrace their steps homeward. So that was decided by all but one man by the name of Warner, a man of about 40 years of age, who had crossed the plains in 46 to Oregon, [and] had gone back to Illinois to visit his old home in the fall of '51. On hearing of the Turners making

preparations to emigrate to Oregon, he [had] hired [on] to the old
Mr. Turner [the Deacon] to drive one of his teams. In fact, I think
he was the instigator of the move of the whole Turner family. His
people lived in their neighborhood and he told such glowing accounts of the far western country that it excited the Turners into
action. They sold their farms and made preparation to move to Oregon where they could get donation claims of 160 acres apiece. They,
like everybody, thought all one had to do was to take up a claim and
go to plowing. . . . No one was expected to get sick and die [and] that
all would be in our favor. As for our party, no one persuaded us to
start. My brother William had made preparation to go to California
with a party, [but] as time drew near for them to start, the two men
that were in with him backed out. So my husband and his brother
John concluded it would be a good chance for them to go in company with him. So the matter was talked over and all decided to go
to Oregon and join the Turner train.

  Now . . . back to the scene of our parting with the Turners. . . .
John Turner had been buried with all the solemnity and respect that
a people in like circumstance could bestow. . . . Mr. Warner [of whom]
I have made mention . . . not wishing to turn back, entered into
negotiation with the Boatman boys and Richardson to haul his bedding and provisions. He was to take his turn on guard at night. The
boys thought it best to buy some of their [the Turner's] provisions in
case ours should run short. We did not start with a spade, so we
wanted to buy the one the Turners had, but they said some of them
might die on the way home and then they might need it. Late in the
afternoon both they and we folks concluded it better to move on
from the camp as cholera was such a contagious disease. Now come
the parting with [those] whom we would never meet again in this
life.

The Turners were by no means the only family that decided to turn back
before reaching Oregon. Unruh, in a comprehensive commentary on eastbound travelers, describes two categories—"turnarounds" or "gobacks" such
as the Turners, who for some reason returned eastward before reaching
their destination, and a second group, the eastbound "overlanders," returning after having reached California or Oregon in previous years. Unruh
estimates that in 1852 at least 1,000 westbound travelers turned around
before reaching either California or Oregon.[37]

  Although there were many reasons for abandoning the westward trek,
the most common cause was death in a party. In 1852, with cholera raging

in the Platte River Valley, so many husbands died that a number of families were compelled to turn around with wives driving the teams. Ezra Meeker recalled a train of eleven wagons returning that year with "not a man left in the entire train;—all died, . . . and the women were returning alone."[38] Others returned because Indians had stolen equipment and especially livestock. Some just plain gave up because they could not cope with the adverse conditions.

In most cases, the eastbound overlanders from either California or Oregon were veterans of the westward journey and thus were experienced travelers on the plains. Their reasons for making the return trip usually were for business purposes or to bring family members back to Oregon. This provided further inspiration to the newer westering travelers to go on and seek a new life on the Pacific. Eastbound overlanders also provided important information about trail conditions ahead. And, they took the emigrants' letters back to the United States. In this manner, thousands of notes and messages were sent to families and friends left behind.

Eastbound "turnarounds," like the Turners, had to deal with their own peculiar problems. By the time they decided to return, it usually was well into summer when vast numbers of emigrant livestock already had devoured most of the season's grass, making forage difficult to find. Furthermore, most "turnarounds" still were relatively inexperienced travelers and many began the return trip alone or in small groups, without the protection of being in larger trains. However, many were fortunate enough to team up with other "gobacks" or experienced overlanders from California or Oregon, who provided added security and experience.[39]

Notes

1. The date might have been about May 28 or 29. According to other diaries, it took five or six days to travel some eighty miles from the Missouri River to the Loup Fork.
2. It is ironic, but apparently coincidental, that two people with the name William Buck should appear in the May 1852 chronicles. However, Ezra Meeker's partner, William Buck, was a bachelor.
3. Polly Coon, "Journal of a Journey over the Rocky Mountains," in *Covered Wagon Women: Diaries and Letters from the Western Trails*, 1852, vol. 5, edited and compiled by Kenneth L. Holmes and David C. Duniway (Glendale, California: Arthur H. Clark, 1986), 187–89.
4. Eliza Ann McAuley, "Iowa to the 'Land of Gold,'" in *Covered Wagon Women: Diaries and Letters from the Western Trails*, 1852, vol. 4, edited and compiled by Kenneth L. Holmes (Glendale, California: Arthur H. Clark, 1985), 38.
5. Stanley B. Kimball, editor, *The Latter-Day Saints' Emigrants' Guide: Being a Table of Distances, Showing all the Springs, Creeks, River, Hills, Mountains, Camping Places, and*

all other Notable Places, from Council Bluffs to the Valley of the Great Salt Lake, by W. Clayton (St. Louis, Missouri: Patrice Press, 1983), 45.

6. McAuley, 49–52.
7. Will Bagley, editor, "The Pioneer Camp of the Saints: The 1846 and 1847 Mormon Trail Journals of Thomas Bullock," in *Kingdom in the West: The Mormon American Frontier*, vol. 1 (Spokane, Washington: Arthur H. Clark, 1997), 128.
8. Dorothy Dustin and Charles Martin, unpublished trail guide along the Loup River to Wood River, 1944, 6, supplied by Helen Sundell.
9. Bagley, 128–29.
10. Kimball, 49.
11. McAuley, 51–52.
12. Martha S. Read, "A History of Our Journey," in *Covered Wagon Women: Diaries and Letters from the Western Trails*, 1852, vol. 5, edited and compiled by Kenneth L. Holmes and David C. Duniway (Glendale, California: Arthur H. Clark, 1986), 220–23.
13. Ibid., 221.
14. Bagley, 129, 131.
15. Read, 221.
16. Kimball, 45.
17. Enoch W. Conyers, "The Diary of E.W. Conyers, a Pioneer of 1852," in *Transactions of the Thirty-third Annual Reunion of the Oregon Pioneer Association* (Portland, Oregon, 1905), 438.
18. Ibid., 438–39.
19. Ibid., 439–40.
20. John D. Unruh Jr., *The Plains Across: The Overland Emigrants and the Trans-Mississippi West, 1840–60*, paperback edition (Urbana, Chicago, and London: University of Illinois Press, 1982), 34.
21. Merrill J. Mattes, *The Great Platte River Road: The Covered Wagon Mainline Via Fort Kearny to Fort Laramie*, Nebraska State Historical Society, vol. 25 (1969), 864; and Peter D. Olich, "Treading the Elephant's Tail: Medical Problems on the Overland Trails," in *Overland Journal* vol. 6, no. 1 (1988), 26–27; published by the Oregon-California Trails Association, Independence, Missouri.
22. Herbert C. Milikien, "Dead of the Bloody Flux, Cholera Stalks the Emigrant Trail," in *Overland Journal*, vol. 14, no. 3 (1996), 4–5; published by the Oregon-California Trails Association, Independence, Missouri.
23. Mattes, 83–84.
24. Ezra Meeker, *Personal Experiences on the Oregon Trail: The Tragedy of Leschi*, fifth reprint (Seattle, Washington: Meeker, 1912), 27–29.
25. Mattes, 85.
26. Meeker, 28.
27. If the Boatmans had left the Missouri on May 24, they could have reached the sandy ridges just beyond the upper Loup River ford about May 31. This estimate is based on eight days of travel and at a rate of about seventeen miles per day. It is unknown if they rested on Sunday. Considering that travel conditions were probably quite good in this area, this would have been a reasonable pace, particularly since the Boatmans started with fresh teams.
28. On this day they crossed Elk Creek, which indeed suggests that they were in elk country.
29. McAuley, 48.
30. If Turner's final resting place is in these rolling "sandy hills," it leads one to speculate if his grave or that of other emigrants might be included in a small, obscure, and

unkempt cemetery in the northeast corner of Section 33, T14N, R8W. According to available information, this lonely graveyard sits immediately adjacent to the trail between the Upper Loup River Ford and the Platte River, and about a mile north of the Prairie Slough crossing (Dorothy Dustin and Charles Martin, unpublished trail guide, Loup River to Wood River, 1944). Although the author, on a visit to this quaint cemetery, did not find marked graves that were old enough to be those of emigrants, it does seem more than coincidental that this graveyard is situated next to the trail, and miles away from any town of today. Perhaps, because Turner or other emigrants might have been buried here, this site eventually became regarded as a community burial ground for later settlers in this locality. Over time, the older, poorly marked, and largely unattended emigrant graves might have become obscure and memory of them was lost. Although this is conjecture, it is fascinating to ponder. It is of interest to note that many other cemeteries lie in close proximity to the Oregon Trail. It seems plausible that some of these may have originated around clusters of emigrant graves.

31. They could have been camping at or near the Prairie Creek Crossing.
32. The identity of this stream has not been determined. However, a fair day's travel from Prairie Creek would have placed them somewhere just west of today's Grand Island, Nebraska.
33. Although Deacon Turner took sick two days before, he did not die until the following morning.
34. Thus, according to Mary Ann's account of the order of events, it can be presumed that Deacon Turner took sick on May 31 and died June 1. The known death of Mary Ann's brother, on June 10, also assists in establishing dates and locations pertaining to the Boatmans during this period.
35. Coon, 189.
36. Ibid.
37. Unruh, 86–94.
38. Meeker, 31.
39. Unruh, 85–96.

Chimney Rock with an old cemetery in the foreground. *W.W. Rau*

Chapter Four

Platte River Valley

Then came the hardest thing that I ever had to do in my life; that was to bury one that was so near and dear to us. . . . I took some of the side boards off my wagon box and made a box, rolled him up in a feather bed and gave him as good a burial as I could under the circumstances. —Willis Boatman

F ROM ELM CREEK, the Boatmans continued their westward trek along the north side of the Platte and the North Platte, eventually reaching Fort Laramie in today's eastern Wyoming. On the average, it took emigrants about seventeen days to cover this distance. Because Mary Ann or Willis seldom mention landmarks, it only can be estimated, based on expected day-by-day traveling distances, where events occurred.

For some considerable distance, the "north-siders" traveled over the rather flat expanse of the broad Platte River Valley, where most diarists mention little regarding the scenery. Their comments were confined largely to the road conditions. They describe sandy or muddy terrain, swamp lands, and crossing the Platte's various tributaries. Weather, too, was a common subject. They recorded rain, storms, or wind, and the hot, dry, or sultry times. The vegetation intrigued some, particularly when wild flowers were blooming in early summer.

Martha Read, while near the Ancient Bluff Ruins, wrote: "we find numerous kinds of flowers. A great many of them resemble our tame flowers such as: fox glove, lark spur, rose moss, China oyster, wax flower, and in some places the ground is covered with prickly pear with a beautiful large yellow bloom on them."[1]

The attractiveness of the prickly pear was offset by the hazard its spiny needles caused for those stepping on the tenacious cactus. Many, of course, also noted the numerous fresh graves and the sicknesses that afflicted the 1852 travelers along the Platte.

In places, sand dunes made travel difficult, particularly for the oxen. A mile or so trace of such road is preserved today about a mile north of Sutherland, Nebraska. Many north-siders mention a "Lone Tree," which actually was the last of three such trees that were noted along the north side of the Platte. It was located some 150 miles west of Elm Creek and a couple of miles east of today's Lewellen, Nebraska. Apparently, it could be viewed from a considerable distance.

The Oregon-bound Reverend John McAllister, who left Louisiana, Missouri, on April 13, 1852, wrote, "lone tree . . . has its top branches cut off . . . is 2½ feet at the butt in diameter and 12 feet high." However, he further stated, "this tree may be consumed by the emigrants in a short time."[2]

Many north-side travelers also mentioned seeing cedar bluffs and Ash Hollow on the opposite side of the North Platte. Ash Hollow was a major stopover point for south-side travelers.

As the emigrants continued to move up the North Platte, the flat lands gave way to rolling hills. In western Nebraska, north-side travelers came upon the picturesque Ancient Bluff Ruins, which were the first of a series of great, colorful rock outcrops encountered along this part of the trail. On June 11, Eliza Ann McAuley described the formation: "a picturesque mass of rocks resembling castles and fortifications in ruins. Here a crumbley turret, there a bastion, and in other places portions of a wall, with portholes, making the illusion complete."[3]

At about the same time, north-siders got their first glimpse of the isolated erosional remnants of Courthouse Rock and Jailhouse Rock on the south side. Then, in a short distance, Chimney Rock came into view, also on the south side of the river. On July 3, 1852, Cecelia Adams wrote this regarding what is perhaps the most celebrated monolith in the valley.

> Today we come to the river opposite Chimney Rock which has been visible most of the way for the last 35 miles It is said to be 3 miles from the opposite side of the river but on these level prairies we cannot judge much of distances by the eye It does not appear more than a half a mile It consists of a large square column of clay and sand mixed together with a base of conical form apparently composed of sand, round base cone. and appears as if the column had been set up and the sand heaped round it to sustain it.[4]

Finally, Scotts Bluff, the largest of the south-side rock masses, came into view across the North Platte. It was an amazing sight to travelers, and nearly all diarists mention it. Particularly descriptive is the observation by Mariett Foster Cummings from Plainfield, Illinois, who was traveling with her husband William (no children) to California.

> Made our noon halt opposite Scott's Bluff, altogether the most symmetrical in form and the most stupendous in size of any we have yet seen. One of them is close in its resemblance to the dome of the capitol at Washington.
>
> There is a pass through that is guarded on one side by Sugar Loaf Rock, on the other by one that resembles a square house with an observatory. . . . Away up on the top is a green spot of earth and cedar trees are clinging to its rocky sides and covering its lofty crest.[5]

The change in scenery was a welcome sight to the westward travelers, after passing over nearly level, rather featureless terrain for hundreds of miles. For many, viewing the massive rock outcrops led them to speculate and wonder as to how these isolated splendors may have been formed.

Modern geologists have revealed that these monoliths are erosional remnants of a series of water-lain and windblown sedimentary deposits. The source of these deposits came from the weathering of highlands to the west where siltstone, sandstone, and volcanic ash had been laid down some thirty to forty million years ago, blanketing much of the interior of the North American continent. Western Nebraska's prominent rock features were formed after the Rocky Mountains were first uplifted four or five million years ago. When the rate of erosion began to exceed that of sedimentation, the ancient high plains succumbed to massive erosion by the Platte River and its numerous tributaries. Eventually, only remnants of the older surface remained, such as Scotts Bluff and similar features. In recent times, the rate of sedimentation versus uplift has somewhat stabilized. The newer, lower surface—formed several hundred feet below the ancient and now nearly gone higher prairie—makes up most of today's Great Plains.[6]

The fifty or so miles from Scotts Bluff to Fort Laramie in today's eastern Wyoming took the emigrants about three days to traverse. Northsiders passed along the base of low bluffs just before crossing into Wyoming. Shortly thereafter, they were awed by their first view of Laramie Peak, rising in the distance above what then were called the Black Hills, but today are known as the Laramie Mountains. This was the emigrants' first sighting of real mountains. Another day or so of travel brought them to the Fort Laramie vicinity near the confluence of the Laramie and North Platte rivers. Here, numerous Indians and white traders anxious to do business greeted them.

∞ ∞

With this introduction to the trail from Elm Creek to Fort Laramie, the Boatman saga resumes with Mary Ann relating events experienced before reaching the post.

They [the Turners] [had] turned the teams homeward [and] we continued westward, [as] night soon overtook us. We camped in a[s] lonely [a] place as we could find, not wishing to attach ourselves to some strange train, not knowing what the result might be.[7] Our aim was to try and overtake the train that had gone on, as we had got acquainted with them and too, Mrs. Scott was so kind and good to me. If I imagined I was sick she did all she could to dispel my thoughts [and] at the same time [would] administer . . . to my need of food and care in general. She was a motherly woman in every respect. As I have said, we camped alone, and yet not alone in person, but alone in companionship.

That night we all slept good as brother was on the road to recovery. . . . Mr. Warner cheered us up with his narrative and adventures of crossing the plains in '46, assuring us that we would not have any trouble with the Indians, as he knew the Chinook language and could talk to them and that would be in our favor. At midnight the guards came in [and] reported the cattle quiet [and] lying down, so all was in the best of spirits.

At an early hour everything was in readiness to start on our journey. We got an early start, driving the cattle as fast as they could travel over the dusty roads, until late in the evening when we came to a low swampy prairie which was covered with tall coarse grass.[8] There were camp fires to be seen in every direction, and cattle grazing in all directions. Everybody was [a] stranger to us as we had not overtaken our train that had gone on ahead. Brother Will told the boys to go and take care of the team and allow him to get wood and water for the night as he had been laid up so long . . . he thought it would give him an appetite for . . . supper. So, according to his request, they consented to leave the work of kindling the fire to him. He was assisting me about cooking supper [and] was holding the long handled frying pan over the fire frying bacon for the evening meal. On looking up he exclaimed "Oh, look at that big black wolf." It was only a few yards away. He got the gun as quick as he could and fired a shot at him, but Mr. Wolf soon hid himself in the tall grass. It had no doubt been attracted to our camp by the scent of the meat frying over the camp fire.

That night was a very pleasant one. About sundown a fog raised making it very dark. As the grass was plentiful the cattle soon filled themselves and laid down to rest. The greatest fear was that wolves might attack them after they had laid down. No, nothing occurred that night to mar our happiness. But little did we know what would be our next sorrow. . . . All fear of death had gone out of our little family as I wish to call it. The evening was spent in social conversation, with now and then making mention of loved ones left behind and wondering how long it would take us to make a fortune in a new country that we would soon be occupying with its abundance of everything. Mr. Warner . . . told of how he had trapped the beaver that dammed the small streams and the exorbitant price received for their fur and what an easy task it was to capture a big fat bear whose hide would make a covering for a bed, and the oil suffice to fry all the potatoes and make pie crust for at least six months, besides plenty to make soap for a family washing [for] a year at least. Of course, if a woman did not wash any oftener than he did, one pound would last a year. [He told] how easy it was for any person to get their meat for the winter. All a man had to do to get his years supply of meat was to take the gun on his shoulder and go out in the woods and shoot a big fat deer or two and salt them down, [and] kill grouse and pheasant. Wild geese and ducks [would] help along the meat supply [and furnish] feathers sufficient to make beds and pillows for all time to come. . . . It would be an easy thing for us to build houses. All that would be necessary to do would be to cut down some timber and build a comfortable house on our donation claim. These kinds of stories occupied the time until quite late. Of course brother Will and myself were the audience whom he was addressing [as] the Boatman boys were on duty that night. Chatting the evening away up to a seasonable bedtime we retired. My bed was in the wagon; brother and Mr. Warner occupied the tent. Long after we retired I could hear Mr. Warner talking of how easy it was to make money by trapping the fur animals in the winter season and trade them off at some trading post, as there were men buying furs to ship to England. [Also] how easy it would be to trade off what we could raise on our farms to the Indians for horses and cattle. . . . That is not all, just think of the fish so plentiful, [one] could almost pick them up on dry land after a raise of high water in the spring.

Now Dear reader, pause for one moment and think. Do you wonder that our child like minds were carried beyond all else by the thought of reaching a promise land like this elderly gentleman had described to us on that last happy evening . . . we all spent together?

At midnight the boys came in [and] Mr. Warner went out alone. Nothing disturbed our rest that night. Early in the morning [June 9] all was on the stir [as we] wanted to make a long drive with the hope of overtaking our train. Brother Will was, as all thought, out of danger, and for the rest of us, we had no thoughts of being sick. He wanted to walk and take his turn driving but the boys said, no, he must ride with me. Oh, what a pleasant forenoon we spent in talking over our plans for the future. He said that we would all take our claims adjoining [and] build one long house on the line of each claim so he and John could be with us and live as one family. As soon as we got everything going nicely we [would] send father and mother word what a paradise we had found in the far west. In like conversation we two spent the forenoon with child like gabble. We called a halt for noon; all ate a hearty dinner.

The cattle were much fatigued, [because] the road was cut [with] deep sand holes [and] we were traveling at a pretty good speed to try and overtake our train. That was more than brother Will could bare to think; the other men having all the work to do and he apparently well, and too, the road was so sandy it made hard for the oxen to haul the heavy wagon with its heavy load. In spite of all our entreaty he would walk. For quite a distance I walked by his side with our arms locked, I thinking, probably that I could be of some help to him and maybe he would consent to get in the wagon, but no, he walked on in advance of the wagon until he came to a spring of cold water. He being thirsty and tired drank a good quantity of the cold beverage, then gathered up some wood for camp fire[s and] sat down to wait our arrival. On coming up we were greeted with "Hello boys, I have found an ideal camping place; the grass knee high, wood and water plentiful."

Inasmuch as they began early in the morning hoping to make a long day's drive, they probably traveled twenty or more miles that day. This possibly would have placed them somewhere in the vicinity of today's Brady, Nebraska.

The oxen were unyoked and driven to the spring and, after quenching their thirst, lost no time in making their way to the spot so bountifully supplied with long coarse grass, such as grew in swampy land. As the fire had been burning long enough for the wood to be burnt into coals, I soon had our evening meal ready. We all gathered around the table and ate with a coming appetite.

Now dear reader, I presume you would like to know what I mean by saying "table." I'll try and explain it. Our table was two boards nailed together with a narrow cleat at each end, about three feet and a half long and three feet wide. The way we set it up for use was by laying two ox yokes on the ground, one for each end to rest on, then we sat on the ground while we appeased our appetites. Our dishes were made of the unbreakable material, the tinsmith having done a good job on them.

With respect to preparing meals on the trail, Mrs. M.E. (Bonney) Shorey recalled how useful a dutch oven proved in baking bread and cooking stews, meats, and an occasional prairie chicken. When baking bread, the dutch oven was set on a bed of coals and additional coals were put on the lid. With care, a "nicely browned loaf of bread could be turned out."[9]

Jane Kellogg added that buffalo chips were used for fuel in many of the cooking fires.[10] Milk was churned into butter by the motion of the wagon during a day's travel, and the table was an oilcloth spread on the ground with ox yokes for seats. The utensils were of metal, as were Mary Ann Boatman's.

Francis Sawyer described a Fourth of July celebration feast at present-day Soda Springs, Idaho, which actually was prepared on the 5th because they had been traveling all day on the 4th. The menu included canned vegetables, freshly caught fish, rice cakes, "and other little dishes." Because it had been a particularly cold night, they had the luxury of adding ice to their drinking water.[11]

Francis Sawyer, twenty-one, and her husband Thomas, thirty, were in company with two young friends, Burk Hall and Benjamin Sampson. They had left Cloverport, Kentucky, for California in April 1852 and crossed the Missouri River on May 20. Uniquely, Francis rode in a one-horse carriage furnished with a feather bed and pulled by a mule.[12]

Mary Ann's story continues:

As I have said, the last few days and evenings had been spent in happy communion one with the other. No trouble entered our minds except the thought of the loved ones at home, as Mr. Warner had dispelled all our dread of a long dangerous journey of 2000 miles. Why I should have been so foolish for one moment to think we were out of danger of sickness, is more than I can understand. When I look back, . . . we were constantly passing new made graves and, not only that, but passing trains of 15 or 20 wagons with people sick and dying.

. . . return[ing] to our evening meal, the time was spent in pleasant conversation up to a reasonable bedtime. My husband and my bother, and I retired, while Mr. Warner and John went out on guard. At midnight they came into camp, reported all quiet, cattle all lying down and if anything should disturb them the bell could be heard at camp, as they were but a short distance away. So all lay down to wait for daylight and were soon sound asleep. Daylight began to break at 3 o'clock [June 10]. My husband woke and on getting up, started out to look after the cattle. He had gone but a short distance when he heard brother Will driving the oxen and calling them by their names. On coming up to him he saw at a glance that poor Will was only partly dressed and had been to the spring of cold water of which I have spoken of before and drunk all he could. . . . then [he] was trying to drive the oxen up to have them drink. On asking him what he was out there for he said, "I want old Duke and Dime to have a good drink." That was his yoke of oxen. Mr. Boatman, at one glance, saw that he was out of his mind and was again attacked with the dreaded disease cholera. . . . taking hold of him [he said] "We go to camp, then I [will] come and see that the cattle are watered from the spring." On reaching the camp he at once came to the wagon, saying "Get up as quick as you can and do something for Will." Saying at the same time, "He is very sick and I found him out with the cattle in that wet swampy ground with only his underclothes and socks on. He['s] chilled through." In a short time a bright fire was burning with a teakettle full of hot water and hot rocks to put around him as soon as we could persuade him to go to bed. We applied hot cloths [and] hot rocks to his feet, gave medicines such as we had, but all we could do did not alleviate his suffering. With patience and prayer he bore his pain without a murmur. All his answers to our questions were kind. Oh, I never can forget his last words he spoke to me nor do I want to. All tho it has been more than fifty years my dear brother's dying words are today ringing in my ears as if it were but yesterday. . . . As I knelt down on his bed, which was on the ground, . . . taking his cold hand in mine, he looked me in the face and said "I must die." I, like a frantic child cried out, saying "Oh, Will you must not go!" He said "My suffering is more than I can endure any longer." Then, with a look of agony on his death set feature[s] . . . said in a low sweet voice "Jesus receive my spirit." Oh, I felt as if I could not let him go, but that enemy to mankind stood at the door of our tent with his flaming sword, and that was death. I said "Brother won't you try once more to take another drink of medicine?" He nodded, "yes" but no sound came from his lips. I gently raised his head while my kind husband tried to give him the medicine that he had prepared, but alas, it was too late; the breat[h] had gone. The spirit had taken its flight. Oh, what were we to do? No one but ourselves to close his sightless eyes and clasp his cold and clammy hands across his lifeless breast. No coffin, no board of any kind to make a rough coffin out of, no spade to dig the grave with. The only thing to do was to wait until some train came along. I never will forget how kind the men were. They stopped their teams, got their spades out and helped dig a grave by the roadside. With sadness in our hearts and tearful eyes they bore him to his last resting place [with] only a winding sheet to protect that dear body from the rough rock and earth; no one to offer up a prayer, no one to say a sympathetic word to help us bear the sorrows. It was then five o'clock in the evening [June 10, 1852,] all that could be done for our loved one was done.

   We hitched up and moved a mile on to get away from unpleasant scenes. Close by the roadside in the Platte River valley lies one that I love. Oh so well he sleeps, sweetly sleeps near the rocky hills.

Willis, too, describes the death and burial of his brother-in-law, William Richardson.

We traveled alone, passing train after train for about two weeks. During this time the cholera had struck the emigration train on the Platte River and we were in the midst of it. . . . William Richardson, my wife's brother was taken sick in the night of the ninth of June and died the next day.

William Richardson's death on June 10 is one of the few dates that both Willis or Mary Ann mention. As with the June 2 storm, however, it helps verify dates for other events as well. Willis continues:

Then came the hardest thing that I ever had to do in my life; that was to bury one that was so near and dear to us. We gave him as decent a burial as we could. A person may imagine the feelings of a parent, brother or sister that has to perform such a sad duty as that so far from civilization, without even a stick or rock to mark the resting place. I took some of the side boards off my wagon box and made a box, rolled him up in a feather bed and gave him as good a burial as I could under the circumstances.

Obviously, Mary Ann's description of the preparation of the body for burial differs from that presented by Willis. It probably never will be known which version is correct. Perhaps Willis confused another burial—possibly one of the Turners—with that of his brother-in-law. At any rate, they both graphically describe how burials were conducted along the Platte during the days of overland travel.

Although the precise location of William Richardson's grave probably will remain unknown, it is possible to speculate about where he may have been laid to rest, based on Mary Ann's account of their daily travels. Starting from Elm Creek, presumably on June 7, and estimating the distance traveled for two and one-half days to June 9 when they made camp prior to William's death, they most likely were in the vicinity of today's Brady, Nebraska. Mary Ann's description of the gravesite, "close by the roadside in the Platte River Valley . . . near the rocky hills," generally describes the terrain beginning near present-day Gothenburg and extending westward to Brady and beyond.

In this area, the valley floor is somewhat restricted with rolling hills extending almost to the river. Therefore, the emigrants no longer were traveling on the broad flood plain of the Platte, but instead, they were beginning to encounter rolling hills. Assuming that Mary Ann's brother was buried in the Brady area, could his grave, together with those of other early travelers, have been the beginning of a present-day cemetery? It is of interest to note that a small, quaint and well-kept cemetery is situated on a hilly slope less than a mile north of Brady. It is one of many that line the trace of the trail along the north side of the Platte River Valley. Could it be that William Richardson rests here?

Notes

1. Martha S. Read, "A History of Our Journey," in *Covered Wagon Women: Diaries and Letters from the Western Trails*, 1852, vol. 5, edited and compiled by Kenneth L. Holmes and David C. Duniway (Glendale, California: Arthur H. Clark, 1986), 226.

2. John McAllister, "The Diary of Rev. John McAllister," in *Transactions of the Fiftieth Annual Reunion of the Oregon Pioneer Association* (Portland, Oregon, 1922), 479. Historian Merrill J. Mattes is convinced that Nehemiah Sandusky McAllister actually wrote the original diary. The version by the Reverend John McAllister appearing in the *Transactions of the Fiftieth Annual Reunion of the Oregon Pioneer Association* (1922) is virtually identical. Mattes could not conclude why the original diary was duplicated under the name of Reverend John McAllister. Because the latter version was the only one available to the author, it is used here. See Merrill J. Mattes, *Platte River Road Narratives* (Urbana and Chicago, Illinois: University of Illinois Press, 1988), 373–74.

3. Eliza Ann McAuley, "Iowa to the 'Land of Gold,'" in *Covered Wagon Women: Diaries and Letter from the Western Trails*, 1852, vol. 4, edited and compiled by Kenneth L. Holmes (Glendale, California: Arthur H. Clark, 1985), 54.

4. Twenty-three-year-old Cecelia Adams and her twin sister Parthenia Blank, together with their husbands William Adams and Steven Blank, left Illinois in May 1852 for

Oregon. Joseph McMillen, father of the twins, and Calvin H. Adams, the brother of William, accompanied them. Joseph had left his wife, Ruth, and three young children in Illinois. The group planned to join an older brother, James, who had immigrated to Oregon in 1845. Joseph returned for the rest of his family in 1856. Cecelia Adams, "Twin Sisters on the Oregon Trail: Cecelia Adams and Parthenia Blank," in *Covered Wagon Women: Diaries and Letters from the Western Trails*, 1852, vol. 5, edited and compiled by Kenneth L. Holmes and David C. Duniway (Glendale, California: Arthur H. Clark, 1986), 253–55, 271.

5. Mariett Foster Cummings, "A Trip across the Continent," in *Covered Wagon Women: Diaries and Letters from the Western Trails*, 1852, vol. 4, edited and compiled by Kenneth L. Holmes (Glendale, California: Arthur H. Clark, 1985), 118, 137–38.

6. "Scotts Bluff National Monument, Nebraska," National Park Service, U.S. Department of Interior, 1988 (brochure).

7. Since John Turner was buried in the afternoon, apparently on Elm Creek, the Boatmans probably had a short day of travel, perhaps six or eight miles to the vicinity of the Buffalo Creek crossing,

8. A hard day's travel of perhaps twenty miles would have placed them about halfway between the present towns of Lexington and Cozad, Nebraska.

9. M.E. (Bonney) Shorey, "A Pioneer Story," in *History of Pierce County*, vol. 2, by W.P. Bonney (Chicago, Illinois: Pioneer Historical Publishing, 1927), 1226–29.

10. Jane D. Kellogg, "Memories of Jane D. Kellogg," in *Transactions of the Forty-first Annual Reunion of the Oregon Pioneer Association* (Portland, Oregon, 1913), 87–88.

11. Francis Sawyer, "Kentucky to California by Carriage and Feather Bed," in *Covered Wagon Women: Diaries and Letters from the Western Trails*, 1852, vol. 4, edited and compiled by Kenneth L. Holmes (Glendale, California: Arthur H. Clark, 1985), 103.

12. Ibid., 83, 85, 88–89.

Looking east from Mitchell Pass in the Scotts Bluff area on the south side of the North Platte River. Note the deep trail swales in the foreground. *W.W. Rau*

Chapter Five

On to Fort Laramie

When we overtook William Scott, one of the main leaders of the original party, he was alone. The rest of the party had gone and left him, and we concluded to stay together, which we did till we got to Portland. —Willis Boatman

T HE ROUTE WEST proved to be a testing ground of personal character. Mary Ann's following commentary illustrates how within one small group, traits of meanness, thoughtlessness, and selfishness were displayed by some, while others were kind and caring. Overall, in spite of the mean-spirited and cantankerous acts of some, there probably were many more that displayed compassion and empathy.

This is the closing of the 10th day of June in the year of 1852. We had been on the road two months and thirteen days. Dear reader, look back and see what those two months and thirteen days had done to mar our happiness and to make us dread the long trip in advance of us, not knowing what casualty might befall us by the hands of the savage that was roving all over the country, almost as inhuman as the wolves and with much more treachery. On the morning of the 11th we again hitched up and moved on hoping to overtake our train that had left us on the morning that I mad[e] mention of before. We traveled as brisk as the team could stand it, traveling lat[e] and early for about a week [before we] came upon them [the Scott family] one evening after they had camped for the night.

I presume you wonder why we wer[e] so anxious to overtake the people that had left us to our fate, no matter what that might be. We had got acquainted with them and no better women than Mrs. Scott and her daughter Eliza ever crossed the plains. . . . The men folks were good and kind, but Mr. Scott was one of [those] "I know

it all[s]." Poor man, he couldn't help that he was born with red hair
and as cross grain[ed] as a sycamore plank! . . . All his life [he had]
ruled the entire family and did all the crowing. In fact, in his own
opinion, he knew more than all the rest of [the] entire population
that was at that time on that long route 2,000 miles long. . . . Our
reason for being so desirous to over take our old train [was that]
Mrs. Scott was like a mother and the men folks said for my sake,
they thought it better to put up with Mr. Scott's disagreeable conduct, so I could be in company with Mrs. Scott and her daughter. . . .
It proved to be of great benefit to all three of us women folks as she
was a mother in acts of kindness to us all, especially to me as I was
often sick and not able to get up. She, dear good soul, would see that
I was cared for before she retired.

Mary Ann's need for the companionship of other women can well be
understood. As a young woman away from her mother and family for the
first time in her life and only having been recently married, she suddenly
found herself alone with men, even though one was her husband—it must
have been somewhat discomforting for her. Furthermore, as will be revealed, her illness most likely was morning sickness because she probably
had been pregnant since the beginning of the journey. Until the Scotts
went ahead, she had enjoyed the motherly support of Mrs. Scott, and was
able to consult with her on matters that would be of concern to a young
woman in her condition. Also, the privacy required at times by women
would have been difficult to achieve without the presence of at least one
other woman. The wide expanses, nearly flat terrain, and little or no vegetation behind which to seek privacy must have been a major concern to a
modest young woman.

In this regard, historian Lillian Schlissel presents a poignant discussion on women's need for female companionship. Not only did women
enjoy "comfortable conversations and the sharing of chores with female
kin and friends," but at times, when personal privacy was required, a cur-
tain of modesty was provided behind the long skirts of at least one and
preferably several women standing together or in a circle.[1] It therefore is
understandable why Mary Ann was anxious to reunite with the Scott family where she would find female support and Mrs. Scott's motherly security.

As I have said, all three women folks, I wish to be understood by
saying us three. I myself was sometimes a little help to Mrs. Scott
and her daughter, as on several occasions Mr. Scott would get angry
at someone, then he would take his spite out on his step-daughter,
whom he would forbid to ride in his wagons. On an occasion like

that, she would ride with me in our wagon. On one occasion he demanded her mother to have Eliza gather all her belongings together and place them in her trunk. So, at night the mother told Eliza to do as her lord and master had commanded. The poor girl, obeying his orders, had spent the night in tears, not knowing what his wrath might terminate in. Next morning he got in the wagon that Eliza's trunk was in and called to one of his hired men to come and help him lift the trunk out. The man, supposing he wanted to change it [to] another wagon, [helped him]. But no, he set it down by the roadside and said to his wife, "Eliza can not ride in my wagon any more [and] I don't care what becomes of her." Poor Mrs. Scott came to us in tears, pleading for our boys to take Eliza in with us. Of course our team was getting weak and we had left some of our plunder behind on account of our team not being able to haul it. While we were making room in our wagon for Eliza and her trunk, Scott hitched on to his wagons and drove off, not knowing whether we could haul the girl and her trunk or not. We took her in and hauled her and trunk for a week. She and I walked most of the time. This inhuman act . . . so enraged his hired men that two of them tied their blankets on their backs and left him. They had paid him to take them to Oregon but they said if Eliza had to be left on the plains, it was time for them to start on and let Scott drive his own teams. If Mrs. Scott had been in a country where law could have been enforced, she would have ordered every team turned back eastward as all belonged to her. She was a widow when she married Scott. He had nothing, [but] her husband had left her with plenty. [Even] so, Mr. Scott politely informed her that she had put all her property in his hands and she could not help herself. In about a week, old tiger's anger being somewhat cooled down, consented for Eliza to come back to his camp and take up her abode for awhile.

We moved on for a time, all keeping in moderate health for a short time, oft times passing new made graves by the dozen in one camp ground. On one occasion we passed a camped train that had buried six during the night and [had] six more lying dead in camp. We never knew how many died in that camp. On the south side of the Plat[te] River there was much more cholera than on the north side [therefore] some trains crossed over from the south side to the north. [One train] said they had buried a family of seven in one grave in one day and night. Another lady said that forty of their people in their train died in two nights and one day on the Plat[te] River just before . . . crossing to the north side. Thousands of testimonies like these could be given and some [even] more thrilling. But what is the use of me horrifying the minds of my readers with

such horrid tales of woe. I [will] drop them for awhile and try to find something more cheerful to talk about.

Mary Ann's statements support those of other writers who in 1852 noted that many travelers crossed over to the north side of the Platte in an attempt to escape cholera.[2] Available records indicate that most forded the river some ten miles west of Fort Kearny and just a few miles east of Elm Creek. Other crossings occasionally were made at other places between Fort Kearny and Fort Laramie.

Francis Sawyer and her husband, aforementioned Kentuckians on their way to California, made the crossing on May 30.

> We passed the Fort [Kearny] this morning and kept the bank of the Platte river till we arrived at a point ten miles above, where we forded the stream. The Platte is a mile wide at this point, and our wagons pulled very hard in the quick-sand. Mr. Sawyer went over in the carriage with me. The water was so deep that our mule had to swim in some places. I was greatly frightened and held on tightly to my husband. When we got over Mr. Sawyer took the mule [off] the carriage and went back on her to help the boys over with the wagon. The mules stopped once and the wagon settled down so, that oxen had to be procured to help start it again. At last they got over safe, and as the wagon box had been propped up, everything kept dry, though in this were more fortunate than any others who were crossing today. Many had their effect[s] badly damaged by water.[3]

William and Mariett Cummings forded to the north side in the same general area, also on May 30. Mariett begins the following, when camping at noon on the 29th in sight of Fort Kearny.

> We passed eight miles and camped a short distance from the ferry.
> 30th, Sunday—Broke up camp late to [ford] the Platte, which is one and a half miles. It is impossible to see an eighth of an inch into it and the bottom is quicksand so that an animal can gain no sure footing and a wagon runs as though it were the roughest stones, one constant jar; and the moment it stops settles very deep.
> It took us two hours to cross with one wagon, the box of which was raised a foot. . . . I surely never was so glad to gain "terra firma" before.
> 31st, Monday—Got an early start and went eight or nine miles and crossed Elm Creek.[4]

Mary Ann continues the Boatmans' story:

We moved on as well as it was possible, [considering] our progress became more tedious as the cattle began to fail. The grass had been pastured down so the cattle had to be driven miles from camp at night to get feed, sometimes as far as five miles. On occasions like those all the guards would go and take a blanket; some would sleep the fore part of the night, then change standing on the ground to lying on it the rest of the night. About sunrise we people in camp would hear the bells ringing, cattle bellowing, and the voices of the tired guards coming in. Then all were up, some cooking, some scolding, some swearing, children crying, a general uproar until all got started on the day's journey.

Willis also noted the lack of feed for "late comers."

Finally the cholera subsided, but then came another difficulty for those that were behind . . . that was feed for their teams. . . . There were certain camping places that we all had to make in order to get water. So, of course we parties that had sickness in our trains got behind and the result was our teams nearly died.

Indians were infrequently encountered along the Platte River roads in the early summer of 1852. The cholera devastation gave them cause to give the emigrants and the sickness a wide berth. Only rarely did northside diarists mention seeing Indians in June between the Loup River and nearly to Fort Laramie. Enoch Conyers was among those few who did. On June 11, when within a few miles of the Lone Tree-Ash Hollow area, he wrote: "About 2 o'clock this afternoon we passed a small band of Indians said to be of the Sioux tribe."[5]

Most writers, however, made no mention of meeting Indians until reaching the Fort Laramie area. For example, Eliza Ann McAuley on June 15 recorded: "This morning we met some Indians, the first in four hundred and fifty miles. They are of the Sioux tribe and are much better looking than any we have seen. About 3 o'clock we came opposite Fort Laramie."[6]

Lucy Rutledge Cooke confirmed the paucity of Indians for some distance along the Platte. In a letter to her sister written while close to Fort Laramie on June 9, 1852, she wrote: "We have not seen Indians till now for two or three weeks These are the Sioux & a noble race they seem, not one comes round to beg as all other tribes did and they are well dressed."[7]

Twenty-four-year-old Lucy and her husband William Sutton Cooke, age twenty-five, together with their infant Sarah, had left Dubuque, Iowa, in the spring of 1852 for California. They were part of a Cooke family contingent of ten people accompanied by twelve additional young men.[8]

During the great 1851 Indian treaty council at Horse Creek, some thirty-five miles east of Fort Laramie, the U.S. government had made arrangements with most of the regional Plains tribes allowing for emigrants to pass through the natives' territory.[9] For this and other considerations, the Indians were to receive $50,000 in merchandise annually for fifty years. However, the number of years originally agreed upon was reduced and the arrangement lasted only about three years. The treaty probably protected travelers in 1852 as well as, or better, than it did emigrants of the following years.

It was tempting for Indians to test entrepreneurship and forbearance on the thousands of emigrants who were bringing relatively substantial wealth in material goods to the frontier. Sometimes it was a matter of a simple and honest trade, such as exchanging moccasins for a mirror, beads, or a piece of metal. Other times, Indians asked to be fed, a request that within reason usually was fulfilled. On other occasions, emigrants found some of their cattle missing.

Some enterprising tribesmen attempted to sell services—most common among these endeavors was charging tolls to cross bridges that the Indians may or may not have constructed themselves. Others assisted with fording procedures for which they usually were modestly paid. In general, the emigrants of 1852 learned not to fear Indians in the Platte River Valley. Although somewhat mischievous, sometimes resentful, and not always trustworthy according to the emigrants' standards, they were nevertheless friendly and meant no harm to white travelers.

Mary Ann describes their first contact and ensuing experiences with Indians. Based on her general statements, they too probably were nearing the Fort Laramie area.

> Things and time went on about the same for a couple of weeks or more. One morning we started on our way [and] had gone about five miles when we met some Indians on horseback, the first that had made their appearance since we had come in[to] the cholera stricken district. They made us understand by broken English language that a river or some kind of stream of water and quicksand had to be crossed with[in] a mile or more and gave us to understand it could not be forded, and they had built a bridge over it and we must pay for crossing . . . it. So, our company told them that they would do the fair thing by them, but would not pay until they got to the stream and found out about the bridge and ford, but the Indians

seemed dissatisfied. On arriving at the stream we found other trains waiting to cross. The white people had built the bridge by cutting down some trees and placing them across the stream, then covering the logs with smaller timber and brush so the oxen and wagons would not sink in the quicksand. As some of the wagons had passed over and the bridge had become weakened, all hands [had] taken hold and repaired it. So, by the middle of the afternoon all were safely over, . . . no thanks to Mr. Indian.

We continued our journey until late that evening. We had come to a convenient place to camp where wood and water [were] obtainable and had supper ready. Just [then] as all . . . [sat] around on the ground or ox-yokes or anything obtainable to sit on, perhaps a bucket or kettle turned bottom up for a stool, talking and laughing at some nonsense of foolish expression some one or other had made; to our great surprise . . . about twenty Indians came walking into camp, all begging for something to eat. So, every camp gave them something to eat. Of course, we felt a little afraid of them. That night part of the men guarded the cattle and part guarded the camp, but all went well that night. In the morning as the sun was sending out its golden rays to gladden all living with light and warmth, who should come strolling into camp [but] twenty more Indians, all hungry. On being informed that we did not run an Indian hash shop, they then wanted a cow, but soon found to their surprise that cow-beef was not on [the] market, [and] soon strolled off in the brush. As hastily as possible all was [made] ready to move on, but to our great surprise on collecting the stock together one of the cows could not be found. As she was not used in the yoke, it was decided that all of the wagons and loose stock should move on and three men remain to search for the missing cow. On making a complete search they discovered two Indians in a ditch with the cow, one at her head and the other at her heels. They demanded the cow and soon came driving her up to the train. That was the last we saw of the Indians for some days.

Now all that were sick had regained their health and the dissatisfied ones had become cheerful. Our company now seemed so small as we traveled alone as much as possible, more for convenience than selfishness, as we had been delayed so much on our journey and too, we were a little shy for fear we should come in contact with some contagious disease. all went well for a month or more.

Because of Mary Ann's vagueness in reference to dates, it is unclear where the Boatmans were when the following fateful event occurred. However, inasmuch as she had not yet made reference to Fort Laramie, they probably were somewhere just east of the fort.

one morning to our great surprise on rising, we learned the old black-smith was very sick. His son and his hired man had been caring for him. He had been feeling quite ill since midnight, but objected to any disturbance being made, saying his ailment was only a slight attack of cholera morbus and would soon be better. [He] would not consent for all to lay by, said we were so far behind and feed so poor for the stock and [he] could lie in the wagon and be as comfortable as if lying still. As he was the oldest man in the train since the Deacon had passed on, his demand was obeyed. All journeyed on [with] the old blacksmith in advance of the train. At noon, as it was custom for the head team to call a halt, when the train came up we were all much surprised to find the blacksmith dead. He had given his son instructions to bury him as quickly as possible and move on. Poor boy, I can see him in my mind's eye as his dear father was lowered in that rough grave, no mother, no sister, or brother [or] anyone he had ever known to say one word of consolation. He was buried as hundreds of others were, no winding sheet, no coffin to protect the body from earth and rock. In a short time the dear father was hid from the eyes of the weeping son. All is over and the body left to return to Mother Earth while the spirit has gone to an unseen world. We hitch up, drove a few miles, camped for the night. This happening cast a new gloom over our little band. We had hoped that sickness and death had forsaken us for a while.

Mr. Scott's family did not have any sickness or death in it. He made things so disagreeable for them that they had no time to think about getting sick. The dying father had instructed his son and hired man to push on and try to reach [a] settlement somewhere before winter set in. In a week or so the young men drove on ahead of us and we never saw or heard of them from that day to this, 53 years ago.[10] Perhaps they, like myself, have grown old or perhaps gone to try the reality of an unseen world from whence no traveler ever returns. The old blacksmith was the last death to occur in our company until we reached The Dalles, Oregon.

Mary Ann continues her story with additional descriptions of encounters with Indians, presumably on the approach to Fort Laramie. The Sioux of the central and western Platte River region, of course, were nomadic in nature. As is made apparent in Francis Parkman's account of his 1846 travels with these Indians, entire villages were ready to move when it was necessary to fulfill their needs—whether to harvest wild plant food, to collect lodge poles for tepees, or to hunt buffalo.[11] Buffalo was of primary importance to them, not only as a major food source, but also because the hides provided bedding, clothing, and tepee covers. It was a common sight to see an entire community en route to a hunting ground or other places. The Boatmans encountered bands of these people, as is revealed in Mary Ann's following discussion of the travois, the Indian mode of transport. She also described Indian attire and the trading posts.

> We . . . travel[ed] up the Plat[te] River on the north side, occasionally meet[ing] large companies of Indians moving camp. It was quite a novelty to us to see their mode of traveling. They would take 2 long poles, fasten the large ends at the horse's shoulder in some way, then tie a rope at the other end and one or two more, and then lash the tent poles across the 2 long ones. In this way they could haul all their outfit. Some old squaw or children would ride the pony to guide it aright. Sometimes children that were too small to walk would be piled on top of the load behind the pony. They were very scantily dressed but had strings of beads hung around their necks and waists. Their moccasins and belts were beaded in fine style.

Dogs also were used as pack animals, as earlier related by Conyers shortly before reaching the Lone Tree-Ash Hollow area. "About 2 o'clock this afternoon [June 11, 1852] we passed a small band of Indians. . . . They had a very large white dog. . . . They had him packed with about 100 pounds."[12]

> There were trading posts along the route [where] the Indians traded off their furs and got beads and blankets. Those traders were a set of cutthroats, more to be dreaded than the Indians. They would take advantage of the Indians, cheat, and steal their cattle and horses. Then the Indians would take their revenge out on the innocent emigrants who had no thought of doing them any harm at all.

Since leaving the Missouri, nearly a month had passed and some 500 miles had been traversed before reaching Fort Laramie. This was a major milepost in the journey and regarded as the gateway to the mountains. Up to this point, even though the emigrants had negotiated occasional hilly regions, they had yet to encounter real mountains. They now realized that the Great Plains were behind them and, with formidable Laramie Peak in full view, rugged ranges lay ahead.

Fort Laramie was a bustling place during the early summer of 1852. Indians were set up for selling or trading along the roads on both sides of the North Platte. Moccasins seemed to be the most popular commodity. Also present were white traders, usually with Indian wives, who according to some emigrants were less than trustworthy and somewhat lacking in moral integrity.

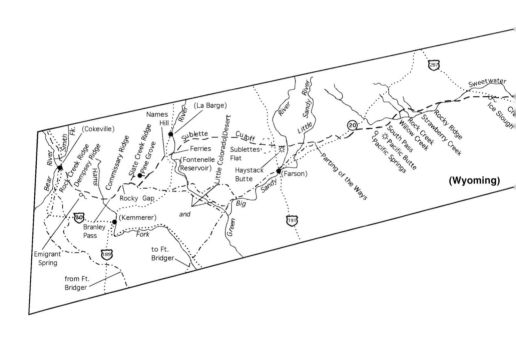

(Wyoming)

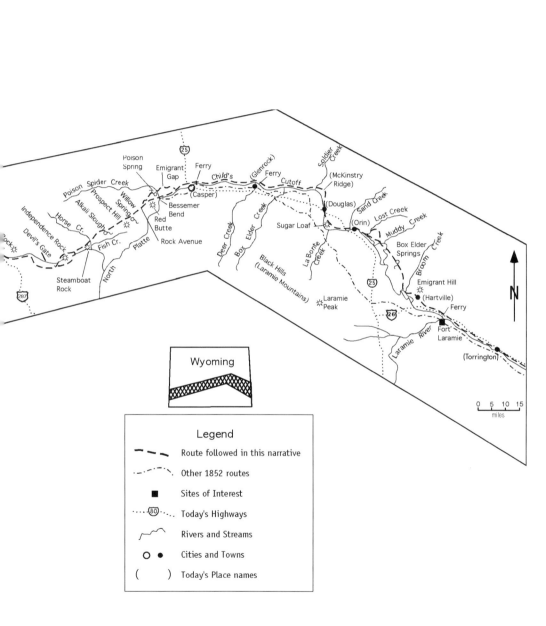

Poison
Spring
Poison Spider Creek
Emigrant
Gap
Ferry
25
Child's
(Glenrock)
Ferry
Cutoff
Solider Creek
(McKinstry
Ridge)
Willow
Prospect Hill
Spring
(Casper)
(Douglas)
Sand Creek
Lost Creek
Alkali Slough
Bessemer
Bend
Deer Creek
Box Elder Creek
Sugar Loaf
(Orin)
Muddy Creek
Horse Cr.
Red
Butte
Independence Rock
Rock Avenue
La Bonte Creek
Box Elder
Springs
Broom Creek
Fish Cr.
Devil's Gate
Black Hills
(Laramie Mountains)
Emigrant Hill
25
(Hartville)
ock
Steamboat
Rock
North
Platte
Laramie
Peak
Ferry
287
26
Fort
Laramie
N
Laramie River
(Torrington)

Wyoming

0 5 10 15
miles

Legend

– – –   Route followed in this narrative

–·–·–   Other 1852 routes

■   Sites of Interest

······(80)······   Today's Highways

Rivers and Streams

O ●   Cities and Towns

(   )   Today's Place names

The fort stood on higher ground some two miles south of the North Platte River. During the mid-nineteenth century, it was in full view to north-side travelers, but today the scene is obstructed somewhat by tall cottonwood trees, which did not grow in dense numbers here during the days of emigrant travel. Today's lush growth along the Platte and other Plains rivers is due to stream flow stabilization for irrigation purposes.[13]

By 1852, many north-side travelers did not bother to visit the fort. There was no compelling reason to cross the river, except to trade, nor did they have to continue the journey on the south side as was done before 1850. In that year, an emigrant route was developed that continued on the north side, eventually known as Child's Cutoff. The new route avoided two crossings of the North Platte—one at Fort Laramie, and the other near today's Casper, Wyoming. Those who did cross the river usually wanted supplies, because as Mattes points out, "here was the only shopping center of consequence for 800 miles between Fort Kearny and Salt Lake City."[14]

The arrival at Fort Laramie usually was a welcomed event. Many emigrants were amazed to see buildings so far from civilization and surprised by the abundance and variety of goods, although at high prices. Lucy Cooke, in a letter to her sister Marianne, recorded a typical reaction on June 9, 1852.

> Oh what a treat it does seem to see buildings again My dear husband has just been over to the store . . . he's come back loaded with good things for which he has had to buy exorbitantly he's brought 2 bottles lemon syrup at $1¼ each a can of preserved quinces 24 Seidlitz powders 24 Soda do & packet of candy & a bottle of ink the latter is a 10 cent bottle but here it was 30 he says they have a splendid store with ever thing & everything that can be called for Oh it seems astonishing to meet with such a place out here away from all the world the store was full of folks & clerks were as busy as they could be . . . There are some 6 or 8 buildings here at the Fort, Warehouses Bakery's &c &c.[15]

The Boatmans probably arrived in the Fort Laramie area sometime during the latter part of June. The distance from the vicinity of Brady, Nebraska, where Mary Ann's brother probably died on June 10, to Fort Laramie is approximately 250 miles. If they averaged a reasonable rate of fifteen miles each day, it would have taken at least two weeks to complete this part of the journey, placing them near the fort in the last week of the month.

We have now got as far on our journey as Fort Laramie. The fort was on the south side of the Platt[e] River. We arrived there about 10:00

o'clock a.m. [and] the men folks wanted to visit the fort. The women, not caring to cross the river in a flat boat, [remained behind]. Besides, [it cost] 25 cents a head. We amused ourselves [by] calling on the Indian women that were living in wigwams along the bank of the river. Their husbands were white face men that said they were traders.

We had passed the lone tree.

Apparently the last statement was an afterthought; something she forgot to mention earlier. They had passed the Lone Tree some eight or nine days previously.

Notes

1. Lillian Schlissel, *Women's Diaries of the Westward Journey* (New York: Schocken Books, 1982), 98–99.
2. Gregory M. Franzwa, *Maps of the Oregon Trail* (Gerald, Missouri: Patrice Press, 1982), 74.
3. Francis H. Sawyer, "Kentucky to California by Carriage and a Feather Bed," in *Covered Wagon Women: Diaries and Letters from the Western Trails*, 1852, vol. 4, edited and compiled by Kenneth L. Holmes (Glendale, California: Arthur H. Clark, 1985), 92.
4. Mariett Foster Cummings, "A Trip across the Continent," in *Covered Wagon Women: Diaries and Letters from the Western Trails*, 1852, vol. 4, edited and compiled by Kenneth L. Holmes (Glendale, California: Arthur H. Clark, 1985), 135.
5. Enoch W. Conyers, "The Diary of E.W. Conyers, a Pioneer of 1852," in *Transactions of the Thirty-third Annual Reunion of the Oregon Pioneer Association* (Portland, Oregon, 1905), 441.
6. Eliza Ann McAuley, "Iowa to the 'Land of Gold,'" in *Covered Wagon Women: Diaries and Letters from the Western Trails*, 1852, vol. 4, edited and compiled by Kenneth L. Holmes (Glendale, California: Arthur H. Clark, 1985), 55–56.
7. Lucy Rutledge Cooke, "The Letters of Lucy R. Cooke," in *Covered Wagon Women: Diaries and Letters from the Western Trails*, 1852, vol. 4, edited and compiled by Kenneth L. Holmes (Glendale, California: Arthur H. Clark, 1985), 241–42.
8. Kenneth L. Holmes, "Letters on the Way to California–Lucy Rutledge Cooke," in *Covered Wagon Women: Diaries and Letters from the Western Trails*, 1852, vol. 4, edited and compiled by Kenneth L. Holmes (Glendale, California: Arthur H. Clark, 1985), 210–11.
9. John D. Unruh Jr., *The Plains Across: The Overland Emigrants and the Trans-Mississippi West, 1840–60*, paperback edition (Urbana, Chicago, and London: University of Illinois Press, 1982), 178.
10. This is another statement indicating that Mary Ann prepared her story in 1905.
11. Francis Parkman Jr., *The Oregon Trail*, edited with an introduction by Bernard Rosenthal (Oxford, New York: Oxford University Press, 1996), 346.
12. Conyers, 423.
13. Merrill J. Mattes, *The Great Platte River Road: The Covered Wagon Mainline Via Fort Kearny to Fort Laramie,* Nebraska State Historical Society, vol. 25 (1969), 507.
14. Ibid., 513.
15. Cooke, 240.

A modern view of deep trail ruts cut in limy sandstone on Child's Cutoff about a mile north of U.S. Route 26 and four miles west of Fort Laramie. Local Oregon Trail expert Randy Brown has named these the "Smith Ruts" after the landowner. The two young persons are Brown's students who have assisted with trail and grave preservation efforts. *Randy Brown*

Chapter Six

Child's Cutoff

As we ascend the Platte . . . . the scenery is grand and high ranges of hills on each side adorned with cedars and pine, while numerous wild flowers and pl(a)nts of erry description adorn the valleys below gives alike beauty and variety to the scenery. —Margaret Ann Scott

ABOUT A WEEK OR TEN DAYS of travel remained along the North Platte River from Fort Laramie to the vicinity of today's Casper, Wyoming. Shortly beyond this segment, the roads on each side of the river eventually merged and, leading west, would leave the North Platte Valley essentially along a single route. With the exception of an event that Mary Ann described much later in her story, but which probably happened along the upper Platte, she mentions nothing regarding their last week or two along the river. It is known that they continued along the north side because she stated that only the men in the party had crossed over to visit Fort Laramie.

The north-side route from Fort Laramie to Casper, known today as Child's Cutoff or Child's Route, was a new segment in the Platte River Valley road system. Indians, trappers, and traders, of course, had used the route for years. Until 1850, however, north-side travelers (including the Mormons) upon reaching Fort Laramie had crossed over to continue on the south-side trail. Up to this time, it was believed that the north side was fraught with obstacles such as high mountains, steep ravines, and deep sand, all of which eventually was proven to be untrue. Some believed that the negative rumors regarding the north side were promoted by those likely to gain monetarily from the operation of the ferries at Fort Laramie and upstream in the Deer Creek vicinity and near Casper.[1]

In spite of the supposed hazards, on June 22, 1850, a party of nineteen wagons of two combined companies, the Wisconsin Blues and the

Upper Mississippi Ox Company, decided to take the risk and attempt the north-side route. Increased traffic, cholera, and particularly the high ferry fees probably played a role in their decision. Within a week, they arrived opposite the upper North Platte ferry without encountering any difficulty and were pleased to learn that they had gained several days on south-side travelers.[2] Many more followed their lead that summer.

By 1852, the road was well established as a primary route. Child's Cutoff was named after Andrew Child, an officer in the Upper Mississippi Ox Company, who returned east and in 1852 published a guidebook that, for the first time, described the north-side route from Fort Laramie. The term Child's Cutoff, however, apparently was coined in later times because the emigrants referred to the trail simply as the North Bank Road or Council Bluffs' Road.[3]

Child's guidebook had not yet been widely circulated in 1852. This is evident in a statement made by Eliza McAuley on June 18 indicating her party was using a different traveler's directory: "our guide book crosses to the south side of the River at Fort Laramie, . . . [But] we keep to the north side, we are following the trail without knowing what is ahead of us."[4]

Travelers on this route in late June and early July 1852 usually followed along the river for five or six miles beyond Fort Laramie. Then they began an ascent out of the valley. At this point, they were compelled to proceed northerly away from the river because, in a short distance, the North Platte canyon became impassable to wagons.

Today, U.S. Route 26 crosses the original route some eight miles beyond the fort. Here the Oregon-California Trails Association (OCTA) has identified wagon swales where they can be seen emerging from the valley. The trail also is marked on the north side of the highway threading its way toward Emigrant Hill. A short interval of deep ruts cut into solid limestone may yet be seen here.

Probably the most frequently discussed subject by diarists as they ascended into the hills was the scenery. The change from flat terrain to mountain-like slopes, together with the distinct change in foliage, gave them much to ponder about. Margaret Ann (Meg) Scott's entry on June 18, 1852, is typical. She was from Illinois and, together with her sister Abigail and father Tucker Scott, kept a family diary on the journey to Oregon.

> As we ascent the Platte the scenery is more beautiful than any we have seen for some time. . . .
>
> The scenery is grand and high ranges of hills on each side adorned with cedars and pine, while numerous wild flowers and pl(a)nts of erry description adorn the valleys below gives alike beauty and variety to the scenery.[5]

On June 13, 1852, Mariett Cummings recorded her impressions. "The hills were almost mountainous and the sides covered with cedar and pine trees in the most fantastical shape imaginable, giving them from a distance a black appearance."[6]

Enoch W. Conyers on June 22 noted: "Cedar and pine is found growing on the side of the hills and quite small and scattered. Some of the emigrants tried their hand at manufacturing a small quantity of tar from the pine knots with very good results."[7]

After having turned northward from the river bottom and climbing for some ten miles, north-side travelers passed through Rocky Pass just beyond present-day Hartville, Wyoming, and then ascended Emigrant Hill. It was a cloudy, rainy day on June 23, 1852, when little Elva Ingram was laid to rest on top of this hill. Nineteen-year-old James Akin Jr., a member of the wagon train, simply noted in his diary: "Elva Ingram, child of James and Retta Ann Ingram, died."[8]

The small headstone with its original inscription still marks the grave.

> Elva Ingram
> died June 23rd '52
> Age 4 yr 6 mo from
> Salem Iowa

In 1985, OCTA fenced the grave and later placed a bronze plaque describing the incident at the site.

Grave of 4½-year-old Elva Ingram from Salem, Iowa, who was buried here on Emigrant Hill, June 23, 1852. Randy Brown and his students constructed the fence and the Oregon-California Trails Association placed the plaque here. *W. W. Rau*

For those travelers passing here during the last week in June 1852 and shortly thereafter, which probably included the Boatmans, Elva's grave would have been another of the newly made burials frequently mentioned by diarists. At least two additional emigrant graves have been located on Emigrant Hill, but their identity or date of burial remains unknown.[9] From Emigrant Hill, the trail descended westward for a few miles where it rejoined the North Platte near the Broom Creek confluence. For many, this was the first place where they camped after leaving the Fort Laramie vicinity.

According to Conyers, it was in the Broom Creek vicinity that two brutal murders occurred in 1852. He states on June 22: "at this camp an emigrant, who with his wife was traveling with another family, murdered the man and his wife. He then took possession of the man's team, clothing and provisions and with his wife started on their return trip for the Missouri River."[10]

When the bodies of the murdered persons were found, the military at Fort Laramie pursued and apprehended the guilty couple. Reportedly they were tried, convicted, and hung at Fort Laramie. Conyers further states that he never learned the names of the murderers.

On June 20, two days before reaching the upper ferry near Casper, Eliza McAuley perhaps noted the same incident: "tonight we heard that the body of a woman, who had been murdered, was found hidden in a clump of rose buses near where we had been."[11]

Apparently, another killing was committed somewhere on the south-side trail. On June 23, a day beyond the upper ferry, Eliza recorded:

> We heard today the particulars about the tragedy across the River. There were two men and a women concerned. The woman's husband attacked the other man and stabbed him to death. He was tried, convicted and hung, and the woman was sent back to the fort.[12]

Francis Sawyer also learned of carnage. On June 18, just one day before passing the upper ferry, she wrote:

> We heard to-day that a murdered man had been found in a deep hollow a short distance from the road. . . .
>
> He had a wife and one child. Great must be their sorrow to be thus so cruelly deprived of a dear friend and protector, and left alone in this wild and friendless country. Some men have gone in pursuit of the murderers.[13]

The following date, June 19—the day her party passed the upper ferry—Francis noted: "We heard of another murdered man to-day. In this case, as in yesterday's, the man was murdered by a man in his own company, but proof in this instance was positive, and the murderer was hung to a tree, by the indignant emigrants."[14]

This may well have been the killing of T. Miller by Lafayette Tate. Tate was captured after trying to escape, given a quick trial, and hung on the banks of LaBonte Creek.[15]

Polly Coon continues the litany on June 29. "We stopped to noon near the river where 3 graves which a tree in the neighborhood stated were the graves of a Man Woman & boy who were found near there with their throats cut from ear to ear, the cause or the perpratrators of so bad a deed were unknown."[16]

Although Polly did not specifically indicate where they were on that date, she did note that they had left the mouth of the Laramie River at noon on June 25, and arrived at this scene at noon four days later. Based on an average travel rate of fifteen miles a day, they probably had proceeded some sixty miles. This would have placed them roughly between Orin and Douglas, Wyoming.

Polly Coon continued with the same theme on the following day, June 30:

> It seems that we are in a fated region—we had not recovered from the shock we felt from learning of the murder above stated when we passed a company from which 2 men had just been drowned in trying to swim their cattle over the river, nor had we ceased to talk about this before we came to a grove of trees where a man had just been hung by his Co for shooting his brotherinlaw It seems that there are some demon spirits near us & the reflection is not very pleasing.[17]

Though some of these accounts might describe the same incidents, it nevertheless appears that uncontrolled tempers, thievery, and other causes resulted in an unusual number of fatal acts along the North Platte in late June 1852.

After leaving the Broom Creek campground, the next day's travel on the north-side route was in a northerly direction, generally over rolling hills and through broad grassy valleys, but with little available water. As they proceeded on in the morning, travelers frequently noted a red coloration in the terrain, as indicated by John McAllister for July 5: "ascend red hill . . . the soil looks red till you cross this rise. On the East are some red sandstone bluffs."[18] The coloration is due to red sandstone and claystone outcrops of the Hartville Formation, a very old rock unit deposited 300 million years ago.[19]

By noontime or shortly thereafter, many emigrants reached Box Elder Springs where they obtained their first good water since leaving Broom Creek that morning. In the afternoon, the road led through a steep, narrow ravine, then climbed a bluff, and finally descended a long, gentle incline to Spring Creek. Here, according to John McAllister, they found, "a cold spring rising on the East side out of the rocks[. The] water cant be beat for coldness and purity."[20]

Somewhere along this section of Child's Cutoff, Ann Roelofson Scott, mother of Abigail and Maggie Scott, died "with a violent dierrehea" on June 20, 1852.[21] Although the location of her grave reportedly is lost, it seems likely based on mileage recorded in the Scotts' diary, and the fact that they were camped "near some excellent springs which seem to gush from the rocks," that she was buried close to Box Elder Springs. A modern-day local historian, Randy Brown, who has conducted extensive research along Child's Cutoff, also has come to this conclusion.[22]

Abigail described the gravesite as,

> situated on an eminence which overlooks a ravine intersected with (*groves of*) small pine and cedar trees.; In about the centre of this ravine or basin, there wells forth from a kind of bank a spring of icy coldness, clear as crystal. . . . In the outskirts of this basin clusters of wild roses and various other wild flowers grow in abundance. . . .
> We call the place Laramie's Point or Castle Hill.[23]

A footnote in the Scott diary further states, "the grave [was] protected from the wolves by stones heaped upon it," a fact that might facilitate a modern-day investigator in finding it.[24]

In the next day's travel beyond Spring Creek, emigrants crossed Willow and Muddy creeks. Today, the Glendo Reservoir has flooded much of this area. There was a choice of routes to be taken shortly after leaving Muddy Creek—one in a westerly direction near the Converse-Platte county line, then northward to a ford of Lost Creek; and another heading northerly for three or four miles, then southwest down Lost Creek Valley. The latter route has been marked with OCTA trail markers.

Byron McKinstry, who was with the first train over the route in 1850, described "interesting looking hills on each side of us, some of them rising nearly perpendicular out of the plain to considerable height."[25] Regardless of which route they took to Lost Creek, most travelers next camped along the North Platte River—some before and others after reaching Lost Creek, a few miles east of today's Orin, Wyoming. In this vicinity, the high, soft sandstone bluffs looming up from the river bottom reminded McKinstry of "Chimney Rock and Bluff Ruins—a second edition of the latter."[26]

The rocks exposed in these bluffs are part of the White River Formation, which are relatively young sedimentary rocks, 30 to 35 million years old. They are, in fact, a geological equivalent to Chimney Rock and the Ancient Bluff Ruins.[27]

Occasional encounters with Indians were reported in this locality by some 1852 travelers. Although generally friendly, they could be somewhat confrontational. In the Lost Creek vicinity, Martha Read recorded a typical incident on July 1.

> We were met by 15 Indians today well armed which gave us somewhat of a start. They paraded themselves across the road ahead of us and would not give the road. They wanted we should give them something but we did not. There were about 17 wagons along at the time. We turned out and went on and left them. Some [of] them followed us a piece and that was the last we saw of them.[28]

The route continued from the Orin vicinity in a westward direction for about five miles to Sand Creek, which the trail crossed at a point between the North Platte shore and today's Burlington Northern and the Chicago and Northwestern railroad tracks. From there, the trail turned northwest, and today is followed by the railway lines and the Irvine Road to Douglas, Wyoming.

In this vicinity, travelers encountered steep bluffs and isolated buttes, with Sugar Loaf Hill being particularly striking. The first record of its name appears in Byron McKinstry's 1850 diary.

> I ascended a high mound that stands in the bottom and had one of the finest views imaginable. I could trace the Platte to the westward and see the teams on the S. side a great way off up the valley of a creek [Bed Tick Creek]. This Sugar Loaf was some 3 or 4 hundred feet high and difficult to climb on account of steepness.[29]

Subsequent diarists also applied the designation, such as John McAllister on July 7, 1852.

> After crossing several ravines you descend gray sand & Clay bluffs in-
> places little jump offs after decending you can see bluffs & mounds of
> the same composition some of them are quite novel observed one in
> the shape of a sugar loaf with a large sandstone on top of it.[30]

The gray, soft claystone and sandstone strata of Sugar Loaf Hill and the
surrounding bluffs also are part of the same White River Formation, 30 to
35 million years old, mentioned for the Orin locality.[31]

From Douglas, the route continued almost due north for about six
miles to what is known today as McKinstry Ridge. Along this section, the
trail may yet be traced in places; for instance, deep ruts are visible at Harvey
Gulch. McKinstry Ridge is a modern name applied by Oregon Trail experts, Troy Gray and Randy Brown, in the early 1980s. It honors the 1850
diarist Byron McKinstry, a member of the Upper Mississippi Ox Company, and his grandson Bruce McKinstry.[32] Over a period of years, Bruce
McKinstry retraced his grandfather's journey. In 1975, Bruce published
his detailed observations of the trail, along with his grandfather's original
diary.[33]

In this vicinity, particularly at McKinstry Ridge, peculiar formations
of cylindrical rocks are scattered about on the terrain. The first known
diarist to describe them was Byron McKinstry on June 27, 1850.

> We passed some rock pillars as nearly round as possible, from 30 to 40
> feet in length and 18 to 20 inches in diameter. . . . most of them
> broken into sections from 8 to 10 ft. long. They were of hard greyish
> or bluish rock, perhaps limestone and look as if they had been turned.
> Some suppose them to be petrified wood.[34]

Although many persons speculated that these curious rock formations were petrified logs, geologists today have concluded that they are
"pipy or log-like concretions." Some of the concretions are as much as 3½
feet in diameter and 130 feet in length. Geologist believe they are formed
by the precipitation of calcium carbonate from ground water flowing
through highly permeable and porous sandstone that is enclosed within
less permeable rock, such as shale. Weathering of the overall rock formation leaves the more resistant sandstone (pipy concretions) resting on the
land surface. These concretions were formed in sedimentary deposits dating from 40 to 50 million years ago in the Eocene Epoch.[35]

From McKinstry Ridge, the trail turned westward and descended a
long gradual grade to the river near the mouth of Fetterman Creek. This
was the next campsite for many. The following day's journey from Fetterman
Creek followed a route similar to that of today's Burlington Northern

railroad, passing close by the riverbank in places. Steep, gray-colored bluffs continue for a considerable distance.

On the night of June 23, the John Tucker Scott family camped on the North Platte nearly opposite to the mouth of Box Elder Creek.[36] A longer day's journey, however, would bring others to, or within a few miles of, a major crossing of the upper Platte. South-side travelers crossing to the north bank primarily used this ferry in the vicinity of present-day Glenrock, Wyoming, although some south-side travelers already had crossed the Platte at various places below. This was the first major crossing point on the upper North Platte. At this juncture, south-side travelers in great numbers began merging with journeyers on the north bank.

Near the mouth of Deer Creek, a stream draining into the North Platte from the south, many 1852 travelers were enticed into interrupting their tight travel schedule to seek mineral wealth. Abigail Scott, who passed here on June 24, noted on the following day:

> It is rumored that gold mines of considerable value have been discovered on the South side on a stream called Deer creek and that some three hundred teams have stopped and are digging for the precious ore. In order to ascertain the truth of this two of our company left the train on horseback this morning with the intention of crossing the Platte and going to the diggins.

In this vicinity, Abigail was impressed with the scenery, writing a fantasizing description of the bluffs lining the North Platte.

> We had a grand and altogether romantic view of a range of bluffs on the South side of the river: They appeared as a city of dome shaped houses churches and every manner of public buildings the whole of which wore a imposing appearance on account of being surrounded by an impenetrable looking fortress.[37]

In places, emigrant inscriptions yet may be seen on these sandstone bluffs.

The final day along the North Platte usually was a long and hard one, passing over numerous hills and through much sand. Mariett Cummings noted: "Passed over the worst hills we have seen; came at noon to the south ferry and went up on the side of the worst sandhill for 200 miles."[38]

In 1852, there were at least two ferries operating near today's Casper, Wyoming. Mariett Cummings described the first as the "south ferry." John McAllister, on the other hand, identified it as the "second ferry which is several canoes fastened together about ½ mile above is a ford most of the emigrants Cross here none at the ferry."[39]

McAllister referred to the uppermost ferry as the "third ferry," consisting of two boats.[40] The location of this site is not precisely known today. However, it likely was situated some four miles upstream in the vicinity of where Fort Caspar later was established (1858) at the Upper Platte or Guinard's bridge.[41]

In the Casper area, most of the 1852 travelers bid farewell to the North Platte. Although another route remained close to the south side of the river for the next few miles, shortly beyond this point most of the travelers would essentially combine (see map). This was a major milepost, and many diarists recorded their impressions about having reached this point in the journey.

Francis Sawyer arrived at the upper ferry on June 19, and expressed satisfaction at already being on the north side. "We passed opposite the ferry on the North Fork of the Platte. Numerous emigrants were there waiting to get over, but we were saved the trouble and expense of ferrying now by having forded the main Platte several days ago."[42]

On June 28, John Kerns briefly recorded an interesting statistic, a tragedy, and his personal feelings about leaving the river.

> Passed the upper ferry on Platte River. 2369 teams have crossed previous to this day. One man was drowned to-day in swimming horses across. We have now made the last camp on Platte River and are glad of it too. I hope I shall never see it again.

He added: "There are a great many Indians at this ferry and some French and Spanish. They all trade for cattle."[43]

On June 16, Lucy Cooke noted the ferry fee. "There's a ferry near by on the Platte which is the last we pass. The charges crossing are enormous $5 for each waggon & extra for our horses & cattle We however have no desire to go on the south side."[44]

While camped near the upper ferry on July 21, Sarah Pratt recorded more shocking statistics: "account of death at ford. said to be 40 drowned dead bodies below ford."[45]

The McAuleys, traveling with the Ezra Meeker family and the bachelor William Buck, had passed the upper ferry at noon on June 23. Eliza McAuley expressed satisfaction that "we now have the use of our guide book again."[46]

⣿⣿

As these accounts reveal, the upper North Platte trails and crossings were bustling in late June and early July 1852 at the height of the travel season.

Many already had grown weary on the long trek over the Plains and in crossing the Platte's many tributaries. Everyone was aware, however, that the route became more difficult in the miles ahead. Water and suitable grass for the cattle would be scarce in this arid region and the hot mid-summer sun would add further discomfort.

It was here, before they left the Platte, that the emigrants readied themselves for the forthcoming adversities.

Notes

1. Randy Brown, "Child's Cutoff," in *Overland Journal*, vol. 5, no. 2 (1987), 17–18; published by the Oregon-California Trails Association, Independence, Missouri.
2. Bruce McKinstry, *The California Gold Rush Overland Diary of Byron N. McKinstry, 1850–1852* (Glendale, California: Arthur H. Clark, 1975), 134–46.
3. Brown, 17.
4. Eliza Ann McAuley, "Iowa to the 'Land of Gold,'" in *Covered Wagon Women: Diaries and Letters from the Western Trails*, 1852, vol. 4, edited and compiled by Kenneth L. Holmes (Glendale, California: Arthur H. Clark, 1985), 56.
5. The John Tucker Scott family left their family home near Gravelland, Illinois, on April 2, 1852. The immediate family consisted of John Tucker, 43; his wife Ann Roelofson, 40; and nine children. Mary Frances (Fanny), 19, was the oldest; other children included Abigail Jane (Jenny), 17; Margaret Ann (Meg), 15; Harvey Whitefield (Harv), 14; Catherine Amanda (Kit), 13; Harriet Louise (Etty), 11; John Henry (Sonny), 9; Sarah Maria (Chat), 5; and William Neill (Willie), 3. In addition, there were 15 Roelofson and Scott relatives and some 24 other persons who were either on their own or working their way west. By the time they reached Ash Hollow, Tucker noted that there were 12 wagons and 52 "soules" in their train.

   In later years, the Scott family became renowned in Oregon. Most prominent was Abigail, who became Mrs. Abigail Scott Duniway and famous as a major advocate of women's rights through her numerous books and particularly her newspaper, the *New Northwest*. Her brother Harvey W. Scott, who disagreed with many of Abigail's ideas, was for forty years editor of the *Oregonian* in Portland and a leader in the Republican Party. Abigail's sister Catherine Scott Coburn shared in editing both papers.

   Margaret Ann Scott, "Journal of a Trip to Oregon by Abigail Jane Scott, with Introduction by David C. Duniway," in *Covered Wagon Women: Diaries and Letters from the Western Trails*, 1852, vol. 5, edited and compiled by Kenneth L. Holmes and David C. Duniway (Glendale, California: Arthur H. Clark, 1986), 21–32, 68.
6. Mariett Foster Cummings, "A Trip across the Continent," in *Covered Wagon Women: Diaries and Letters from the Western Trails*, 1852, vol. 4, edited and compiled by Kenneth L. Holmes (Glendale, California: Arthur H. Clark, 1985), 139.
7. Enoch W. Conyers, "Diary of E.W. Conyers, a Pioneer of 1852," in *Transactions of the Thirty-third Annual Reunion of the Oregon Pioneer Association* (Portland, Oregon, 1905), 444.
8. James Akin Jr., *The Oregon Trail Diary of James Akin Jr. in 1852: The Unabridged Diary with Introduction and Contemporary Comments by Bert Webber* (Medford, Oregon: Webb Research Group, Pacific Northwest Books, 1989), 33.
9. Randy Brown, personal communication, 1994.
10. Conyers, 444.

11. McAuley, 57–58.

12. Ibid., 58.

13. Francis Sawyer, "Kentucky to California by Carriage and a Feather Bed," in *Covered Wagon Women: Diaries and Letters from the Western Trails*, 1852, vol. 4, edited and compiled by Kenneth L. Holmes (Glendale, California: Arthur H. Clark, 1985), 97.

14. Ibid.

15. Reg P. Duffin, "The Miller-Tate Murder and John F. Miller Grave," in *Overland Journal* vol. 5, no. 4 (1987), 24–31; published by the Oregon-California Trails Association, Independence, Missouri.

16. Polly Coon, "Journal of a Journey over the Rocky Mountains," in *Covered Wagon Women: Diaries and Letters from the Western Trails*, 1852, vol. 5, edited and compiled by Kenneth L. Holmes and David C. Duniway (Glendale, California: Arthur H. Clark, 1986), 192.

17. Ibid.

18. John McAllister, "Diary of Rev. John McAllister," in *Transactions of the Fiftieth Annual Reunion of the Oregon Pioneer Association* (Portland, Oregon, 1922), 482; see additional information under note 2 in chapter four.

19. J.D. Love and A.C. Christiansen, *Geologic Map of Wyoming*, scale 1:500,000, 3 sheets, U.S. Geological Survey and Geological Survey of Wyoming, 1985.

20. McAllister, 482.

21. Abigail Jane Scott [Duniway], "Journal of a Trip to Oregon," in *Covered Wagon Women: Diaries and Letters from the Western Trails,* 1852, vol. 5, edited and compiled by Kenneth L. Holmes and David C. Duniway (Glendale, California: Arthur H. Clark, 1986), 71.

22. Randy Brown, written communication, 1994.

23. Abigail Scott, 71–72.

24. Ibid., 72.

25. McKinstry, 139.

26. Ibid., 140.

27. Love and Christiansen.

28. Martha S. Read, "A History of Our Journey," in *Covered Wagon Women: Diaries and Letters from the Western Trails*, 1852, vol. 5, edited and compiled by Kenneth L. Holmes and David C. Duniway (Glendale, California: Arthur H. Clark, 1986), 228.

29. McKinstry, 142.

30. McAllister, 493.

31. Love and Christiansen.

32. Brown, 19.

33. McKinstry.

34. Ibid., 144.

35. Carol Waite Connor, "The Lance Formation: Petrography and Stratigraphy, Powder River Basin, Wyoming and Montana," in U.S. Geological Survey Bulletin 1917-I (1992), 15–18.

36. Leslie M. Scott, *History of the Oregon Country by Harvey W. Scott,* compiler's appendix 3 (Cambridge: Riverside Press, 1924), 273.

37. Abigail Scott, 75.

38. Cummings, 145.

39. McAllister, 484.

40. Ibid.

41. Aubrey L. Haines, *Historic Sites along the Oregon Trail*, third edition (St. Louis, Missouri: Patrice Press, 1987), 186.

42. Sawyer, 97.

43. John T. Kerns, "Journal of Crossing the Plains to Oregon in 1852," in *Transactions of the Forty-second Annual Reunion of the Oregon Pioneer Association* (Portland, Oregon, 1914), 168.

44. Lucy Rutledge Cooke, "The Letters of Lucy R. Cooke," in *Covered Wagon Women: Diaries and Letters from the Western Trails*, 1852, vol. 4, edited and compiled by Kenneth L. Holmes (Glendale, California: Arthur H. Clark, 1985), 246.

45. Sarah Pratt, "The Daily Notes of Sarah Pratt," in *Covered Wagon Women: Diaries and Letters from the Western Trails*, 1852, 4, edited and compiled by Kenneth L. Holmes and David C. Duniway (Glendale, California: Arthur H. Clark, 1985), 188.

46. McAuley, 57.

Devil's Gate, located a few miles west of Independence Rock, was a curiosity to early travelers, who often camped nearby. Here, the Sweetwater River has channeled its way down through granitic rock. *W.W. Rau*

Chapter Seven

Sweetwater Valley

We . . . began to ascend the Sweetwater Mountains as they were called in our guide book. The hill proved to be a steep and long one. . . . In some places looked as if the wagons and oxen would fall backwards. —Mary Ann Boatman

BEFORE REACHING THE NEXT major drainage, the Sweetwater River Valley, it was necessary to traverse nearly fifty miles of a desert-like sagebrush country. What little water could be found mostly was confined to alkali ponds and streams. Attempts to lighten loads had been ongoing prior to arriving at the upper Platte crossing, as was apparent from the supplies, equipment, and personal effects left along the way. But upon leaving the North Platte, the quantity of discarded items significantly increased.

The comments of Captain Howard Stansbury of the U.S. Army Corps of Topographical Engineers are particularly descriptive in this regard. In 1850, he was being sent on a surveying expedition to the Great Salt Lake Valley. On arriving at the upper Platte ferry near Deer Creek on July 25, he recorded: "Property of every description was strewn about in all directions, and in much greater quantities than we had yet seen."[1]

Further on, as he left the North Platte River on July 27, Stansbury observed:

The road has been literally strewn with articles that had been thrown away. Bar-iron and steel, large blacksmiths' anvils and bellows, crowbars, drills, augers, gold washers, chisels, axes, lead, trunks, spades, ploughs, large grindstones, baking-ovens, cooking stoves without number, kegs, barrels, harness, clothing, bacon, and beans, were found along the road.[2]

It is apparent that many emigrants were reducing their loads to the bare essentials. Traveling a distance of twenty-four miles on July 27, Stansbury also noted, "the relics of seventeen wagons and the carcasses of twenty-seven dead oxen."[3]

In 1852, two primary routes north of the river led westward from a point beyond the Casper area (see map). One followed along the north side of the North Platte for nearly ten miles to Bessemer Bend, near the colorful Red Buttes and the mouth of Poison Spider Creek. According to Abigail Scott, this road was considered to be new, as she indicated on June 27, 1852. "We took a new road this morning and traveled along the Platte until noon . . . and prepared to rest until evening; We are now opposite the Red Buttes."[4]

From Bessemer Bend, this route continued west for five miles on an older section of trail that was part of the original route that followed along the river's south side to a ford at Bessemer Bend.[5] This trail, which Abigail Scott's party followed, merged with the older, more northerly Poison Spider road that left the North Platte at the upper crossings.

In 1852, the Poison Spider road was the most popular of the two routes. It led almost due west from the Casper area for eight miles over nearly flat terrain to a rise known as Emigrant Gap. From this high ground, travelers had an excellent view eastward, bidding a final farewell to the North Platte. In the next few miles, the trail crossed through desert lands to Poison Spider Creek, continued on by Poison Spring (usually called Mineral Spring or Mineral Lake by emigrants), and in a few miles merged with the road from Bessemer Bend.

Two more miles brought the immigrants to what John McAllister referred to as "a chain of rocks making a right angle with the road."[6] This geologic feature consists of a series of upturned, largely sandstone beds of Cretaceous age, 65 to 136 million years old. It frequently was referred to as "Rock Avenue."

After continuing another seven miles through desolate country, travelers reached Willow Spring, the first source of good water beyond the North Platte. McAllister arrived here on July 17, describing the spring as, "right of the road [where] it boiled up from the south bank good cold water [but] the willows are nearly all cut down."[7] This usually was a crowded campsite during the height of the travel season because many parties made it their first overnight stop beyond the North Platte.

After resting at Willow Spring, next came a long, hard pull up Prospect Hill, followed by eight miles over more barren land, including Alkali Slough and along Fish Creek. On arriving at Horse Creek (usually called Greasewood Creek by emigrants), good water once again was available. Ten more miles across nearly flat sagebrush prairie and past Steamboat Rock off to the left, travelers arrived at the banks of the Sweetwater River. Nearby was the impressive monolith known as Independence Rock.

Just a mile or so before reaching the Sweetwater on June 21, Mariett Cummings described "several lakes near the road and one of them was for a distance of six or seven yards encrusted with saleratus in a crystallized form."[8]

On July 18, John McAllister also mentioned a "Salearatus Lake the water has a crust of salearatus on it This lake is left of the road a few spaces in a basin."[9] These ponds essentially are unchanged today.

Following is Mary Ann's description of the Boatmans' trek through the arid country from the North Platte to the Sweetwater River and Independence Rock.

> We now leave the Platte River [to] go across the Sand Hill Plains. It is well named, for it was one plain of sand. No grass to speak of [and] no fuel but buffalo chips or some dry sage brush. As far as one could see on all sides were sand hills dotted here and there with sage brush. Occasionally a sage hen would fly through the air. The poor lonely bird would usually come to the earth at the report of some man's gun to be stripped of its pretty coat of spotted feathers and make an appetizing supper for some hungry family. Ofttimes . . . [we had] to travel until late at night to reach a watering place. . . . all were on the look out for fuel. Usually each family had gathered a little of some kind of fuel to make a fire to boil a kettle of water and fry a few slices of bacon. The bread was usually baked of a morning to last all day. So in this way we trudged on over sand hills for several days. Then crossed a shallow stream called in the guide book Little Sanday [probably today's Horse Creek], thence on through Alki Plain [probably the Alkali Slough area]. The ground was white as if it were covered with snow. Some of the people gathered it up an put it in bottles to use in place of soda. The next thing of interest was the

Independent Rock, a large round rock with hundreds of names cut in its side.

The arrival at the Sweetwater River near the base of Independence Rock normally was a joyous occasion. The emigrants and their livestock were refreshed by the cool, clear waters of the stream. Independence Rock, which had been in view for several miles during the approach, was a geologic oddity piquing their curiosity. This granitic, turtle-shaped, erosional remnant of the earth's interior is geologically ancient, representing magma that cooled deep within the crust during pre-Cambrian times prior to 570 million years ago. Over many eons, the overlying rock eroded away exposing this feature. It measures 1,900 feet long, 700 feet wide, and rises 128 feet above the valley floor.[10]

The origin of its name remains uncertain, but according to historian Aubrey L. Haines, it "probably dates from the sojourn of [mountain men] Thomas Fitzpatrick and companions at its base on July 4, 1824."[11] Most emigrants took time to examine the ancient monolith, and many recorded their names on it in some fashion. In fact, some thought it should be called "Registry Rock."

Enoch Conyers, after having climbed to the top, recorded on July 2:

> Here we had a splendid view of the surrounding country for miles. We found the rock literally covered with names of emigrants. . . . Some of these names were written with white or red chalk; some were cut in the rock with a cold chisel, whilst others were written with tar—and, in fact, were written in every conceivable manner.[12]

While camped one-half mile from Independence Rock on July 6, Polly Coon noted that along with "a multitude of people. . . . We . . . traversed it over & around & enjoyed the excursion very much. Some one had put up a banner the 4th & it still fluttered in the breeze."[13]

For the emigrants, a general rule for gauging their progress on the overland trail was that they reach Independence Rock by July 4. This was believed to be required if the trains expected to pass over the mountain ranges near the trail's end before snow fell. Many travelers achieved this goal, giving added enthusiasm for the numerous Fourth of July celebrations held at or near Independence Rock.

Conyers recorded one of the more detailed accounts of rejoicing—on the seventy-sixth year of American Independence. The party arrived at Independence Rock on July 2, 1852, and added their names "to the great multitude."[14] From there, they drove five miles to Devil's Gate and then south some four miles to a beautiful secluded valley in the Sweetwater Mountains. Here they enjoyed good, cold water and plenty of tall grass for the stock—an excellent place to lay over and celebrate July 4. They had learned about this location from Alfred A. Archambault, or "Schambau" as Conyers identified him. Archambault had joined John C. Fremont's second exploring expedition in 1844 and currently was engaged in building a trading post near Devil's Gate.

The Conyers company spent the entire day on July 3 preparing for a rousing celebration. Wagon beds were "taken to pieces and formed into long tables"; hunters shot antelope, sage hens, and jackrabbits; several women fashioned a flag, "Old Glory," from a sheet, red striped shirt, and blue jacket; and others were engaged in preparing food "on to a late hour in the night."

Just before sunrise, the Fourth "was ushered in with the booming of small arms," and "Old Glory" was nailed to a flagstaff and raised forty feet above the valley floor, after which the company circled around and sang "The Star Spangled Banner." After a reading of the Declaration of Independence, Virgil Y. Ralston rendered a half-hour speech, having been chosen for the deed the day before. In the meantime, however, he had indulged "in a little too much firewater." Nevertheless, some of the boys propped him up on a table where he "delivered, off-hand, an excellent oration."[15]

The feast consisted of game meats prepared in a variety of ways, potatoes from Illinois, baked beans, rice, pickles, and a variety of freshly baked breads and rolls. For desert there was an assortment of cakes including "Sweetwater Mountain cake," together with several kinds of pies. Beverages consisted of coffee, tea, chocolate, and "good cold mountain water." All of this was topped off with a "fine lot of Sweetwater Mountain ice cream" made possible by a large snowball that the boys had carried down from the mountain on a pole. As Conyers summarized: "We passed . . . a Fourth of July on the plains never to be forgotten."[16]

After passing by Independence Rock, Mary Ann continues with a description of their first campsite on the Sweetwater.

> The next thing of interest was crossing [the] Sweetwater. Why it is
> named Sweetwater I can not tell, unless the water is so clear and
> sweet, to be compared with water that people had been compelled to

use. It is a wid[e] shallow stream at the ford. About a quarter of a mile up the river we camped for the night. At that place the river run though [a] narrow tunnel like passage between high rocky bluffs on each side forming a canyon . . . . It was an ideal camping ground at the foot of the Sweetwater Mountains.

This campsite was near Devil's Gate. Since they crossed the river a quarter-mile upstream from this campsite, it is apparent that they did not ford at the popular Independence Rock crossing. Rather, they had continued along the Sweetwater's north side for four miles before fording, less than a mile from Devil's Gate.

There was no timber to be seen. But [it was a pleasure] to be away from alkali plains and get good pure water to use. The men folks [were] all busy, some taking cear [care] of the stock, others looking for fuel an kindling fires. The women folks with soap and towels [were] down at the river washing and combing as if to complete their toilet to attend a first class theater. On our return, fires were sending sparks and smoke high up in the air. The clink of the cow bell [could be] heard on the hill side. The men, some were lazily lounging on the ground while others were climbing up the cragged rocks that formed the canyon that the river ran through hundreds of feet below, looking in the sun set like a thread of silver. Those that were venturesome enough to go to the very highest point and look down said the river did not look larger than a little stream of a foot in width. The rocks come so near together at the top that one could jump from one side to the other. The name of this phenomena is Devils Gate. Why it was named that I cannot say unless some person would be dare devil enough to try to jump from one side to the other and perhaps miss his aim and loose his life. None in our company was foolish enough to try it. In after years I made an acquaintance with a lady who said they thought her brother tried to make the leap but failed and was found dead below.

It hardly seems plausible, of course, that anyone would attempt such a jump since Devil's Gate is "perhaps, 300 feet across at the top at the widest part," and the chasm is from 300 to 500 feet deep, and about 30 feet wide at the bottom.[17] The rock through which the river has carved its narrow passage is the same type of granite formation as Independence Rock, and therefore Devil's Gate has the same geological history. As the river slowly eroded downward in this locality, it eventually encountered the granitic rock and continued cutting into a weak zone in the granite, perhaps a fault, rather than be diverted around the granite.

As the sun . . . shed . . . her last golden ray over the mountain top, the quiet breeze bore away on its zephyr wings the odor of the frugal meal served throughout the various divisions of the camp. The evening was spent in rest, all having been refreshed by natur[e]s bath. Nothing to disturb the quiet of the night but the lowing of some lonely ox and tinkling of bells on the distant hill side keeping time with the noisy cataract that was making its way through the narrow canyon far below. Never did the kings of old rise from their beds of down, covered with the snow white silken sheets to array . . . [themselves in] royal robe[s], appreciate the rising sun [that] shed its golden rays on kingly mansion[s] more than did these humble emigrants, who had a quiet nights rest on their hard and dusty beds.

[We] woke early in the morning refreshed and rested, with the happy thought that we had once more reached a land where pure water could be obtained and fairly good grazing for the stock. It was a beautiful morning in July. Bright and early all was astir. Camp fires sending clouds of smoke and sparks heavenward. The sun pushing up her golden rays as if no cloud could ever obscure the light of the earth again. All were busy, getting ready to move on at an early hour. All were on the march with a good supply of good pure water for our days journey as every canteen and every vessel available was brought in use.

The next segment of Mary Ann's story took place between Devil's Gate and the continental divide (South Pass), a distance of about ninety miles. Even though her recollection was that it took them only a couple of days, the journey actually required at least a week to complete. Before continuing with Mary Ann's account, following here is a summary of the route together with a few incidents, experiences, and scenes recorded by others in June and July 1852. Although Mary Ann only briefly described this part of the journey, the Boatman party probably observed the same sights and events as others.

The trail followed within a mile or two of the river for much of this distance, and Split Rock eventually came into view, a sentinel that emigrants could see from miles away. After passing Split Rock and diverting south of the river, the road continued westerly across a five-mile stretch of desert. Just before reaching the river again, the alternate Deep Sand route led off to the left. This road had been used by earlier travelers and still was utilized by some in 1852. At this fork in the road, however, the trail to the right, or the "Three Crossings" route, proved more desirable to most emigrants than did the sandy left-hand route. In less than a mile from the intersection, the first of three Sweetwater crossings was made within about a two-mile distance. John McAllister, among others, observed that after completing the first ford, "the road runs close to the bluff on the right on the rocks of which are the names of many emigrants."[18]

Following the three crossings, the road forded the river once again (actually the fifth Sweetwater crossing up to this time) and then merged with the Deep Sand road from the south. At the first of the "Three Crossings," swift justice was summoned for a murder on June 29 1852. Although some mention of the incident was made by almost all 1852 diarists that passed this way, probably Origen Thomson, a single man from Indiana, presented one of the more detailed accounts.[19]

Thomson related that the incident occurred "a short time before we came up." It seems that a young man under the employ of an older man had been continually quarreling on their journey. The situation finally culminated in the older man shooting the other while under the pretense of hunting. After "the man acknowledged the act, but boasted that they could not find the body," the dead man was found. In short order,

> a jury was empaneled and the man condemned. They made a gallows by running two or three wagons with their tongues together, so as to make a fork. . . . The culprit was made to stand on some boxes and the rope put on his neck; . . .the sheriff kicked the boxes from under him and he was launched into eternity. This is the way in which justice is meted out on the Plains—without impediment of legal proceedings.[20]

According to Abigail Scott, the murdered man's name was Charles Botsford and the condemned man was Horace Dolley.[21] They were buried side by side.

Another four miles brought the emigrants to a swampy area known as Ice Slough, or Ice Spring. It froze in the severe winters to a considerable depth. When the sun beat down in the summer, however, the spring's thick vegetative cover served as insulation for icy tundra-like deposits. Thus, by digging down a foot or two, it was possible to find frozen ground and ice. Many were skeptical, such as William Byers, a young, single man from Iowa who arrived here on June 28. He penned, "by digging to a depth of over two feet the ice is found which I call no ice. It is a formation resembling ice, compose (I think) of Alum, Salt, Saleratus, etc."[22]

Other early travelers did recover ice. Today, probably due to the lowering of the water table, Ice Slough essentially is dry and little ice forms in winter.[23]

Another ten miles over the rolling, arid terrain brought travelers to the sixth crossing of the Sweetwater River. From here, three more crossings yet lay ahead—the seventh and eighth fords occurred within a short distance, beyond which in eight miles Rocky Ridge was ascended. After observing the view from this vista, emigrants descended into a meadow-like locality and proceeded on to Strawberry Creek, a major tributary of the Sweetwater where trading posts were in operation. Ten more miles brought the wagons to the ninth and final ford of the Sweetwater. From there, with lofty Pacific Butte (known to the emigrants as Table Mountain) looming ahead, they made their final, gradual ascent for ten miles to the broad and nearly imperceptible summit of South Pass, elevation 7,550 feet.

Since most emigrants never before had seen scenery quite like that of the Sweetwater Valley, diarists often attempted to describe the landscape and picturesque campsites. Although frequently rugged and difficult to traverse, the beauty, or at least the oddity, of the terrain captured attention. After having departed Devil's Gate the previous day, John Kerns related his impressions of July 2. "Our road lay along up Sweetwater, surrounded entirely by hills of rocky mountains appearing to be from 400 to 600 feet in height, and with the narrow valleys far below, portrayed some delightful scenery."[24]

On the following day, the Kerns company passed through the Three Crossings area (actually fords two, three, and four) and then to the fifth Sweetwater crossing. Kerns wrote, "our road was mostly hemmed in close to the river, so much so that we were at times compelled to go in the water to get along. . . . The country is about as we have seen for the last few days. Mountains, rocky abrupt, valleys, sandy and gravelly."[25]

While camped on the banks of the Sweetwater some ten miles beyond the seventh crossing, Polly Coon described an apparently crowded campsite, but, nevertheless, a picturesque scene.

> We have a beautiful camping ground on the bank of the S. Water. Clumps of willows thickly tangled with goosebery & wild Rose whose perfume is sweet as "Home" are scattered along its banks. On every side are camped the busy bustling emigrants with their thousand cattle Near us nipping the soft grass is a flock of sheep & were it not for the lofty snow capped mountain peaks which soar aloft towards the blue

heavens on either side one could almost fancy himself back among the scenes of childhood.[26]

She philosophically pondered:

> How different will be the scene in a few weeks—where now are moving daily thousands of white people will be heard nothing but the sound of the savage tongue & the quiet hills which now are speckled with horses oxen & cows, will soon be deserted by all save the wild animals of the country.[27]

Diarists in June and July 1852 noted that snow yet remained on the ground in places along the Sweetwater. Apparently, an unusual amount had fallen in the winter. According to Conyers' account, it must have remained in shaded or high places as far down as the Devil's Gate vicinity because, as previously related, snow was obtained for making ice cream on July 4.[28] Most records, however, indicate that snow banks were prevalent along the trail for a day or two prior to reaching South Pass. John Kerns reported for July 8, "the prairies are covered with snow in many places now."[29] At the time, the party was a day east of South Pass.

Francis Sawyer also mentioned snow on June 25, the day before reaching South Pass. "We pass plenty of snow and had all the ice water that we could use."[30]

Twelve miles west of Willow Creek on June 24, Mariett Cummings noted that Aspen Creek's banks were "covered with snow." When encamped nearby, she also observed that they were next to a "bank of snow 30 feet deep." The next day near the last Sweetwater crossing, she "walked over a snow bank several feet deep and supplied myself with a snowball."[31]

Lucy Cooke noted when writing a letter to her sister sometime in late June, probably near the last crossing: "we [are] bathing by the side of the snow banks & in sight of mountains covered with it."[32] Mary Ann Boatman also would report the presence of snow in the wide, open South Pass locality.

According to diarists, several trading establishments were open along the Sweetwater where a variety of supplies were offered, but always at inflated prices. After leaving the Devil's Gate area on June 30, Abigail Scott noted, "we passed a trading post this morning belonging to a Salt Lake Company; They asked $20 per bbl. for flour $12 per gal. for brandy and other things in proportion."[33]

On July 26, Cecelia Adams recorded after leaving Devil's Gate: "passed a station here we traded off a yoke of oxen for a yoke of cows."[34]

William Byers also mentioned a trading post located about one mile beyond Devil's Gate.[35] Hubert Papin and associates owned the establishment. It was abandoned in 1856.[36]

The trading post that Conyers mentioned earlier, as being built by "Schambau" (Alfred A. Archambault), operated until 1856.[37] It was Archambault, of course, who had directed Conyers' party to the Fourth of July celebration site in the nearby mountains.

Polly Coon on July 11, 1852, mentioned another trading station some ten miles beyond the seventh crossing of the Sweetwater River. This would have been near Spring Creek, south of the Rocky Ridge area. On the same date, she further notes that they were camped near a large site recently "occupied by about 2000 Indians of the Snake & Crow tribe."[38]

There were at least two stations still further west. Cecelia Adams on July 30 passed one shortly before reaching a branch of the Sweetwater, probably either Rock or Willow Creek.

> Here we saw plenty of Indians They seem very friendly They were engaged in dressing some prairie dogs They had several little Pappoos's they look very cunning Some were makeing moccasins for sale they trim them very nice with beads.

Traveling farther, Cecelia related that they came to another station with a blacksmith shop. She also saw a white woman and men "engaged in gambling and playing cards." Apparently, Cecelia's family camped nearby "on a branch of the Sweetwater."[39]

On June 25, Francis Sawyer also passed one of the trading posts. Although she did not specifically state where it stood, according to her party's recorded mileage from Independence Rock, it could well have been in the Rock Creek–Willow Creek area. She referred to the keeper as a "Frenchman." Here, they exchanged their wagon for a lighter one, and traded a stubborn mule for an Indian pony. Well aware that the proprietor got the best of the deal, she philosophically conceded, "when you trade for anything on this trip, you usually give double value for what you get in return."[40]

Mariett Cummings on June 24 likewise referred to "a French trader's post in one of the ravines." He operated a grocery store with "an old squaw and some halfbreed children."[41] This establishment too may have been in the Rock Creek–Willow Creek area, since Mariett's party stopped this day at noon on Strawberry Creek, a few miles to the east. She also noted passing a blacksmith shop on Aspen Creek. It would seem that if the emigrants were willing to pay inflated prices, most of their needs were met along the Sweetwater during the summer of 1852.

In addition to the abandoned Indian camp mentioned by Polly Coon, other diarists referred to the prevalence of Indians along the Sweetwater road. James Akin Jr., probably on the Sweetwater at the fifth crossing, noted on July 5 that a "great many Indians came and camp within two miles of us. Trade some with us."

The next day, after traveling seventeen miles to the sixth crossing of the Sweetwater, Akin wrote, "Indians go with us. . . . Indians camp one mile above us." The next day's travel of fifteen miles placed them in the vicinity of Strawberry Creek. Akin simply stated, "Indians plenty."[42]

John Kerns, having traveled from the sixth crossing to a few miles beyond Strawberry Creek, recorded on July 5: "now among the Shawnee [Shoshone] Indians." He continued with his evaluation of the tribe. "We saw about 500 of them today and they all possess a good countenance, both as to intelligence and neatness. They lack nothing considering their situation."

A few days later on July 8, he referred to the same Shoshone or Snake Indians, but in less glowing terms, stating: "some 300 to 400 Snake Indians came and pitched camp 200 or 300 yards below ours on the same branch." Because most of the emigrant company was out hunting at the time, the Indians alarmed "the few at camp very much." Kerns noted after returning to camp, "we . . . watched the motions of the rascals close."[43]

The experiences recorded by these 1852 diarists probably were the same that the Boatmans and their small company had as they too passed through the Sweetwater corridor to South Pass. Mary Ann's story continues:

> We . . . began to ascend the Sweetwater Mountains as they were called in our guide book. The hill proved to be a steep and long one, teams going on and we women walking. In some places looked as if the wagons and oxen would fall backwards. About 2 o'clock p. m. we reached the summit.

As revealed shortly, this was not the South Pass summit. It may well have been the approach to Rocky Ridge some twenty-five miles east of the pass.

On finding no water for the stock all but the Boatman boys moved on saying they would not stop until they could find water for the cattle. The Boatmans unhitched saying they believed that within a mile north of the road [they] would find the river. So they unhitched and started off in pursuit of water. All of the other teams moved on, so that left me alone. I with fear and trembling, sat for hours by the road side expecting to be carried away by some monster, in what form it would be I could not imagine, as there was nothing to be seen or heard. The longer I waited the greater my fear increased. Another hour passed [and] nobody came. By this time I concluded to arm myself. Not knowing how to handle the rifle, the axe was brought into use. So I sat with axe in hand for another hour. At last I heard a sound and thought my time on earth had ended. With my axe in hand, I picked up courage enough to crawl out of the wagon and look to see what was coming. Dear reader what do you suppose it was, a boy with a horse loaded with water cans. He was going on in search of a camping place. He said the train was 2 or 3 miles back. As my fears had increased and I felt as if I would be murdered or carried away by something I know not what, I resolved to hide. So I went quit[e] away from the road and laid down waiting for my fait whatever it should be. After lying conceal[ed] for a while I heard someone call. Of course I thought it was Indians coming to rob and kill me. So after a few minut[e]s I . . . looked up. The men had come an[d] on finding me gon[e], had feared that the Indians had come and frighten me away as they had seen some on their way to the river. All my fears were for nothing. As to the journey to the river with cattle, it was a long an hard one. Insted of one mile, it proved to be 3 and rough steep hills to climb so that mad[e] us late to the camping ground. It was long after dark when we got to camp. Our comrades greeted us with joy. As the evening wore away to bed time, I amused the women folks by telling them of my [fears that I] would . . . [be] taken captive to spend a life in captivity, if there had been any savage to take me. But as it was, there was nothing except my imagination to be frighten at.

Our camping place proved to be quit a good one plenty of wood and grass not far away. Next morning all was astir bright and early. The air being cool we . . . [donned] our raps and started in advance of the team. On reaching the summit . . . we found snow, so we indulged in a little girls play snowballing for a while.

This summit, of course, was well known South Pass. It is marked today by a couple of monuments, one of which Ezra Meeker placed here in 1906 with the inscription:

OLD
OREGON
TRAIL
1843–57

At noon when we call[ed] a halt to rest and [eat] dinner, [there was] no grass or water for the cattle. After a short rest we moved on. Now came the task of a down hill descent. . . . Some parts of the way [were] very difficult to make. But as the teamster[s] wer[e] all that could be exp[ec]ted in skillfulness of men and driving ox teams there wer[e] no mishaps on the descent.

We have now made the journey over the mountain in safety [and] find a good campground. The plain is comparatively level with a small stream of water fed from a small spring from the mountain. From the appearance, in the winter [this place] would be one boggy marsh. But, as we were late in getting over as it was in July, the ground had dried up [and] was covered with coarse grass. It was an ideal camping ground and all [were] in favor of resting a day, as plenty of fuel could be obtained without much difficulty. Along the little water cours[e], grew, wild currant bushes with their fruit red and yellow, but not very palatable. We women gathered som[e] thinking to surprise the men when they come in from hunting on the mountainside and looking after the stock, with sitting before them a nice currant pie, and of a sure they were surprised and ourselves too. Of all the baking and stirring, the fruit was as ha[r]d as it was when first picked off of the bush. We should have known [they were not] eatable [because] ther[e] would not have been any left as hundreds of emigrants had passed on before us saying nothing about the Indians that rove the country.

The campsite almost certainly was at Pacific Springs, a popular stop-over 2½ miles west of the summit. From this spring, the emigrants first observed water running westward. Bushes still grow along this waterway, presumably Mary Ann's currants. Today, a small ghost town (privately owned) of later years is located here.

Notes

1. Howard Stansbury, "Exploration of the Valley of the Great Salt Lake," in *Exploring the American West*, reprinted 1988 (Washington D.C.: Smithsonian Institution Press, 1988), 60.
2. Ibid., 63.
3. Ibid.

4. Abigail Jane Scott [Duniway], "Journal of a Trip to Oregon," in *Covered Wagon Women: Diaries and Letters from the Western Trails,* 1852, vol. 5, edited and compiled by Kenneth L. Holmes and David C. Duniway (Glendale, California: Arthur H. Clark, 1986), 76.
5. Randy Brown, written communication, 1998.
6. John McAllister, "Diary of Rev. John McAllister," in *Transactions of the Fiftieth Annual Reunion of the Oregon Pioneer Association* (Portland, Oregon, 1922), 485; see additional information under note 2 in chapter four.
7. Ibid.
8. Mariett Foster Cummings, "A Trip across the Continent," in *Covered Wagon Women: Diaries and Letters from the Western Trails,* 1852, vol. 4, edited and compiled by Kenneth L. Holmes (Glendale, California: Arthur H. Clark, 1985), 143.
9. McAllister, 485.
10. Aubrey L. Haines, *Historic Sites along the Oregon Trail,* third edition (St. Louis, Missouri: Patrice Press, 1987), 197.
11. Ibid.
12. Enoch W. Conyers, "Diary of E.W. Conyers, a Pioneer of 1852," in *Transactions of the Thirty-third Annual Reunion of the Oregon Pioneer Association* (Portland, Oregon, 1905), 454.
13. Polly Coon, "Journal of a Journey over the Rocky Mountains," in *Covered Wagon Women: Diaries and Letters from the Western Trails,* 1852, vol. 5, edited and compiled by Kenneth L. Holmes and David C. Duniway (Glendale, California: Arthur H. Clark, 1986), 193.
14. Conyers, 456–58.
15. Ibid., 457–58.
16. Ibid., 458.
17. Gregory M. Franzwa, *The Oregon Trail Revisited,* third edition (Gerald, Missouri: Patrice Press, 1983), 264.
18. McAllister, 486.
19. Origen Thomson, in company with his recently married sister Camilla Thomson Donnell and her husband Zelik M. Donnell, was a member of a large Oregon-bound train consisting of nearly 100 persons, mostly from Dector and Rush counties, Indiana, together with others from Ohio and Illinois. In Oregon, Thomson surveyed much of the Umpqua country and was active in Republican politics. He returned to Indiana in 1858, married Zilla McCay, and apparently remained there until his death in 1882. Origen Thomson, *Crossing the Plains* (Fairfield, Washington: Ye Galleon Press, 1983), 7–9.
20. Ibid., 44.
21. Scott, 79.
22. William N. Byers had surveying experience and started out with a California-bound train from Dubuque, Iowa, but switched to the Mohoska County Company for Oregon at the Green River Crossing. In Oregon, he was active in the timber business and became a Deputy U.S. Surveyor for Oregon Territory. He soon returned to the states and married Mary Elizabeth Summers in 1854. During a short stay in the new town of Omaha, Nebraska Territory, he entered the newspaper business. By 1858, he had moved to Denver, Colorado, where he became a strong defender of law and order, and founded the *Rocky Mountain News,* a newspaper yet in operation today. William N. Byers, "The Odyssey of William N. Byers," edited by Merrill J. Mattes, in *Overland Journal,* vol. 1, no. 1 (1983), 14–16; vol. 1, no. 2 (1983), 15; published by the Oregon-California Trails Association, Independence, Missouri.

23. Haines, 221–22.
24. John T. Kerns, "Journal of Crossing the Plains to Oregon in 1852," in *Transactions of the Forty-second Annual Reunion of the Oregon Pioneer Association* (Portland, Oregon, 1914), 169.
25. Ibid.
26. Coon, 194.
27. Ibid., 194–95.
28. Conyers, 457.
29. Kerns, 171.
30. Francis Sawyer, "Kentucky to California by Carriage and a Feather Bed," in *Covered Wagon Women: Diaries and Letters from the Western Trails,* 1852, vol. 4, edited and compiled by Kenneth L. Holmes (Glendale, California: Arthur H. Clark, 1985), 100.
31. Cummings, 145.
32. Lucy Rutledge Cooke, "The Letters of Lucy R. Cooke," in *Covered Wagon Women: Diaries and Letters from the Western Trails,* 1852, vol. 4, edited and compiled by Kenneth L. Holmes (Glendale, California: Arthur H. Clark, 1985), 250.
33. Scott, 79.
34. Cecelia Adams, "Twin Sisters on the Oregon Trail: Cecelia Adams and Parthenia Blank," in *Covered Wagon Women: Diaries and Letters from the Western Trails,* 1852, vol. 5, edited and compiled by Kenneth L. Holmes and David C. Duniway (Glendale, California: Arthur H. Clark, 1986), 276.
35. Byers, vol. 1, no. 2 (1983), 14.
36. Noted Nebraska researcher Eli S. Ricker's interview with Magloire A. Mousseau revealed that Hubert Papin and Associates established a trading post one mile beyond Devil's Gate in 1852. Mousseau began clerking there at the time. Magloire Alexis Mousseau, October 30, 1906, Tablet 28, 16–17, Ricker Tablets, MS 8, Eli Seavey Ricker Collection, Nebraska State Historical Society, Lincoln, Nebraska.
37. "Documents and letters," in *Annals of Wyoming,* vol. 15, no. 3 (1943), 229–33.
38. Coon, 194.
39. Adams, 277.
40. Sawyer, 145.
41. Cummings, 145.
42. James Akin Jr., *The Oregon Trail Diary of James Akin Jr. in 1852: The Unabridged Diary with Introduction and Contemporary Comments by Bert Webber* (Medford, Oregon: Webb Research Group, Pacific Northwest Books, 1989), 38.
43. Kerns, 170.

Emigrant names are carved in sandstone east of the Green River at Steed Canyon. Could W.R. Walker be a little Addie Walker's folk? *W.W. Rau*

Chapter Eight

Sublette Cutoff

Now comes the 60 miles of desert to be cross[ed]. After eating our dinners and letting [the] cattle eat and drink all they would, every canteen, . . . keg, bottle, and vessel . . . that would hold water was brought in use. —Mary Ann Boatman

R EACHING THE CONTINENTAL DIVIDE was a major benchmark for emigrants. For weeks they had toiled over hills and valleys in a gradual ascent of the Rocky Mountains. At South Pass, elevation 7,550 feet, the climb was completed. The wide, nearly flat expanse of South Pass, however, gave them little sense of having reached a summit, but the westward flow of water from Pacific Springs, three miles further on, assured them that they were on western slopes. At the pass, William Byers commented that the "gentle rolling prairie surrounded it on every side. In short it seems nature intended this as a gateway of great highway of nations."[1]

For some, the arrival at South Pass was a place and time in their journey to reflect on the past as well as ponder the future. Origen Thomson decided to climb a nearby mountain (probably Pacific Butte) from which, "as far as my vision could extend wagon followed wagon until the foremost one dwindled into insignificance." He noted that he was standing on the divide, "separating the east from west, on the one side was home with all its endearments, on the other was hope with all its allurements." After musing over the past and future, Thomson "plucked a flower that grew on the summit, descended and joined the train."[2]

At Pacific Springs, many took time to rest livestock, reorganize loads, and repair wagons. Arid country and rugged mountains had yet to be traversed. Still, at this "halfway" point in the journey, their confidence was high and they were ready for whatever challenges lay ahead.

From Pacific Springs, the road descended for a few miles to a relatively flat and sparse sagebrush plain. Fifteen miles west of Pacific Springs, the road divided —with one trail leading to the southwest, and the other continuing almost straight ahead on a nearly due west course. This major junction, known as the "Parting of the Ways," remains clearly visible today. Both roads continue far off into the distance across the vast empty plain.

The left-hand road was the original route of the Oregon Trail. In a short distance, it crossed Little Sandy Creek, followed by the Big Sandy River, and eventually the Green River and Hams Fork before reaching Fort Bridger. There, emigrants bound for Salt Lake and some for California continued in a southwesterly direction. Those proceeding to Oregon and the remaining portion of the California-bound travelers went northwest. The Fort Bridger route was relatively easy traveling, following along watercourses and crossing a minimal amount of mountainous and arid terrain.

The right-hand road leading directly west from the "Parting of the Ways" became known as the Sublette Cutoff, having been initially traversed by fur-trader William Sublette in 1826. It is believed that wagons first took the route in 1844 when an old mountain man, Caleb Greenwood, led a train this way.[3] Consequently, the trail was known as the Greenwood Cutoff until 1849. The name Sublette Cutoff first appeared in *The Emigrants' Guide to California* (1849) by Joseph Ware, who had obtained information from John C. Fremont and William Sublette's younger brother Solomon.

This route of about a hundred miles generally traversed westward to rejoin the main Oregon Trail at the Bear River near today's Cokeville, Wyoming. Being more direct than the southward looping Fort Bridger route, it saved as much as seventy to eighty miles in distance, but there were tradeoffs.[4] The adversities were greater. Travelers first encountered fifty miles of high, waterless plains, known to the emigrants as the Little Colorado Desert. Beyond that, and almost over the same distance, a mountainous country had to be negotiated before the wagons finally reached succor in the Bear River Valley. The numerous steep ascents and descents in terrain sometimes exceeding 8,000 feet in elevation were challenging. Furthermore, the opportunity to rest, resupply, and refurbish at Fort Bridger was missed by taking the Sublette Cutoff.

The choice made by travelers at the "Parting of the Ways" was largely based on whether cutting distance and time was more desirable, or whether a stop at Fort Bridger was required. Key considerations included the condition of livestock and the emigrants themselves, and the state of the supplies and equipment. Also, reports about conditions along the routes ahead were evaluated, including the availability of grazing for livestock.[5]

By 1852, additional options were available to travelers not wishing to take the extra time to complete the longer Fort Bridger loop. The Kinney and Slate Creek cutoffs departed from the Fort Bridger road thirty to thirty-five miles west of the "Parting of the Ways." After crossing the Green River, these routes took a northwesterly course and eventually merged into a single road before joining the Sublette Cutoff. These variations became popular, mainly because they followed along watercourses and avoided much of the Little Colorado Desert. In 1852, these perhaps were more heavily traveled than the original cutoff leading west from the "Parting of the Ways."

For whatever reasons, the Boatmans followed the Sublette Cutoff. Perhaps the decision was made by tempestuous William Scott, who seemed to be in charge and in a hurry, regardless of the party's possible needs. On the other hand, it probably took little encouragement to convince the young, adventuresome Boatman brothers to take the gamble in spite of the known adversities ahead. Mary Ann and the Scott women perhaps would have preferred an opportunity to rest and shop at Fort Bridger, but they probably had little influence in the matter. Mary Ann did not identify which

A major decision had to be made at the "Parting of the Ways." The road at the left led to supplies and recuperation at Fort Bridger, whereas the Sublette Cutoff to the right was a shorter but a far more rigorous route through the desert and mountains. The person in the picture is the author. *Richard Klein*

route they took, but it becomes apparent in her account when crossing the desert beyond the Big Sandy River that they were on the Sublette Cutoff.

Among others taking the Sublette Cutoff in 1852 was the Clifton and Martha Read family, passing the intersection on July 20 and camping on Little Sandy Creek that evening.[6] The Reverend John Spencer family likewise selected this route, camping at the Little Sandy on July 27.[7] Scars on the landscape left by the emigrant wagons and livestock are yet evident today where trains descended or ascended in the Little Sandy watershed. On July 11, the Akin family also chose the right-hand road and managed to reach the Big Sandy River on the same day.[8]

The young McAuley clan, too, spent most of July 4 traveling from the "Parting of the Ways" along the Sublette Cutoff. Eliza McAuley recorded the following:

> Four miles brought us to the forks of the Salt Lake and California roads. We took the Sublette Cut-off, leaving Salt Lake to the south. Made eighteen miles today and camped on Big Sandy. Had to drive the Cattle about six miles toward the hills for grass. It has been so windy and dusty that some times we could scarcely see the length of the team, and it blows so tonight that we cannot set the tent or get any supper, so we take a cold bite and go to bed in the wagon. The wagons are anchored by driving stakes in the ground and fastening the wagon wheels to them with ox chains.[9]

Wind and dust often were bothersome along the flat, arid segment of road leading to the Big Sandy River. Many teams, already weakened by the long, hard pull up to the Continental Divide, were unable to cope with the harsh conditions and succumbed along the way. Reportedly, during some years the entire road from Pacific Springs to the Big Sandy River became "one vast graveyard of sick and dying cattle."[10] The stench of dead animals on the desert winds added to the misery of crossing this wasteland.

After camping at or near Pacific Springs just west of South Pass, Mary Ann's story continues to the Big Sandy River.

> **We now take up our march for a long and weary journey of which seems as if there is no end. To[i]ling on and on, nothing out of every days occurrence happening to be worth mention, only tired and foot sore, all most wishing at time[s] that we had not been car[ri]ed away with fairy stories told by money makers of the far western country**

and, of its great recourse, making [for] homes to spring up in one night like Jonas gourd. We pushed on through sand, up hill and down. Nothing unusual occurring more than now and then a dispute about some nonsensical thing that no one paid any attention to. About the first of August, if my memory serves me correct, we came to a wide shallow sluggish stream of water called the Big Sandy. . . . [Because] it run through quick sand . . . it [was] unsafe for a team to cross, [except] only in one place. As . . . the men had become use to all kind of precaution, a man was selected to ride across on horse back to try the bottom of the stream, as quick sand often changes it[s] course. It was found by going up stream and driving down stream for a hundred yards and then mak[ing] for the opposite bank, [it] would be safe. Only one team at a time was allowed to drive in for fear that something would go wrong. It was 10 clock A. M. By noon all was safely landed over.

Today the Big Sandy ford is far less formidable. A visit here by the author in July 1994 found the watercourse to be only about fifteen-feet wide and little more than ankle deep. The Big Sandy Reservoir located immediately upstream probably accounts for much of today's reduced flow.

In addition to difficulties in fording the river, apparently by July 1852 all of the grass was gone in the vicinity. As indicated by Eliza McAuley, as early as July 4 cattle were driven some six miles from camp to find grazing.[11] Other wayfarers shortly verified this inconvenience. Martha Read recorded on July 21 that they went eight miles upstream for grazing,[12] and John Spencer on July 29 "moved up B Sandy 6 or 7 miles to better grass."[13]

It was important that cattle were well fed and watered at the Big Sandy, as the next fifty miles to the Green River continued over a barren, waterless land. Many spent a full day in the vicinity, resting and feeding the cattle before beginning the long, arid trek to the Green River. To avoid the heat of day as much as possible, they usually traveled at least part of the distance in the cool of night.

On July 30, the Spencers "started across the desert at 2 o'clock P.M. Stoped an hour for supper after traveling some 10 miles. Then moved on and stoped at 3 o'clock A. M. next morning. Had a hard night."[14] They reached the Green River at two o'clock in the afternoon.

On July 6, the McAuleys "started about noon, crossed Big Sandy and traveled part of the night before stopping to camp." The next day, they "started before daylight and traveled until sunrise, when we found good grass and stopped to get breakfast. . . . At sundown we arrived at the Green River."[15]

The Akins family departed the Big Sandy at 10 A.M. on July 14 and traveled until dark, at which time they stopped for supper. They then continued the journey until midnight. After an hour of rest, their travel resumed until daylight when grass was found for their cattle. Continuing on, they arrived at the Green River at noon on July 15.[16]

After crossing the Big Sandy River and ascending onto the flat plain, Haystack Butte came into view two miles away, About seventy-five feet high and perhaps a hundred feet across, this looming erosional remnant was a beckoning guidepost upon which the emigrants aimed their westward course. In the parched Sublettes Flat, dust reportedly stood from one to twelve inches deep at times.[17] The clouds of suffocating dust billowed about and covered everything, making it difficult to see, let alone protect the eyes.

Other than the steep and challenging dry gulches at Buckhorn Canyon and West Buckhorn Draw, the road continued through relatively flat country. Within a few miles of the Green River, however, a steep and difficult descent from the desert tableland led down Steed Canyon to the valley floor, dropping almost 400 feet along a sandstone bluff. It was another three miles to the banks of the cool, clear Green River.[18] Here, livestock and humans alike wasted no time quenching their thirst.

In Mary Ann's description of the journey across this parched landscape, she states that the distance traveled was sixty miles, but it actually was about fifty. Perhaps she counted the miles from the "Parting of the Ways," which would have been nearer sixty miles—and, of course, all across very arid terrain.

> Now comes the 60 miles of desert to be cross[ed]. After eating our dinners and letting [the] cattle eat and drink all they would, every canteen . . . keg, bottle, and vessel of every kind that would hold water was brought in use. It was the last watering place for 60 miles. We are off, all of the men and women walking, some with buckets filled with water carrying them in hand. Late in the evening a halt was call[ed] and the teams unhitched and guarded while they grazed an hour. We human animals eat our lunch. Then all was ready to make another start. The children and women wer[e] stowed away in the wagons, that is all that felt like riding after the oxen in the dark. I for one choose to walk most of the night. About mid night the teams got tired and restless. One teamster drove his team on a side hill and upset. Poor fellow, he may have gon to sleep for all any body knew. When the hinder teams come up he had the oxen unhitched and [was] trying to right the wagon down side up. Our wagon came

next to his. As luck was on his side, no person was in his wagon. He drove the provision and camp out fit for Scott. After an hour of work for all hands the wagon was rite side up and all moved on until daybreak. By this time both man and beast wer[e] both tired and thursta. We hurriedly gathered together a few buffalo chips, built a fire, boiled some water, made our coffee, fried some bacon, ate a hasty breakfast, let the teams rest a while, not durst to unyok for fear they would run away on the desert. [It] was so dry that no grass grew. At night no dew fell to moisten the earth. We did not see a living thing that made the wilderness it[s] home. No not as much as a reptile.

Now we have taken up our march again: men tired and sleepy, women dragging behind declaring that end of the road will never come, or we would never find it. The poor cattle almost unmanageable. About 3 o'clock in the afternoon the cattle began to snuff the air as if they smelled something that excited them. In a moment it was thought that water must be near. A man was sent on to see how far it was to water. He galloped a way as fast as the poor gaded horse could go, returning as speedly as he could, sa[i]d it was 2 miles at the least and that a quarter of a mile before the river was reached [there] was a alkali pool that cattle would run in and drink and then die or be sick and be no use. The banks of it wer[e] cover[e]d with dead cattle and bones. Now what could be done. It was impossible to control them any longer. So every man but one to a team was detail[ed] to go on and guard the pool so the cattle would not get to the alkali water. They pushed on as speedily as it was possible for them to do. But oh what a time the men had that were taking care of the oxen that was hitched to the wagons. They became wild and mad [and] could not be controled. So it was decided to unhitch as it was a sure fact that they would stampede. So all [were] unhitched from the wagons, but could not get them unyoked. As they started on the run, snorting and bellowing like a frighten band of buffalo, went t[e]aring down to the alkali pool. The man on horse back rode in the lake to try to keep the cattle from drinking the lye water, as it was an tasted like strong lye. But they could not possibly keep them all from drinking some of the lye water, but few drank enough to hurt them. One of Boatmans wheel oxen, old Duke was his name, got enough to lay him up for repairs for a few days. By giving him bacon greas[e] and salt he got better but not well for 2 weeks. one of the lead oxen got to much and died in a few weeks. It looked discouraging to be thousands of mile from no where and your team begins giving out an dying and not knowing what perils was a head of us.

Today, alkali ponds yet remain near the mouth of Steed Canyon. Although Mary Ann did not explain how they finally got the cattle to the river, they obviously were successful in doing so. From a trader he met near Devil's Gate, Enoch Conyers learned of an alkali poisoning remedy that was similar to the cure used by the Boatmans on their livestock. "Take one-half pint each of lard and syrup; warm just sufficient to mix good, and if the animal is bloated, add one-half pint of good vinegar and drench them immediately."[19] By using this remedy, Conyers claimed he never again lost livestock because of alkali or other poisons.

> **The cattle and men have all quench their thirst. the next thing to do was to drive the oxen back to their wagons and bring them down to the river. As I have said, we were compeled to unhitch a mile from the river. It is now late in the evening all are at the river, a crooked swift stream. It must be forded like all that we had crossed.**

The Green River was one of the swiftest and most treacherous streams along the entire Oregon Trail. Reportedly, at least a hundred yards wide and, at times, nearly ten-feet deep, it had an estimated current of twelve to fifteen miles per hour.[20] Emigrants forded or ferried the river at a number of points between Steed and Anderson canyons, a distance of about seven miles. However, most crossed at just a few designated places. Although the details of the 1852 crossings are not fully known, the following fords probably were primarily used.

An uppermost crossing at the mouth of Steed Canyon was popular for many years, since it was on a direct line from Steed Canyon. The Boatmans perhaps forded here, as this was the shortest route to the river. Another frequently used ford crossed less than a half-mile downstream, just north of today's oil company bridge.[21] An Upper Ferry operated a short distance downstream from the bridge and directly across from the mouth of Delaney Canyon.[22] This may have been where William Byers crossed on the morning of July 8, observing "four good ferry boats here. Ferriage $6. per wagon."[23]

A third major crossing, both a ferry and ford, was situated two-and-one-half miles downstream from Steed Canyon in the immediate vicinity of Names Hill. It was known by some as the Mountain Men's Ferry, and by others as the Middle Ferry.[24] Two additional ferry sites were used, particularly in the early years of travel. One was located two miles south of Names Hill at Muddy Creek, and the second, known as the Mormon Ferry, was three miles further downstream at the mouth of Anderson Canyon. The two sites now are submerged beneath Fontenelle Reservoir.[25]

The McAuleys probably used the Upper Ferry because Eliza noted, after ferrying across and camping, that the next day, July 8, they traveled two miles downstream to where "thousands of names [were] cut in the soft rock." This was Names Hill. She also noted, "ferriage, six dollars per wagon."[26] The Reads likewise "crossed in a ferry Boat. Paid 20 shilling a wagon and swam our cattle."[27]

Mary Ann Boatman verifies the perils of fording the Green River.

> They [the men] decided it better to cross over that evening as we would be a way from the alkali water and that the grass would be more plentiful, as the stock had not had anything to eat for 36 hours. So it was decided to cross the river. The man on horse back rode in to try it[s] depth, and [found] it so deep and swift that if every precaution were not taken that some of the wagons and its contents would be lost. It was decided to run rope from the top of one standard to the other and put the wagon box on top to keep it from floating and to keep the contents dry. In a short time all was redy to start. The man on horse back went a head of the team as it went in the swift cold water. The Boatman boys went first. Oh, that hour of horror as I have always expressed it in my long life time. We were . . . all loaded in the wagon box up to the top of the standard, Willis Boatman, John Boatman, Mr. Warner, and myself. As the oxen got

The site of a Green River ferry crossing at the mouth of Delaney Canyon on the Sublette Cutoff. The trace of the trail can be seen passing through the trees at the left. *W. W. Rau*

mid way of the swift stream it was so deep and swift that the cattle had to swim and started down stream. Every moment we expected to be up set. John Boatman, dear boy, being the small one of the men, pull[ed] off his shoes and coat and run out on the tongue of the wagon and on the cha[i]n that held the 2 lead yoke of oxen. . . . [By] taking one of the lead steers by his horn [and] drop[ping] himself in the water, holding to the horn of the swimming ox, [he] talked and slaped him on the cheek and finely suceeded in turning the team upstream. The water was so swift it washed John's pants and socks off. Poor boy he was all out of breath and said he could [not] have kept his hold much longer. Now do you wonder that I look back and think of it in any other light but horrible.

Now all [were] over that part of the stream. It [was] sun down and the moving city once more set up for the night. It was decided to lay bye a day and rest both man and beast, as there was grass for the cattle, altho they had to be [driven] quit[e] a ways from camp to find good grazing. Plenty of wood and water as timber grew on the banks of the stream. We soon found out that this stream had to be crossed nine times, as we had crossed it one time only eight more times for us to cross, but none was so deep and swift as the first one. If I remember correct, our guide book called it Green River.

Mary Ann is wrong in respect to crossing the Green River "nine times." Almost certainly, she mistakenly remembered the crossings of the Sweetwater River already negotiated some distance back. Travelers on the Sublette Cutoff forded the Green River just once.

While the men [were] looking after the stock, the women folk [were] washing up dirty clothes and baking bread for another day. So you see all had his or her duty to preform. All slept sound that night but the guards who made ther regular change at midnight.

I will now try to expla[i]n why the river had to be crossed so often. The river made its corse down a canyon and the wagon road followed the canyon. . . . As the canyon was narrow, the river shifted from one side to the other. So, in some places the river would [be] on one side of the canyon, then cross on the other side. So that accounts for so often crossing [the] stream.

To reiterate, she most likely recalled the Sweetwater fords, particularly Three Crossings, where emigrants encountered restrictive canyon walls forcing them to cross three times in two miles. At any rate, Mary Ann's description could not have been of the Green River.

Now all are once more on the rough and tirsom[e[journey. The road through the canyon is very rough. We toiled on all day and made about 10 miles, the cattle being so fagged out from the drive across the desert that it was prudent to take as good cear [care] of them as it was possible to do. [Then came the] hard drive to make the ascent out of the canyon that we had been traveling down for so many miles. Day after day we toiled on some times trav[e]ling after night when the moon give light so the road could be followed. Now the progress down is completed.

Mary Ann's recollections in the above paragraph are unclear. If it is assumed that the canyon she describes was encountered after crossing the Green River, it probably was located somewhere along the remaining section of the Sublette Cutoff, and prior to reaching the Bear River.

After days of hard toil for man and beast, we now find a little stream to the left of the road, winding in and out through the rocks [a] silvery . . . thread. A halt was called [and] all with joy, greeted its refreshing beverage. O reader, on reaching its bank what pang of sudden fright met our gaze. There were three new graves, and on a sheet of writing paper wer[e] written these words, "We a company of emigrants of five wagons called a halt here yesterday noon finding a man about 40 years old, woman about 35, with front teeth filled with gold, a swcingle around her neck, been dragged down to waters edg[e]. A boy about 10 years old all have their throats cut from ear to ear. Advising all that coming to be on the look out for Indians." As to who had comited [this] crime, no one knew as there was no sign of anything left but the dead bodies [and] wagons. . . . The cattle were gone. It was all a mystery who had [committed the] crime. . . . Though no pleasant task to bring this sad after part to the notice of the reader, it is nevertheless a tail that may be interesting for him to ponder . . . and give him some idea . . . of what misfortunes can bef[a]ll those who first traversed that long and dangerous journey 2,000 miles through a wilderness its chief inhabitants inhuman savages that rove over hill and plain seeking whom he might devour. . . . Frequently small scouts of Indians pass us scantly dressed, if it could be called dress at all. What little they wore was shockingly indecent, being stolen from the wild animals, but not so graceful fitting as whe[n] belonging to its former . . . owner.

This story of horror is strikingly similar to one related earlier on June 29 by Polly Coon while traveling along the North Platte near Douglas, Wyoming. The three graves—of a man, woman, and boy—together with a similar note on a tree, suggest that Polly's and Mary Ann's observations were of the same incident. Regardless of where the Boatmans actually approached the scene of these dreadful murders, the event became well etched in Mary Ann's memory, though she may not have remembered the correct location. This encounter nevertheless impacted their thinking and actions:

> We wer[e] now in a state of confusion as we all knew the Oatman family had been way laid in 1851 one year before, [and] part of the family taken in captivity. 9 in all. Two girls [were] taken in captivity 7 left for dead. Lorenzo, a boy of 14 revived after the heartless savages had gone. Knowing of this, we wer[e] at a loss to know what to do. It was finely decided to move on, not wishing to shear the same fate, not know[ing] but the savage and murderous fiends . . . might return to [the] scen[e] of slaughter and treat us in the same manner.

The well-publicized Oatman incident significantly contributed to instilling a fear of Indians in the minds of many westward travelers in 1852.[28] It took place in Arizona on March 19, 1851, near the Gila River about seventy miles east of Fort Yuma. Royse Oatman, along with his pregnant wife Mary Ann and their seven children, originally were in a company led by James C. Brewster, the head of a Mormon sect. They were on their way to establishing what they believed would be a utopian settlement in the wilderness. All in the company eventually gave up the trek except the Oatmans, who pressed on alone.

With supplies nearly gone, their animals giving out, and nearly exhausted themselves, the Oatmans were overtaken and assaulted by a band of Indians, probably Yavapais. The attackers first struck down fourteen-year-old Lorenzo, then murdered Royse, his wife, and four other children, but spared sixteen-year-old Olive and a younger sister, Mary Ann. The two girls were forced to walk some 200 miles to the Indians' mountain camp and were held captive for a year, after which time they were sold to the Mojave tribe. Although treated somewhat better, Mary Ann died during the winter of 1852–53.

Young Lorenzo Oatman, who remarkably had survived the attack, eventually would begin a search for the girls. Through the efforts of a compassionate carpenter at Fort Yuma named Henry Grinnell and a contact in the Catholic church, a ransom was promised for the girls' release, together with the threat of force from an imaginary expedition if they were not freed. On February 20, 1856, Olive was released near Fort Yuma. She had been tattooed on the chin and arms and was in poor physical and mental condition. However, she recovered and in 1865 married John B. Fairchild, had children, and apparently lived happily in the Red River country of North Texas until her death in 1903.

Mary Ann's story continues:

After considering the circumstance, it was decided to move on a few mil[e]s and keep gurare [guards], both on cattle and camp. After eating a cold lunch and watering the teams, filling all the canteens with pure water, all was on the march again. Sometime between dark and midnight a halt was called. Some train a head of us had abandon a wagon. The night being dark and no fuel for fire the men . . . took it apart to build fires [and] to get our suppers with. A hasty meal . . . was eaten, cattle unyoked, guard station[ed] around camp and cattle. [The] men [were] almost exhausted and [the] women [were] all excited for fear of an attack of some kind. On knowledge of what it would be, no[body] could sleep through the temporary city that night but the small children. Ere yet twilight had lifted the deepes[t] shades of night from the plain and hill side on the morning of the next day, there was a stir and a bustle and hurryin to and fro through out the camp. As beautiful a sunrise as ever mantled the east or threw its first purest glories upon a long and gladdened west, found all thing[s] in order . . . the colony arranged [and] prepared for march, all glad that his or her scalp was not taken off. Through the long weary night perhaps all of the precaution taken was unnecessary, as no intruder of any kind molested us. But as human power is weak and what little strength he has so weakened by toil and lack of proper nourishment that it takes but little to discourage.

The moving city crept on at snail fashion for day after day. Nothing unusual occurring more than everyday a like up hill and down through sand and alkali dust and water, scarcity of grass for the stock and fuel for fire. After weeks of toil we had come to the Snake River.

As mentioned, a portion of Mary Ann's account might not be in proper chronological order and her descriptions sometimes are vague and brief. However, much of her commentary obviously does actually depict the party's experiences between the Green and Snake rivers, a considerable distance of about 170 miles. To gain a fuller understanding of this segment of trail, the records of other 1852 travelers are presented here and in chapter nine.

A sandstone bluff now called Names Hill is among the points of interest just west of the Green River crossing. As previously mentioned, Eliza McAuley noted on July 8, after traveling two miles downstream from camp, "we had to climb a very sharp bluff. On the bluff along the road are thousands of names cut in the soft rock. . . . of course [we] left our own record.[29]

Today, U.S. Route 189 passes by the foot of this bluff where numerous emigrant names and dates yet remain etched in the sandstone. Not only did early white travelers leave their mark here, but also, in places, there are much older Native American petroglyphs beneath the mid-nineteenth century carvings. The steep climb up the "sharp bluff" mentioned by Eliza McAuley, though modified in recent years, still remains apparent.

From the top of Names Hill, the trail led southward for a hilly twelve miles to Fontenelle Creek. The most notable feature along this section was Holden Hill where emigrants again carved inscriptions on a prominent sandstone outcrop. Switchbacks had to be negotiated when descending into the green Fontenelle Creek Valley. A welcome sight to emigrants, this was a pleasant stopping place to feed cattle, indulge in fishing, conduct trade with white traders and Indians, and rest and reorganize for the challenges ahead.

From here, the trail continued in a southwesterly direction for thirteen miles over low, barren ridges to what was called Pine Grove Campground. This was a popular site for wayfarers. The pines and Sheep Creek were an oasis surrounded by a much less hospitable landscape. According to Eliza McAuley, here on the evening of July 10, "our old traveling companions Buck and the Meekers came up and camped with us. We left them on the Platte River and have not seen them since. Ezra has been sick with the mountain fever, but is better now."[30]

From the Pine Grove Campground, the journey continued southwesterly on a steep, long ascent to the top of Slate Creek Ridge, a rise of over a thousand feet, and reaching 8,250 feet above sea level. This was one of the high points along the Sublette Cutoff, and the first in a series of north-south trending ridges encountered before reaching the Bear River.

At this point, emigrants were entering what geologists refer to today as the Overthrust Belt.[31] This formidable series of high ridges and deep valleys largely extends between the Green and Bear river valleys. These features resulted from a foreshortening of the earth's crust along lengthy, north-south trending faults. Limestone, sandstone, and shale have been thrust up and pushed eastward over each other. Subsequent erosion has differentially formed an uplifted land surface, with high ridges consisting of resistant sandstone or limestone, and valleys composed of less resistant, softer rock such as shale.

In addition to Slate Creek Ridge, other major topographic features in this region include Commissary, Dempsey, and Rock Creek ridges and the Pomeroy Basin, Hams Fork, and Rock Creek valleys, all of which had to be negotiated before reaching the Bear River. In regard to one of these ridges, Abigail Scott observed on July 13, "on the summit we found plenty of excellent looking lime-stone rock and some specimens of quartz."[32]

From the top of Slate Creek Ridge, the trail descended steeply southwest, some 700 feet in a mile, to a narrow tributary valley of Slate Creek. From there it was only a short distance to Rocky Gap, a natural pass through Oyster Ridge. Within a mile before reaching the gap, the Slate Creek and Kinney cutoff from the Fort Bridger route approached from the southeast and joined the Sublette Cutoff. Thus, the travelers who at the "Parting of the Ways" had chosen to go southwest to the Kinney and Slate Creek cutoffs were again joined with those who took the Sublette trail (see map).

Willow Creek in the Rocky Gap vicinity provided an excellent camping place and an abundance of grass along a clear stream and several springs. Some who investigated the cliffs found large, fossilized oyster shells.[33]

Over the years, there were several choices of roads to take from Rocky Gap. One route led almost due west across Wheat Creek, over Commissary Ridge, and then southwest down Trail Creek to Hams Fork. Beginning in 1854, the Dempsey Cutoff branched off from this road in the upper reaches of Trail Creek and continued nearly due west to the Bear River Valley. This was the most direct route from Rocky Gap. Another trail led southwest from Rocky Gap across Pomeroy Basin and several branches of Willow Creek, over Commissary Ridge, through Branley Pass, and on to Hams Fork. This route appears to have been the most popular one in 1852 as indicated by the numerous diary accounts of that year.[34]

Apparently, several routes were developed through Pomeroy Basin over the years, all of which continued on to Branley Pass. The road over Commissary Ridge was steep and difficult, especially the descent from Branley Pass into the Hams Fork Valley. Wheels had to be locked and some wagons were controlled by men holding ropes attached to the rear of wagons. Once over the pass, there were several roads leading to the river.[35]

The fertile Hams Fork Valley was an excellent stopover point with an abundance of fine water and dense willow growth. Indians and traders also made use of this comfortable setting. The Adams and Blank party arrived here on July 9. Cecelia Adams wrote, "encamp to night on Ham's Fork here is an Indian village it consists of some 40 or 50 tents covered with buffalo skins. . . . Find good grass and a beautiful camp ground." The following day, they remained in camp until noon to rest the cattle, pick berries, and catch "some speckled trout."[36]

Several roads led westward from Hams Fork, all of which ascended steep White Hill. Eliza McAuley departing Hams Fork on July 12 recorded: "we have a very long, steep mountain to cross, two miles to the summit. In places it is very steep and difficult and we see the wrecks of several wagons and carriages that have broken down in attempting it."[37]

Reaching the top of White Hill, emigrants found themselves on an undulating upland between two east-west drainages of the Hams Fork Plateau. After traveling westward through lush grasses for six or seven miles, wayfarers arrived at Emigrant Spring, sometimes referred to as Quaking Asp Grove, situated a short distance below the Dempsey Ridge summit. The pine, aspen, and spring located here made this another favorite stopping place.

John McAllister noted a "tolerably good road to Quaking Asp grove & spring a beautiful grove left of the road the spring is at the north end." He assessed the locality, saying: "good soil a nice situation for a farm."[38] As a reminder of the adversities and risks of the times, the protected graves of Nancy Jane Hill (died July 1852), Alfred Corum, and others unknown are visible today flanking the trail's deep swales just east of Emigrant Spring.

Leaving Emigrant Spring, the road continued northward some two miles, climbing about 200 feet to the summit of Dempsey Ridge (elevation exceeding 8,200 feet above sea level), possibly the highest point on the Oregon Trail.[39] In this area, the trail passed through an impressive stand of timber, described by Eliza McAuley on July 12. "This afternoon we passed through a beautiful grove of fir and quaking aspen. Shortly after that we had some very steep rough road, mostly descending."[40]

At times, there were two choices in making the descent from Dempsey Ridge. One route continued northward along the summit for about four miles, where it joined the Dempsey Cutoff and descended the ridge. In 1852, however, this northern trail may not yet have been used. At any rate, the diarists suggest that another route was preferred, if not used exclusively. It began to descend a short distance after passing through the timber grove. The two-mile descent, with a 700-foot drop, was particularly steep, winding, and difficult, as confirmed by Eliza McAuley above. As in previous abrupt descents, wagon wheels were locked and men pulled back on ropes attached to the rear of the wagons. In spite of precautions, there were many accidents resulting in "the remnants of numerous wagons near the foot of the mountain."[41]

The descent brought travelers to narrow Rock Creek Valley, sometimes referred to as Stony Creek. After negotiating the stream, they ascended

1½ miles up Rock Creek Ridge to about 7,500 feet, which was considerably less elevation than the previous ridge. The final descent into the Bear River Valley also was steep and dangerous, as noted by Abigail Scott on July 13.

> In the afternoon we descended a very long steep hill from whose summit we viewed the Bear River Valley Creek: We traveled two miles without unlocking the wagon wheels and in many places men held back the wagon in addition to having both wheels locked. . . . We camped near a small stream with a tolerable good spring adjacent to it.[42]

A view of the wide Bear River Valley from atop the final ridge was a welcome sight to the tired wayfarers. The steep descent off Rock Creek Ridge to Sublette Creek or another tributary completed the torturous journey over the Sublette Cutoff. At this juncture in the Bear River Valley near present-day Cokeville, Wyoming, all of the Oregon bound travelers on the Sublette Cutoff and the Fort Bridger loop merged again on a single course.

Notes

1. William N. Byers, "The Odyssey of William N. Byers," edited by Merrill J. Mattes, in *Overland Journal*, vol. 1, no. 2 (1983), 15; published by the Oregon-California Trails Association, Independence, Missouri.
2. Origen Thomson, *Crossing the Plains* (Fairfield, Washington: Ye Galleon Press, 1983), 46.
3. Mike W. Brown, "'Cutoffs' and the Parting of the Ways," in *Headed West: Historic Trails in Southwest Wyoming*, edited by Mike W. Brown and Beverly Gorny (Salt Lake City, Utah: Artistic Printing, 1992), 71; published for the Oregon-California Trails Association Tenth Annual Convention, Rock Springs, Wyoming.
4. Ross L. Jensen, "The Greenwood-Sublette Cutoff of the Oregon Trail," University of Utah, Department of History, M.A. thesis, 1975, vi.
5. Brown, 70–72.
6. Martha S. Read, "A History of Our Journey," in *Covered Wagon Women: Diaries and Letters from the Western Trails*, 1852, vol. 5, edited and compiled by Kenneth L. Holmes and David C. Duniway (Glendale, California: Arthur H. Clark, 1986), 232.
7. On April 8, 1852, fifty-year-old John Spencer with his wife and children left Wellsville, Ohio, aboard the steamer *Paris*. At St. Louis on April 15, they boarded the steamboat *El Paso* and continued to St. Joseph, Missouri, where they began the overland trek to Oregon. Spencer became captain of a train consisting of eight wagons, two other families, and a number of single men. John Spencer, "Daily Journal Kept by John Spencer, 1852 from Wellsville, Ohio to Portland, Oregon," typescript manuscript, Oregon Historical Society, Portland, Oregon, 1–6, 14; Merrill J. Mattes, *Platte River Road Narratives* (Urbana and Chicago, Illinois: University of Illinois Press, 1988), 359 (entry 1179), 388 (entry 1287).
8. James Akin Jr., *The Oregon Trail Diary of James Akin Jr. in 1852: The Unabridged Diary with Introduction and Contemporary Comments by Bert Webber* (Medford, Oregon: Webb Research Group, Pacific Northwest Books, 1989), 39.

9. Eliza Ann McAuley, "Iowa to the 'Land of Gold,'" in *Covered Wagon Women: Diaries and Letters from the Western Trails*, 1852, vol. 4, edited and compiled by Kenneth L. Holmes (Glendale, California: Arthur H. Clark, 1985), 60.
10. Jensen, 28.
11. McAuley, 60.
12. Read, 232.
13. Spencer, 14.
14. Ibid.
15. McAuley, 61.
16. Akin, 41.
17. Jensen, 99.
18. Ibid., 11–12.
19. Enoch W. Conyers, "Diary of E.W. Conyers, a Pioneer of 1852," in *Transactions of the Thirty-third Annual Reunion of the Oregon Pioneer Association* (Portland, Oregon, 1905), 455.
20. Jensen, 116.
21. Bob and Karen Rennells, personal communication, 1996.
22. Ibid.
23. Byers, 16.
24. Jensen, 124–25.
25. Rennells; Jensen, 126–27.
26. McAuley, 62.
27. Read, 233.
28. Richard H. Dillon, "The Ordeal of Olive Oatman," in *American History*, September 1995, 30–32, 70–71; Royal B. Stratton, *Captivity of the Oatman Girls*, third edition, paperback (Lincoln, Nebraska: University of Nebraska Press, 1983), 290 pp.
29. McAuley, 62.
30. Ibid.
31. J.D. Love and A.C. Christiansen, *Geologic Map of Wyoming*, scale 1:500,000, 3 sheets, U.S. Geological Survey and Geological Survey of Wyoming, 1985.
32. Abigail Jane Scott [Duniway], "Journal of a Trip to Oregon," in *Covered Wagon Women: Diaries and Letters from the Western Trails*, 1852, vol. 5, edited and compiled by Kenneth L. Holmes and David C. Duniway (Glendale, California: Arthur H. Clark, 1986), 85.
33. Jensen, 190–91.
34. Ibid., 194–95.
35. Ibid., 197.
36. Cecelia Adams, "Twin Sisters on the Oregon Trail: Cecelia Adams and Parthenia Blank," in *Covered Wagon Women: Diaries and Letters from the Western Trails*, 1852, vol. 5, edited and compiled by Kenneth L. Holmes and David C. Duniway (Glendale, California: Arthur H. Clark, 1986), 273.
37. McAuley, 63.
38. John McAllister, "Diary of Rev. John McAllister," in *Transactions of the Fiftieth Annual Reunion of the Oregon Pioneer Association* (Portland, Oregon, 1922), 489; see additional information under note 2 in chapter four.
39. Jensen, 226.
40. McAuley, 63.
41. Jensen, 237.
42. Scott, 86.

Chapter Nine

Bear River to Fort Hall

[Fort Hall] was built 20 years ago . . . of Spanish Brick or adobe. it is 4 squar
[about 60 feet]. on the west line it is raised 2 storys. the other 3 walls are about
15 ft high. —Dr. Thomas White

UPON REACHING THE BEAR RIVER and joining with the travelers coming from Fort Bridger, the wagon parties continued northwest along
the luxuriant valley for sixty miles, enjoying an abundance of game, good
water, and knee-high grass. For the Sublette Cutoff wayfarers, many made
their first camp near the mouth of Smiths Fork. Here, they usually rested a
day after their rigorous travels.

On July 2, Francis Sawyer recorded, "came to the main Bear River today, and forded Smith's Fork. It was a very rocky and dangerous ford." In
camp, they soon learned that not all was serene in the valley: "the mosquitoes were so thick, so brave and resolute, that all our time was occupied in
fighting them off. . . . The grass is good here, but our mules could not eat
any until 8 o'clock. or after, when the mosquitoes left us."[1]

Shortly, a bridge was built across Smiths Fork. Eliza McAuley's party
on July 14, 1852, "crossed Smith's Fork of the Bear River on a toll bridge
which was just completed that morning."[2] The charge was fifty cents a
wagon. William Byers also crossed this bridge on the same day.[3]

Another eleven miles brought emigrants to the Thomas Fork crossing, two miles west of today's Wyoming-Idaho border, and one-half mile
north of U.S. Route 30. Thomas Fork also could be crossed on a toll bridge,
which was made of poles. According to John McAllister, the structure was
"tolerably substantial [where] the river [was] 70 feet wide 5 feet deep." He
further noted a ford located nine miles upstream.[4] The Sawyers, who crossed

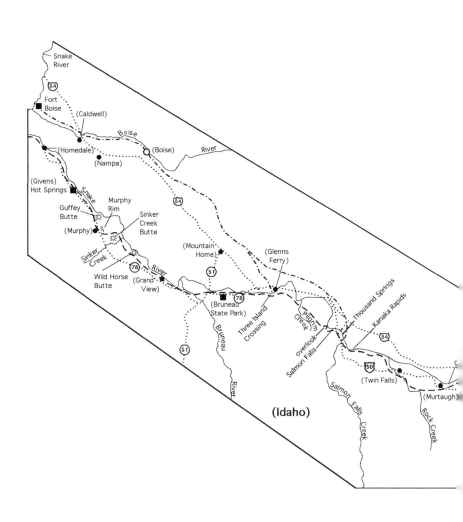

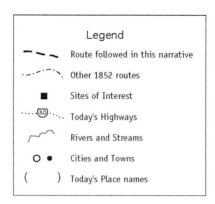

Legend

— — — Route followed in this narrative

·—··—·· Other 1852 routes

■ Sites of Interest

····(80)···· Today's Highways

‿‿‿ Rivers and Streams

○ ● Cities and Towns

( ) Today's Place names

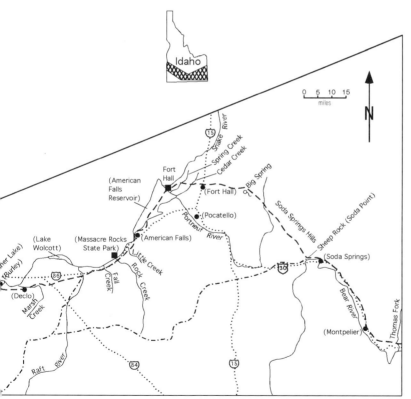

Idaho

0 5 10 15
miles

N

Snake River

(15)

Spring Creek

Cedar Creek

Fort Hall

Big Spring

Soda Springs Hills

(American Falls Reservoir)

●(Fort Hall)

Sheep Rock (Soda Point)

●(Pocatello)

Portneuf River

(Lake Wolcott)

(Massacre Rocks State Park)

●(American Falls)

(Soda Springs)

(30)

(Burley)

(86)

Little Creek

Rock Creek

Fall Creek

Bear River

(Declo)

Marsh Creek

Raft River

(84)

(15)

(Montpelier)

Thomas Fork

the bridge on July 3, paid "$1.00 per wagon."[5] Byers, however, took the ford, proclaiming it to be a "good ford four rods wide, two feet deep."[6]

A short distance beyond Thomas Fork, the trail ascended into the Bear River Mountains to bypass a large bend of the Bear River. Seven miles later the road descended back to the river a few miles south of present-day Montpelier, Idaho. Today's U.S. Route 30 follows the trail's same general course into town.

In this vicinity on July 15, the McAuleys "discovered a pass, by which the mountain [could] be avoided by doing a little road building." They remained here for two weeks while the men constructed a trail that enabled future travelers to avoid the mountainous route. On July 17, the Oregon-bound Meekers left the group.

However, Ezra's partner William Buck remained behind to assist with the road construction. By July 19, the McAuleys settled down to regular housekeeping, "washing cloths, baking, and drying fruit." During the stay, they befriended a local Indian named Poro. He taught them some of his language and traded moccasins for which Eliza gave a "gay plaid shawl." However, Poro's son, having accompanied his father, thought the shawl was pretty, but he wanted food. The McAuleys complied with his wishes.[7] After completing the road, Thomas McAuley and William Buck remained for a time and collected a toll to help defray construction expenses.

On August 7, John McAllister took the new route, stating, "by going it you avoid a long ascent, [and] a long steep & rough dangerous descent."[8] Cecelia Adams wrote on August 13, "the new road is two miles farther but saves very high mountains."[9] In 1992, the Oregon-California Trails Association placed a placard here to commemorate the road building story and the "initiative and thought of a group of young Americans in the year 1852."

From the Montpelier area, early travelers continued their trek along the Bear River Valley for thirty miles to the present-day Soda Springs, Idaho, locality. In spite of dust, ever-present mosquitoes, and other insects, travel conditions were favorable on the relatively flat trail, closely followed today by U.S. Route 30. In respect to insects, Cecilia Adams observed on August 14, "The grasshoppers are so thick that they look like snow in the air coming very fast."[10]

The waters of Soda Springs fascinated most early travelers. John Kerns, arriving here on July 22, declared it was "the greatest natural curiosity I ever saw."[11] Likewise impressed, Enoch Conyers stated on the same day, "these springs are indeed a great curiosity."[12] He continued with a vivid and comprehensive observation of the phenomenon.

> hollow cones nearly three feet in diameter and four feet high are formed by the mineral water. At times these cones will be filled with water and strongly impregnated with soda; in a short time the water in the cones will disappear, leaving nothing but a reddish-colored sediment in the bottom of the cone. there are over twenty of these cones in this vicinity. A number of them are extinct. . . . Many of the emigrants relish the taste of this sodawater and drink freely of it, but I cannot endure it. . . . We came on one mile to . . . where, a short distance from the trail, . . . is the famous Steamboat Spring. . . . This spring is also strongly impregnated with soda, and, in fact, the Bear River itself is strongly impregnated with soda at this place. The water from this spring is emitted through an oblong crevice in a large, flat rock of basalt formation. The water in this spring recedes for a few minutes until no water can be seen in the crevice, and within a few minutes more the water begins to flow again, continually gaining in force and finally emitting the water with great force to the height of about four feet and making noise resembling steam escaping from an exhaust pipe—hence called Steamboat Spring.[13]

Conyers recorded a playful incident demonstrating the force with which Steamboat Spring ejected water. R.L. Doyle wagered he could stop the flow by sitting on the crevice. When he put the boast to a test, however, he needed several others to assist in holding him down. Doyle finally cried out, "Boys, there is no use trying to hold the devil down, It can't be did."[14]

At Soda Springs, Martha Read saw "a large tribe of Indians and a trading post."[15] William Byers, arriving on July 19, also recorded "a number of trading establishments, Blacksmith Shop, etc."[16] This was a popular trading center for whites and Indians. Martha further stated, "there were about 30 wagons campt here for the night."

The forces of nature producing Soda Springs were an unexplained wonderment to early wayfarers. Today, geologists and other scientists suggest that a hot intrusive body, lying here at a relatively shallow depth, sits beneath fractured, very old, rocks of the Overthrust Belt. These rocks, in turn, have been overlain by much younger basaltic lava flows. Groundwater continually supplied by crevices in the rocks is heated by the intrusive source. Steam subsequently forms, forcing hot water to the surface through the crevices in the basaltic rock cap. Minerals and gases, including carbon dioxide, sulfur dioxide, and sodium silicate, too are dissolved by the steam and hot water from the older rocks that lie beneath. These gases give the water its "soda" or sulfur characteristics, and the precipitated minerals form colorful, shaped deposits.[17]

Geological processes also have been responsible for interesting changes in the Bear River's course. At one time, the river flowed northwest through Portneuf Canyon to the Snake River. Approximately 30,000 years ago, however, extruding lava flows formed a dam blocking the Bear River's channel to the Snake. During that time, a large inland sea (Lake Bonneville) had formed, covering much of Utah during a period when the climate was wetter. The diversion of the Bear River into huge Lake Bonneville contributed to its eventual overflowing into the Snake River. When the climate became drier about 8,000 years ago, the lake receded and the Bear River continued in its new channel to Lake Bonneville's smaller successor, the Great Salt Lake. However, the Portneuf River, which originally was a tributary to the Bear River, continued its course down the Bear River's old channel to the Snake.[18]

Four miles down the valley from Steamboat Spring, emigrants came to a divide in the road where many of the California-bound wayfarers went in a westerly direction, leaving the others to continue on a northwest course. Both roads departed from the Bear River, the channel of which diverts nearly due south around Soda Point (frequently referred to as Sheep Rock), a prominent mountain looming above the valley floor.

Enoch Conyers, as well as other 1852 travelers, referred to the California road as the "Myers' Cutoff, leading into the Humbolt Valley."[19] The route eventually became known as the Hudspeth Cutoff. Conyers describes the setting: "On our left is an abrupt termination of the mountain range in a rocky peak, around which Bear River makes a sharp curve to the left, the Oregon Trail turning to the right around the point of the mountain." Among those who bid farewell here to proceed toward the Golden State included Francis Sawyer and her husband, and Lucy and William Cooke.

For others, the goal was Fort Hall on the Snake River, about sixty miles northwest and several days' travel away. The first miles traversed a wide, flat region, which actually is a low-lying divide between the Bear

River draining to the Great Basin and the Portneuf River flowing into the Snake River. Soda Springs Hills flanks this area on the east. Here on July 22, Enoch Conyers observed,

> several crevices in the earth formed by volcanic eruptions. They were from two to three feet wide and no knowing how deep. A rock the size of ones fist dropped into one of these crevices could be heard for hundreds of feet as it struck the walls of the crevice on either side. These crevices were nearly covered by the growing grass, and it is a great wonder that our cattle escaped falling into one of them.[20]

Apparently, Conyers had observed fractures in a young basaltic lava formation. John McAllister, while passing on August 10, also reported, "many crevices in the earth and rocks also huge masses of burned rock."[21] He noted a "Beer spring" and other soda springs in the immediate area, confirming that the Soda Springs phenomenon extended well down the valley.

In a few miles, travelers had reached the Portneuf River, the first stream encountered that drains into the Snake River (i.e., the Columbia watershed). They followed the Portneuf for about ten miles, eventually crossing its upper reaches. (Later, after leaving Fort Hall, they would cross it again in a few miles, near its mouth.)

Next came an uphill, eight-mile pull along a tributary to a summit. Conyers recorded on July 24 that this was "a rough, ragged mountainous country."[22] John McAllister on August 11 stated, "the road is very rough but not steep dry & green quaking asp in abundance some grass in the groves. . . . The road winds its way up a large hollow among quaking asp nearly all the way to the summit of the mountain."[23]

When William Byers arrived atop the Portneuf Range he recorded his impressions. "Here what a sight! Worlds of mountains, and we seem to be in the very midst. . . . Stupendous mountain spurs transverse the country in every direction."[24]

A few miles beyond the summit, many camped near what Conyers described as a "good spring of water at the foot of the mountain."[25] This probably was in the Big Spring vicinity on the Ross Fork headwaters. The road from the spring nearly to Fort Hall followed down the Ross Fork drainage. It was regarded by most 1852 wayfarers as good travelling, although Conyers described part of it near Fort Hall as a "very heavy, sandy road, the dust flying so thick at times I could not see my head oxen." He also wrote at camp, when within five miles of the fort (probably at Clear Creek), "the mosquitos—my oh my, they are in great abundance."[26]

Leading westward over the broad bottomland of the Snake River Valley, the route closely followed today's Sheepskin Road, crossing Clear, Spring, and Jimmy creeks. The last four miles continued southwest along the Snake River. Prominent swales of the old trail are still visible in places here.

For miles on approaching Fort Hall, travelers caught occasional glimpses of the trading post's nearly white adobe walls. Many looked forward to restocking provisions and repairing wagons there. However, on arrival they were disappointed to find few supplies or facilities available to travelers. The post had been a major stopover point during the earlier days of the Oregon and California migration, but by 1852 it nearly had been abandoned as a trading post.

Dr. Thomas White, having arrived at Fort Hall on July 2, 1852, later stated in a letter dated April 19, 1853, there were "very few & rather poor goods, & they are few in deed."[27] Origen Thomson likened the fort to "an old boot run down at the heels."[28]

Nathaniel Wyeth, an enterprising New England merchant, established Fort Hall in the summer of 1834. He had come west with supplies and goods with which to acquire pelts from the Rocky Mountain Fur Company, an American firm consisting of traders and beaver-hunting mountain men. To Wyeth's chagrin, the fur company reneged on its original intention to treat with Wyeth and conducted its business elsewhere.

Hoping to take revenge, Wyeth built Fort Hall to peddle his wares and compete against others, including the British traders of the Hudson's Bay Company (HBC). He named the post after Henry Hall, a senior investor in the enterprise. After supplies ran short in 1837, however, the HBC bought the establishment, hoping that their ownership would sustain British claims in this part of the Oregon Country. According to international agreements at the time, the Oregon Country (i.e., today's Idaho, Oregon, Washington, parts of western Montana and Wyoming, and a large portion of British Columbia) was yet jointly occupied by both the British and Americans. By legal arrangement, the fort remained in the hands of the HBC for a time after the Oregon Treaty of 1846 established the international boundary at the 49th parallel, placing Fort Hall and several other British properties within U.S. territory. By 1852, the trading operation at Fort Hall had greatly declined. The post finally was abandoned in 1856.[29]

Among the many 1852 travelers describing Fort Hall, Dr. Thomas White rendered one of the most detailed descriptions. Following is an excerpt:

> It is built of Spanish Bricks or adobe. it is 4 squar [about 60 feet]. on the west line it is raised 2 storys. the other 3 walls are about 15 ft high & inside there are aprartments builded up with the main walls, all around, about 8 ft., toward the center, & perhaps 10 ft against the main wall, except at one corner, there is a magazine which is raised to 18 ft. & about 19 ft. squar, & those inner apartments, are all covered with earth, & nearly flat & the main building covered also with earth, so that a man can stand on top of those inside & be screened from an enemy without, by the main wall, through which there are port holes for small arms, & these look every way & those inner apartments serve for shops & store Houses, & for sleeping apartments &c. there is but one white man at this point & he is in service of the H. B. C. & here are about 125 of the awfulest wagons, then about 8 to 10 cords of ox yokes, & sir those wagons would almost frighten a green Yankey. O what folly in government agents, to contract for such unmanageble things. here to, are loads of log chains, fifth chains, strecher chains, single trees & many other things the property of Uncle Sam, all going to wast.[30]

The government wagons belonged to the Regiment of Mounted Riflemen, who temporarily set up shop here in 1849.[31] This was the first U.S. military force to travel the full length of the Oregon Trail and enter newly established Oregon Territory.

Although somewhat discouraged by the state of Fort Hall, travelers felt satisfaction in finally arriving at the Snake River, a major tributary to the Columbia River. These mighty waterways would lead them to their final destination.

Notes

1. Francis Sawyer, "Kentucky to California by Carriage and a Feather Bed," in *Covered Wagon Women: Diaries and Letters form the Western Trails*, 1852, vol. 4, edited and compiled by Kenneth L. Holmes (Glendale, California: Arthur H. Clark, 1985), 102.
2. Eliza Ann McAuley, "Iowa to the 'Land of Gold,'" in *Covered Wagon Women: Diaries and Letters from the Western Trails*, 1852, vol. 4, edited and compiled by Kenneth L. Holmes (Glendale, California: Arthur H. Clark, 1985), 64.
3. William N. Byers, "The Odyssey of William N. Byers," edited by Merrill J. Mattes, in *Overland Journal*, vol. 1, no. 2 (1983), 18; published by the Oregon-California Trails Association, Independence, Missouri.

4. John McAllister, "Diary of Rev. John McAllister," in *Transactions of the Fiftieth Annual Reunion of the Oregon Pioneer Association* (Portland, Oregon, 1922), 490; see additional information under note 2 in chapter four.

5. Sawyer, 102.

6. Byers, 18.

7. McAuley, 64.

8. McAllister, 490.

9. Cecelia Adams, "Twin Sisters on the Oregon Trail: Cecelia Adams and Parthenia Blank," in *Covered Wagon Women: Diaries and Letters from the Western Trails,* 1852, vol. 5, edited and compiled by Kenneth L. Holmes and David C. Duniway (Glendale, California: Arthur H. Clark, 1986), 281–82.

10. Ibid., 282.

11. John T. Kerns, "Journal of Crossing the Plains to Oregon in 1852," in *Transactions of the Forty-second Annual Reunion of the Oregon Pioneer Association* (Portland, Oregon, 1914), 173.

12. Enoch W. Conyers, "Diary of E.W. Conyers, a Pioneer of 1852," in *Transactions of the Thirty-third Annual Reunion of the Oregon Pioneer Association* (Portland, Oregon, 1905), 423.

13. Ibid., 468–69.

14. Ibid., 469.

15. Martha S. Read, "A History of Our Journey," in *Covered Wagon Women: Diaries and Letters from the Western Trails*, 1852, vol. 5, edited and compiled by Kenneth L. Holmes and David C. Duniway (Glendale, California: Arthur H. Clark, 1986), 236.

16. Byers, 18.

17. Paul K. Link and E. Chilton Phoenix, *Rocks, Rails and Trails* (Pocatello, Idaho: Idaho State University Press, 1994), 81–82.

18. Ibid., 27.

19. Conyers, 469.

20. Ibid., 470.

21. McAllister, 492.

22. Conyers, 470.

23. McAllister, 492.

24. Byers, 19.

25. Conyers, 470.

26. Ibid., 471.

27. Thomas White, "To Oregon in 1852, Letter of Dr. Thomas White," edited by Oscar O. Winther and Gayle Thornbrough (Indianapolis, Indiana: Indiana Historical Society, 1964), 15–16.

28. Origen Thomson, *Crossing the Plains* (Fairfield, Washington: Ye Galleon Press, 1983), 53.

29. Irene D. Paden, *The Wake of the Prairie Schooner*, reprint edition (Gerald, Missouri: Patrice Press, 1985), 279; Bill Carnes, "Fort Hall: Origins of an Oregon Trail Outpost," in *News from the Plains*, vol. 11, no. 3 (1997), 1, 6; newsletter of the Oregon-California Trails Association, Independence, Missouri.

30. White, 15–16.

31. Byers, 19.

Chapter Ten

Along the Snake

*Our train slowly drag[g]ed on, . . . We camped one night on Salmon Falls on the Snake River. There wer[e] a great many emigrants in camp at that place making preparation to cross over the river. —*Mary Ann Boatman

UPON REACHING THE SNAKE RIVER, the early travelers soon realized it would require all the physical and mental fortitude they could muster to survive for the next month. For three hundred miles, the route would follow along this elusive, graphically named river. They also would traverse the adjacent Snake River Plain—a nearly treeless, desolate, flat expanse. By now it was late July or August, when temperatures commonly exceeded 100 degrees.

John Kerns, although usually upbeat and optimistic, had little good to say about the region. On July 30, while camped at the Raft River three days beyond Fort Hall, he declared the Snake "runs through one of the poorest countries in God's world." Five days later near Twin Falls, Idaho (now a thriving, irrigated and fertile locality), he thought the route passed "over as poor a country as ever was put in to fill up."[1]

The Snake River Plain is underlain by a series of nearly flat-lying lava flows, the oldest of which were extruded perhaps only a few million years ago. Many of the exposed flows are indeed very recent, dating from the Pleistocene Epoch (ice age) just a few tens of thousands of years before the present. The Snake has carved its deep, walled channel down through these black basaltic flows.[2] Far too often, early travelers in dire need of water were frustrated because they could see the river several hundred feet below, but could not reach it, or at least found it very difficult to negotiate a way down the canyon walls.

Fort Hall, as sketched by an unknown artist during the march of the Regiment of Mounted Riflemen to Oregon in 1849.

On August 8, Polly Coon described the nature of the river and the effects that it had on travel. "This is one of the most singular rivers in the world being for miles enclosed by perpendicular ledges of rock & thirsty animals are obliged to toil for miles together in the heat & dust with the sound of water in their ears & neither man or beast able to get a drop."[3]

Relatively young sediments blanket much of the landscape. In addition to silts, sand, and cobbles deposited by the Snake River in its narrow valley, ancient lakes that formerly inundated portions of the Snake plain also left quantities of similar materials, plus clay and diatomite. These lakes developed during the ice age's wetter climate or, in some cases, resulted from lava flows damming streams. Such sediments are particularly prevalent between present-day Glenns Ferry and Grand View, Idaho. Today, they continue to be redeposited in wind-formed dunes, as exemplified at Bruneau Dunes State Park located west of Glenns Ferry. Glacial melt water also contributed gravel, sand, silt, and clay at places on the Snake plain. Some of these deposits were the result of floods.

Perhaps the youngest features in the area are the wind-blown soil deposits known as loess. Following the glacial retreat 10,000 to 15,000 years ago, barren expanses of glacial-fluvial materials were exposed. Over time, winds picked up the finer-grained sediments and redeposited them, forming rich soils.[4] Today, loess soils make for some of the best farmland in Idaho. On the Oregon Trail, however, the passing livestock and wagons disturbed these fine-grained, sun-parched particles, creating irritating clouds of dust. The August 13 entry of John Tucker Scott, while in the vicinity of Sinker Creek, is typical. "The dust today and for the last 100 miles or more has been very annoying . . . almost suffocating man and beast."[5]

Often, the Snake River's tributary streams were situated far apart across the sagebrush-dotted plain. The banks could be steep and difficult to negotiate, and the water might be contaminated. Enoch Conyers noted on July 31 while camped at Marsh Creek:

> I went over one-half mile up the creek and every few steps I either found a [dead] horse, mule or ox, and in some places I found three or four in one pile. A scum consisting of all the colors of the rainbow was oozing from them and floating down stream for the benefit of the emigrants. . . . We counted over fifty head of dead oxen, horses and mules lying in the creek above our camp.[6]

Grazing for the livestock was infrequently found in side-stream valleys or on the Snake canyon floor. Often, earlier trains already had consumed any available forage. The faithful livestock weakened from long labor in the searing heat and the lack of adequate nourishment and water. Many died along the way, as testified to by Martha Read, who recorded each day's count of dead animals from Fort Hall to the Snake crossing at Glenns Ferry—there were 133 dead cattle and 8 horses in about 180 miles.[7] This being the first half of the Snake River trek, losses likely were greater in the second part.

The rigors of four months of travel were taking a toll on the emigrants and food supplies were dwindling, adding further strain. Many became ill during this especially trying part of the journey. Among the most frequently mentioned ailments were diarrhea, dysentery, scurvy, and mountain fever—a disease modern authorities have identified as being transmitted by wood ticks. It now is called Colorado Tick Fever, an arbovirus infection.[8] All factors considered, the trek along the Snake River probably was the most disagreeable and demanding part of the journey.

The route from Fort Hall to American Falls, a distance of a little over twenty miles, today is largely inundated by the American Falls Reservoir. After crossing Spring Creek a short distance from Fort Hall, travelers soon came again to the Portneuf River, near its mouth. On July 26, Enoch Conyers described the crossing as "about sixty feet wide and between five and six feet deep, with very steep banks on both sides and very hard for the cattle to climb out." At a ferry here, Conyers noted:"$1 if we ferry our-selves or $2 if they ferry you."[9]

Most, however, forded the stream. Abigail Scott described how many raised their "wagon beds by tying ropes under them, across the stan-dards . . . and managed to keep our goods free from damage."[10] Those who did not do this, according to Conyers, dealt with a foot of water in the wagon boxes.

In this area, Conyers first noted a "large herd of black crickets about one and one-quarter inches long and three-quarters of an inch in diam-eter." He continued by relating how the local "Digger," or Shoshone, Indi-ans added them into root bread.

> They first dig holes in the sandy loam about three feet across and two feet deep, then fill them with sagebrush or willow wood, making a good hot fire, more fuel being added at intervals until the furnace reaches the desired heat. Then all the old bucks, squaws and kids, provided with brush to whip the surrounding grass and soil, circle around a drove of these large, black crickets and make a drive for the heated hole in the center. Very few crickets escape being caught in the furnace. There they sizzle and fry until they swell up and burst like roasted chestnut. The squaws take the cooked crickets and mash them fine, mixing a quantity of roots and herbs and finally rolling them into flat cakes and baking or drying them in the hot sun, thus com-pleting the work towards furnishing the winter supply of bread for the family use.[11]

From the Portneuf crossing, the emigrant road continued along the Snake, sometimes in its narrow canyon and at times on the plain, but normally within a mile or less of the river. About one day's travel brought the emigrants to American Falls. Today, a dam impounds the Snake imme-diately above the falls, forming American Falls Reservoir.[12] At the falls, the river is compressed in an approximately 250-yard-wide gap and drops over a series of short steps about fifty total feet. On July 26, Abigail Scott ob-served, "the water tumbles over rocks and falls forty feet presenting a hand-some appearance, and making a great noise."[13]

Soon after leaving Fort Hall, where the emigrants had found few pro-visions to purchase or trade, they began meeting local Indians who had a plentiful supply of Snake River salmon for which they would willingly barter. John McAllister on August 28 described the Indians trading salmon "for clothing Fish Hooks gun powder shot balls percussion caps etc."[14]

This supply of fresh fish was a welcome addition to the emigrant's depleted food supply and a pleasant change from short rations of bacon, beans, and hardtack. However, the temptation to over-do their consumption of fish sometimes caused sickness and even resulted in death for a few. Some developed an aversion to salmon for the rest of their lives.[15]

In fact, the Boatmans' encounter with Snake River salmon turned out to be unpleasant. Although Mary Ann's suppositions in this regard may be in error, she nevertheless presented strong convictions on the subject.

We now find ourselves camped no great distance from an Indian camp of fishers who[se] business it was to pick up dead salmon along the banks of the river and trade them to the half starved emigrants for clothes or any thing they could get in exchange. The people, being ignorant of how they had obtained the fish, was only too glad to get a square meal of the red meat that looked from appearance that it would satisfy the most fastidious appetite. The swap, as the red skin called it, was soon made at every camp fire and O[h] what a feast of fresh fish all had partaken of. But before morning the story was told on some of us. I for one. O[h] how sick we wer[e]. I though[t] my time had come. The sickness come in the form of cholera morbus. That night it was thought best by all to keep a close watch over the stock. So all the men wer[e] on watch, but no disturbance occurred. The Indians wer[e] peaceable.

We are now in the Snake river valley traveling down the river, the miles we had to travel down before we come to the mountains I do not know. As we traveled down we soon found out the caus[e] for our sickness from eating the salmon that we had got from the siwash [Indians]. At the edge of the water every now and then would be a dead ox or cow that had gone down the steep bank to quench it[s] thurst and, being to weak to make the return up the steep bank, would fall in the river and drown. About those dead carcass's would be dozens of large fish dead. [They] had been eating on the putrid flesh of the dead cattle. So that ended the feast of fish.

From American Falls, the emigrant road proceeded almost entirely along the high rim, but never more than a mile or so from the river, while crossing such tributaries as Little, Rock, and Fall creeks. Prior to reaching Rock Creek, travelers passed what many years later became known as Massacre Rocks. A small group of pioneers were buried here following several bloody clashes with Indians in this vicinity in 1862. At Rock Creek, emigrants were fascinated with the numerous, rounded boulders found in and along the stream, and on which many travelers chiseled, painted, or otherwise left their marks, some of which still are evident today

According to John Tucker Scott, the road to Fall Creek was "very bad; being over an sand and sage plains."[16] Although a few segments of this route are preserved today, most sections have been obliterated by modern highway construction.

Beyond Fall Creek, the Snake eventually begins a broad northward swing. At this place, the emigrant trail departed from the river and continued for eight miles in a west-southwest direction to the Raft River. After crossing this stream, the last of the California-bound travelers turned into a road leading southward up the Raft River toward the Golden State. The Oregon wayfarers continued westward, climbing a steep, basalt bluff to enter a high plain. Today, the Raft River virtually has a dry bed, due largely to modern irrigation. However, at the intersection of these roads during the early travel days, this was a considerable stream and a popular camping place. Although much of the valley now is cultivated, traces of the California and Oregon trails still are visible.

Near the approximate intersection of these roads, three graves have been fenced in with wooden rails by Lyle and Carol Woodbury, the owners of the land. In 1992, the Oregon-California Trails Association placed a plaque here explaining the significance of this fork in the road. The exact identities of those buried here remains uncertain, but they are thought to be Lydia Edmonson, who died August 15, 1847, age 25; Elizabeth Adams, who succumbed August 11, 1862, age 26; and G.W. Sanders, who died July 27, 1862, age 33. Henry Hays, who passed away in August 1852, also is believed buried at a nearby spot.

The next fifteen miles to Marsh Creek crossed over virtually waterless terrain. On July 31, John Kerns referred to it as "a rocky sage brush desert."[17] Because Marsh Creek was the first water reached since leaving the Raft River, the campground here usually was crowded, as confirmed by John Spencer in an August 21 entry: "camped on Marshy Creek among a crowd of trains."[18] As previously mentioned, Enoch Conyers when passing here on July 31 found the stream above polluted with over fifty dead livestock.

From the campground, the road continued down Marsh Creek, crossing it several times before reaching the Snake again near today's Declo, Idaho. From there, the trail followed along the river for several miles, nearly to present-day Burley. Homes now flank the Snake River's Milner Reservoir in this area. Here the river swings north again while the trail continued westward, crossing Goose Creek a mile or so south of Burley. Reportedly, this section of road, other than being dusty, was tolerable. After leaving Goose Creek, the road swung northwest toward the Snake, which it followed nearly to today's Murtaugh.

In this area on August 2, John Kerns wrote, "five head of cattle died last night out of the train, which makes us think the elephant is not far off." Slang-like references to the "elephant" are common in the mid-nineteenth century accounts. Phrases such as "seeing the elephant" or Kerns' "the elephant is not far off" wryly depicted one's involvement in a very trying or unusual situation. Although an American household term during those times, its origin is obscure. Some have suggested that it derived from a person visiting a circus for the first time to see a new and unimaginably big, yet spectacularly real, animal—the elephant. Regardless of its derivation, the expression was well understood and, as historian Merrill J. Mattes aptly states, "it was the poetic imagery of all deadly perils that threatened a westering emigrant."[19]

On July 29, the John Tucker Scott family also camped here along the Snake. Abigail Scott recorded, "the roads this afternoon were very rough and rocky. . . . Some of the work cattle are failing very fast." That afternoon, while sitting on the banks of the Snake observing the Caldron Linn cataract, named by early fur traders, she described the scene.

> The river here runs through a rocky Kanyon The current is remarkably swift and the water tumbles over the rocks with a roaring noise; The scenery here is of a truly wild and romantic description Huge piles of rock rise up in bold array around me.[20]

In the vicinity of today's Murtaugh, the river again swings northward. Here the emigrant road veered away and continued west for about fifteen miles over the usual dusty and rocky, although relatively level, terrain to Rock Creek. John Spencer noted on August 24, "had a horrid time of dust, holes, rocks etc."[21] Rock Creek had cut a formidable canyon in the basalt, forming nearly sheer walls a hundred or more feet high in places. Crossing this stream was a major challenge and restricted to a place used by Indians.[22] Conyers wrote on August 4, "The banks of the creek at this place are very rocky, steep and ragged."[23]

From the Rock Creek crossing, travelers followed along the stream in a northwesterly direction passing through the southern part of modern-day Twin Falls, a distance of about eighteen miles. Today this is a fertile locality due to irrigation. During the emigrant days, of course, it was dry and arid. Conyers noted on August 4, while camped near Rock Creek and just west of today's Twin Falls, "hard in getting down to the water; more so, it seems to us, than any other place since crossing the Missouri River."[24]

The Adams-Blank party avoided the heat of the day here by traveling during the night. On September 1, after crossing Rock Creek, Parthenia Blank noted: "traveled on till after dark and then halted till the moon rose about 9 o'clock and then stared on again. Weather very cold so that a man could not keep warm in walking without an overcoat and my hands suffered with cold."[25]

 Upon arriving at the Snake again on August 5, Enoch Conyers described the difficult effort to obtain water.

> We were obliged to descend a very rough, rocky and steep hill to reach the river, not knowing if we would be able to get our cattle back up the hill or not. Of course we left our wagons on the hill. It required from three-quarters' to one hour's time to water our cattle and return to the place where we left our wagons. It is so steep and bad that many cattle are too weak to climb the hill, therefore are left at the foot of the hill to perish among the big basalt boulders that cover the narrow bottoms of the Snake River.[26]

Today, a reservoir floods this canyon area nearly to its rim.

The trail generally continued on high above the river for several miles in the vicinity of "Fremont's Fishing Falls" and "Kanaka Rapids." Here was a major Indian fishery where many travelers traded for salmon.[27] These may be the rapids that John Kerns referred to on August 6 as, "the great cascade falls of the Snake River," which he claimed fell 600 feet in five miles.[28] Today, as the result of modern dam building, reservoir waters also fill the canyon in this area. According to Parthenia Blank, the trail eventually "passed down the bottom with high rocky banks on each side nearly perpendicular."[29]

It was a short distance to the crossing of Salmon Falls Creek, where Parthenia Blank observed "a fall in the river [creek] about equal to American Falls."[30] Abigail Scott, on August 5, described Salmon Falls Creek as "a clear stream with a rocky bottom . . . about one hundred feet wide, and two one half feet deep."[31]

After the crossing, the trail followed the stream's west bank a mile or so to its confluence with the Snake River. Then, in a short distance, emigrants were treated to the spectacular sight of Thousand Springs gushing from beneath the rim rocks on the north side of the Snake. Nearly all diarists passing here mentioned the scene. Polly Coon recorded on August 16, "passed some of the most beautiful cascades I ever saw on the opposite side of the river. They fell from a springs near the top of the bank where it was nearly one hundred feet high."[32]

A source for a portion of this flow appears to come from the distant Big Lost River, Little Lost River, and Birch Creek drainages. The waters of these streams disappear into the broad, lava plains of the Lost River country many miles away, and, flowing under the surface, reappear at Thousand Springs. In addition to other groundwater contributions from rain and melting snow, in recent years irrigation on the north side of the river has added to the flow. The major source of the water, however, is now believed to be the Snake River itself near Rexburg, Idaho, where much of the river flows underground, to reappear many miles and many years later at Thousand Springs.[33] Much of the water of these springs now is harnessed for power, thus they are greatly reduced.[34]

Reportedly, a river crossing to the north bank was established in 1852 just upstream from these springs, consisting of a ford and a ferry for which a $6 toll was charged. The crossing supposedly accessed a better route that continued over thirty miles downstream to Three Island Crossing and a connection to the well-established north-side trail that continued from that point.[35]

A ferry was established in 1851 several miles downstream from Thousand Springs and a mile or so above Upper Salmon Falls.[36] It appears that more travelers crossed here in 1852 than at the older and now well-known Three Island Crossing located about thirty miles downstream.

On September 4, Cecelia Adams described the Salmon Falls ferry as "consisting of 2 wagon boxes lashed together so as to make a boat and a rope stretched across the river to pull it across." Noting a toll of $3 per wagon, she described the ferry's general location:

> Just below the ferry is another great falls [Salmon Falls]. Just above on the opposite bank very large springs [Thousand Springs] break out high up in the bank and fall into the river with great noise[.] A fine sight.[37]

Polly Coon substantiates the popularity of this crossing in 1852. On August 16, "we only made about 3 miles to Salmon Falls where the most of the emigrants was crossing the river." She too described the ferry as being a pair of wagon boxes coupled together with a rope stretched across the river. The ferry hauled the Coon party, wagons, and luggage, while towing the livestock.[38] Apparently, the ferry toll varied from time to time. Martha Read on August 23 reported they paid $6 per wagon and $2 to tow the cattle.[39]

Salmon Falls was a popular Indian fishery, thus a thriving trade ensued between the Indians and emigrants at this crossing. While waiting to cross the river on September 4, Parthenia Blank related that the Indians had "very nice salmon for sale and we all got a good supply—they will trade them for powder, lead & caps bread, beads, brass nails old shirts or almost anything you have."[40] Today, Salmon Falls and the original channel for a considerable distance upstream has been completely inundated by damming for hydroelectric power generation.

In addition to Polly Coon and the Crandall train, twin sisters Cecelia Adams and Parthenia Blank accompanied by husbands William and Stephen, and the Martha and Clifton Read family, others who reported crossing the Snake above Salmon Falls in 1852 included the John Spencer family and the Reverend John McAllister.

In the Salmon Falls vicinity, some emigrants were enticed by corrupt traders to consider the totally impractical idea of floating downstream in wagon boxes to far-off The Dalles, Oregon. In this regard, Mary Ann related the following experiences of the John M. Hawk family, as later told to her by Mrs. Hawk after arriving in Portland, Oregon. Although Mary Ann did not report that the incident began at Salmon Falls, Al R. Hawk, the eldest of the six Hawk sons, revealed this fact in later years. He was about thirteen when the party attempted to float the Snake.[41]

> We are slowly making our way down the Snake River Valley. One morning about 10 O'clock we come in sight of a little log cabin on the bank of the river and a dozen or two running gears of wagons standing around the place. All wer[e] taken by surprise to see a house in the wilderness. But we soon learned that 2 men occupied the house and wer[e] traders [that] had a few articles to sell, provided one had money enough to pay ten times the value of the desired article. They had established themselves as traders. There aim was to deceive people by tel[l]ing them if they would sell them the[i]r cattle then take the wagon box an make it water proof and put all their belongings in it an put it in the river as a boat, using oars as on any small boat, that, in 4 days, . . . they would be at there journeys end. . . . That was a true saying for many who started down the river in the[i]r wagon boxes come to the[i]r journeys end in a very short time, for I am sorry to say that quit[e] a good many was persuaded to sell them their cattle and take the wagon box for a boat, putting

the[i]r beding and provisions and family in it and started down the river never to be heard of any more.

Now reader just paus[e] for a moment and give it one thought. People tired, foot sore, provisions all most to the last meal gon[e], cattle fatigue[d], lame foot, sore, scarcely able to draw the empty wagon—at the very shortes[t] time to make the end of the journey would [be] by land 2 months with the jaded teams. Knowing nothing of the rapid[s] and falls of the river and the narrow canyons its co[u]rse traversed, [and] supposing those white men, more despicable than Indians that they lived with, had told them the truth, once embarked in the frai[l], make shift of the boat and gon[e] a few miles down the raped [rapid] stream with it[s] abrupt falls and steep banks on both sides, it was an impossibility to turn back. In that way most all that started down was lost. The wagon box was unmanageable in the swift current and steep rapids. In trying to go over the rapids the box would go with such rapidity over the rapids that it would upset or break to pieces and all would be lost. I know one family by the name of Hawk that started down the river in the[i]r wagon box after selling the[i]r team to the traders. . . . going down the river 10 miles [they came] . . . to a rapid and, trying to go over, lost every thing and come near loosing all their lives. The women and children got out on the rock, jumped from one to another, while the men were trying to save the wagon box boat. As good luck or common sense, which ever you are a mind to term . . . it to be, they had only sold part of the team and sent a man on the road with one yoke of oxen and run[n]ing gears of the wagon. After loosing everything but their lives the men started to try to over take the trains that was gone on. Some kindhearted person picked up the women and children and hauled and feed them until they could make some provision for the remainder of the journey. We never met anyone that made the journey down the Snake River to the Columbia River altho some one may have been lucky enough to have guided there frail makeshift of a boat over the many rough, steep abrupt falls.

The Hawk family had left De Kalb County, Indiana, on March 1, 1852, in company with the Samuel Russell family and Mr. Elliot Cline.[42] They took much the same route as the Boatmans, crossing the Missouri River at Kanesville, following the north side of the Platte, and then along the south side of the Snake. Furthermore, as revealed later, the Boatmans and the Hawk party met somewhere along the journey west.

Years later, Al R. Hawk related the Snake River incident, "from the imperfect recollection I have of the trip," adding that his recollections were "aided by information that I got from Mrs. Willis Boatman . . . as told to her by my mother after we arrived in Portland." [43] Following is his version of the adventure.

> There were two miserable white scrubs located at Salmon Falls for the purpose of swindling the emigrants out of their stock. They would induce the pilgrims to sell them their cattle and horses, and convert their wagon beds into boats and float down Snake River to The Dalles. . . .
>
> We converted our wagon bed into a boat, and in order to make it water-tight we took the hides from dead cattle, which were plenty, and covered the bottom of the bed. They were stretched on tight, which gave more strength to the bed and kept it perfectly dry inside. Father would not dispose of his team, for he thought if anything should happen to us we would have something left to help us out of our difficulty. So Mr. Cline took the team and running gear of the wagon and hit the trail for The Dalles, where he expected to find us waiting for him. But the fond hopes and pleasure that we expected to enjoy on the boating trip were never realized. . . . We left Salmon Falls with a full crew. Besides our family of eight, we had Jim Riley and Bob Wallace. We drifted and paddled along where the current seemed the strongest, and were getting along nicely as Riley remarked, on a four-mile current. All seemed to be perfectly satisfied with the boat in preference to the wagon until we got in quick water, when the river seemed to pretty nearly stand on end for about half a mile. It was impossible to make the shore. The boat and all hands were at the mercy of the angry water. But we shot through those waters so quick that it didn't give us much time to realize the danger we were in. From that on the boat hugged the shore pretty closely. We now began to discover the disadvantages of river travel. The river was a continuation of rapids for miles, and it required the greatest care to keep the boat from swamping. And then again for miles it would be without a ripple and but little current. At times we would be near the road and could see along the emigrant trail. . . .
>
> The river seemed to narrow down to half its width, and the current became very swift and terminated in some very dangerous rapids. Mother and children were put ashore to get along the best we could, while the men, with ropes, let the boat down over the rapids, and from that on we had only one day of pleasant boating. It was along a low, flat country, and the footing on the banks was good. . . . The river soon made a change for the worse. . . . The following morning in making a hasty examination of the river below, it was found to be very bad. However, the men started with the boat and mother and children clambered along the steep hillside among the rocks the best we could.

The banks became so steep in places that it was impossible to manage the boat from the shore, so the men had to take to the water and in many places it was from knee to neck deep. The men were compelled to manage the boat that way for days, and over many difficult places we had to take everything out of the boat and let it down empty. Quite often we had to take the boat out and carry it around dangerous places.

An old Indian and his two boys were our only companions. They became very much attached to us. In about ten days, as near as I can remember, our hearts were made glad by the appearance of Mr. Cline and the team. It was the work of a short time to get the water-soaked bed on the wagon again and rolling over the prairie, and we were as happy as a picnic party.[44]

Although there are some discrepancies in the two versions describing this incident, the dangers encountered by those enticed into attempting this mode of travel are clearly understood. While at Salmon Falls, Mary Ann related yet another incident, this time with tragic result. It appears that she observed the accident immediately above the falls and not at the established ferry crossing a mile or so upstream. Furthermore, her description of the makeshift single-wagon arrangement involved in the incident seems distinctly different from that of the two-wagon upstream ferry.

Our train slowly drag[g]ed on, day after day nothing out of every days occurrence. All looking anxious for the end of the journey. We camped one night on Salmon Falls on the Snake River. There wer[e] a great many emigrants in camp at that place making preparation to cross over the river to travel on the north side, expecting to find grass more plentiful for the teams. They had contrived for conveyance to cross the river in, . . . to cork a wagon box so it would be water proof. Then . . . a rop[e] across the river. . . . A[nother] rop[e attached] to each end of the wagon box boat, [to] . . . slide over the one that crossed the river. All went well for a little time. They had landed a few loads on the opsit side. As they wer[e] returning for another load, we heard a scream. On looking what a horible sight met our gaze. The rop[e] had broken and 3 men and a boy with the boat had gone over the falls. The boy was drown or killed, the men, clinging to the rocks, calling for help. In some way they got to shore badly bruised and exhausted almost unto death. They, in some way, managed to recover the boys body. As it was not late that afternoon, our company concluded to hitch up and pull out as we had seen so much sorrow and sufren on the way that we preferd to get away from as much as convenient. Drove a few miles and camped for the night. We never heard from that party dont know how they made crossing if they made it or not. We went about 20 miles down the river and found another ferry boat made of [a] wagon box where some men had taken charge . . . and ferried emigrants over and charged them exorbit prices. As for our company, they did not have money to wast[e]. So we wer[e] willing to let good enough alone and traveled all the way down the Snake River on the south side.

Mary Ann's reference to another ferry "about 20 miles down the river" probably was at today's Glenns Ferry. Furthermore, her statement regarding staying "on the south side" is the only indication as to the route they followed from the Glenns Ferry area.

Near Salmon Falls, the river yet again swings northward. Here, south-side travelers left the Snake in a northwesterly direction, cutting across the broad loop formed by the river. They began with a three-mile pull out of the valley to the upland plain. Near where the road made a final swing onto the heights, there remains today about a quarter-mile of pristine, well-preserved, multi-track swales marked by the OCTA. From the overlook, emigrants were treated to a grand view. Stretching off to the east was the terrain over which they had struggled for the past several days.

For about twenty-five miles, Conyers reported on August 8, "The whole country around here is covered with wild sage."[45] The same day, John Kerns wryly stated, "hot weather and dust are the only authorized subjects of suffrage along here." The next day he reported, "weather and road as usual; a little on the infernal order."[46] Today, this upland area is cultivated for dry land farming, mostly in hay and some grain crops.

A number of emigrants proceeded at night, at least for part of this distance, to avoid the heat of the day. The Akin family "laid by [at Salmon Falls] until sundown then started and traveled until 2 o'clock in the morning."[47] Near a halfway place where the Snake makes a temporary southwest bend in the vicinity of Pilgrim Creek, many travelers detoured to access the river for water. Here, they were forced to make a difficult descent. Conyers recorded on August 8:

> At this place we stopped to water and graze our cattle. We were obliged to descend another very steep hill to get down to the river. . . . many cattle that go down this hill for water never return, being too weak to make the ascent.[48]

The next day at this location, John Kerns "counted forty-eight head of dead stock . . . besides eight wagons left and other things."[49]

Some twelve more miles brought the emigrants to the next river crossing in the vicinity of today's Glenns Ferry. In 1852, no permanent operation was located here, but in 1871 a commercial ferry was established from which the name Glenns Ferry is derived. Most 1852 diarists describe this as a place where travelers crossed in their own wagon boxes. Abigail Scott observed, when passing by on August 7, "emigrants were ferrying in their wagon boxes."[50] The Conyers decided to cross here to avoid further desert traveling and hoping to find better grass for the livestock. On August 9, Enoch "calked two wagon beds and used them as a ferry to cross the river, one tied before the other."[51]

The Akins probably crossed here also, although they possibly forded at Three Island Crossing located four miles downstream.[52] On August 20, James said: "tow[ed] the cattle across the river behind wagon beds. Ferry the wagons over in the evening."[53] By referring only to "ferrying" and not "fording," it seems likely they were at the upper crossing, essentially today's Glenns Ferry.

Two days later while still at the crossing, but on the north side of the river, James Akin Jr.'s mother, Eliza Rickey Akin, passed away. On August 23, she "was buried about 10 o'clock in the morning about 200 yards above the crossing of the river."[54]

On August 10, John Kerns reported the distance between the upper and lower crossings as four miles.[55] The lower ford eventually became known as Three Island Crossing, although only two islands were traversed in fording. While camping here on August 8, Abigail Scott recorded: "About noon a party of ten men and two women passed us going down the river in a boat made of a wagon bed."[56]

Abigail's family and the John Kerns and Boatman groups were among those who bypassed Three Island Crossing, which was considered particularly dangerous. In fact, some regarded it as the most difficult crossing of the entire Oregon Trail. Those who risked fording here did so to seek better forage for livestock, easier access to water, and better trail conditions on the north side.

The north-side travelers crossing at Salmon Falls, Glenns Ferry, or Three Island Crossing continued to the Boise River near modern-day Boise, Idaho. From there, they followed the south side of the Boise River to its confluence with the Snake near Fort Boise, south of present-day Ontario,

Oregon. Meanwhile, travelers who chose not to risk a crossing continued their journey along the arid south side of the Snake River. Another ten days to two weeks of traveling, a distance of about 130 miles, also brought them to near the Snake-Boise confluence.

Beyond Three Island Crossing, south-side travelers suffered in even more dire conditions than previously. In the August heat, they traversed one of the most desolate localities yet encountered. The first day, they continued close to the river in a treacherous rocky canyon, where Abigail Scott related on August 9: "In many places the wagons were held by two or three men or they would [have] been precipitated over the rocks into the river." And, the same day, "again saw some men going down the river in a wagon bed."[57] Today, sections of this south-side trail can be seen from Interstate 84, which passes by on the north bank of the river.

Less precariously, travelers continued largely along the river for another day or so before arriving at Catharine Creek, also known as the Bruneau River. This is in today's C.J. Strike Reservoir area. After arriving at Catharine Creek on August 13, John Kerns recorded: "Road as usual, very dusty, and country a barren, deserted, burnt-to-death waste." He concluded, the "girls look as cross as I feel."[58]

Here, travelers were passing through ancient lake deposits of sand, silt, clay, and diatomite. Kerns graphically describes large clouds of annoying dust arising from wagon wheels and hooves. In places, the deposits are preserved as buttes capped by a thin, resistant cap of basalt.[59] The good grass in the bottom near the Bruneau's mouth provided for a reasonably comfortable campsite despite the dust.

In the days ahead, the trail continued along the river through today's Grandview locality, past Wild Horse Butte, and on to Sinker Creek. On August 14, Kerns wrote that they had traveled "over a dusty road in hot weather, through the poorest of all countries." He further observed, "Dirty faces are as numerous as the stars every evening." While laying by the next day, he declared, "bad luck to the man who is such a sinner as to have to seek refuge in such a country as this."[60]

John Tucker Scott, also complaining about the dust, stated on August 13 while in the vicinity of Sinker Creek, the "country all around is extremely barren interspersed with deep kanyons & high rocky bluffs all blackened . . . doubtless of volcanic formation."[61]

From Sinker Creek, the road soon led away from the river for fourteen miles, traversing an arid divide and passing around basalt-capped Murphy Rim before arriving back at the river, just west of Guffey Butte, which also was basalt-capped. On August 15, while along the river just west of this butte, five men of the John Tucker Scott party caulked two wagon boxes and joined the Snake River flotilla.[62]

Continuing along the Snake, the emigrants next came to a thermal feature known today as Givens Hot Springs. A resort was established here in 1860, but burned in 1914. Today it is a covered swimming facility with a water temperature maintained at 138 degrees.[63] The Kerns party passed just to the right (east) of the springs on August 19. John observed, "the water was nearly boiling heat and run off quite a stream to the river."[64]

From the hot springs, the route continued to the present-day Homedale vicinity. Even though some grazing was available along the river and in the nearby foothills, livestock nevertheless were failing. While camped in the area on August 19, Abigail Scott wrote: "our cattle are much jaded and many of them too nearly worn out to work." She noted considerable sickness in the company, including two in her family. The following day while camped on the banks of the Owyhee River, she continued, "the roads very heavy and hilly and we are all very tired. . . . Some of our folks are yet quite sick . . . none among us . . . can say they are quite well." Diarrhea troubled almost everybody.[65]

Having turned northward with the bending Snake River, they came opposite to Fort Boise, located on the Snake's east shore just above the Boise River's mouth. South-side wayfarers, however, rarely visited the post, as it would require crossing the Snake to do so. Furthermore, by 1852 there was little reason to make the effort, as supplies at Fort Boise were meager at best. Also located here was the Snake River crossings used by the north-side travelers coming down the Boise valley. When getting across, the north-siders soon joined with the south bank travelers to continue northwest along a single trail again into the hills.

The Hudson's Bay Company's Fort Boise, established in 1834, had thrived for some years. By 1852, however, a single trader who had little to offer but sugar, tobacco, and fish occupied it. Following the 1846 Oregon Treaty and the establishment of the international boundary, HBC posts in Oregon Territory were minimally manned. The British were awaiting a negotiated financial settlement for the properties that they had to abandon south of the 49th parallel.

The reason that some immigrants spent time at Fort Boise usually was to graze livestock on a river island just to the north. In 1853, floodwaters severely damaged the old trading post. Today, nothing remains. A concrete monument erected in 1971 marks the approximate site.

North-side travelers coming down the Boise valley, of course, passed by the fort. Arriving here on September 20, Parthenia Blank wrote:

> It is built of unburnt brick a large yard inclosed by a wall some 12 feet high and 2 buildings of the same about 14 feet square and one story high It is tenanted by a rough looking Scotchman and a few indians and squaws. . . . A great many had depended on getting provisions here but failed entirely of getting anything except fish—There is a little sugar for sale here at .75, cents pr pound—Prospects seem to darken around us a good deal for some families are already entirely out of bread and many more will be in the course of one or two weeks.[66]

Earlier, Enoch Conyers had noted earlier on August 19: "Inside the fort are quite a number of Indian women ornamenting moccasins with bead work, for which they charge 25 cents per pair."[67]

Emigrants crossing the Snake River at Fort Boise in 1852 had a choice of fording or ferrying, at least at times. John McAllister, arriving on September 12, described the ford as "1/4 mile below the fort." He advised, after entering the river, to "keep well up to the head of the first sand bar . . . till striking of the next island." From there, it was a short distance to the west bank, noting that the second ford "is not so swift as the first of the fords With great care this may be forded by laying the goods on the top of the wagon Boxes." He added, "there is at times a ferry above the ford made of wagon boxes."[68]

The ferry toll apparently varied through the season. Conyers paid $3 on August 19; James Akin Jr. stated the fee was $2.50 on September 1; and the Reads were charged $5 on September 4.[69] Perhaps these differences were due to fluctuations in the availability of wagon boxes to serve as ferry vessels. At times, they may have been in short supply. Here too, Abigail Scott noted that the men who earlier left their party on August 16 to float down the Snake had arrived at Fort Boise on August 21. The men decided to end their cruise and sold their craft for $25, presumably to be used as a ferry.[70]

From the Snake River, the trail ascended northwestward up Cow Hollow for eight miles before reaching the plain. Ruts still are visible at a number of places along this distance, and are particularly deep and pristine near the top of the climb, known as Lytle or Keeney Pass. In recent years, an interpretive center has been established nearby and the adjacent swales now are protected.

Another five winding, dusty miles through barren country brought the emigrants to the Malheur River crossing at present-day Vale, Oregon.

Although the road between the Snake and Malheur generally was regarded as good, emigrants still were plagued with "intolerable dust."[71] On August 22, while camped on the banks of the Malheur, John Kerns penned yet another quaint observation: "Thanks be to the rewarder of trouble, 460 miles more will get us dirty-faced boys and girls out of this dirty-faced Kingdom."[72]

In this vicinity, many emigrants were fascinated by and made use of the hot springs at the river bank. Dr. Thomas White noted, "there are many hot springs, & some of them boiling hot. some of our company made lumps of dough & put in the spring it cooked them quite done."[73]

After crossing the Malheur River, it was a day's drive up Willow Creek and over dry, rolling grasslands to Alkali Springs, known then as Sulfur Springs. Kerns described the road as "good but some dusty," adding, the "route was up a dry branch and through a beautiful valley most of the day."[74] A major portion of this road exists today, much as it was, and may be driven by automobile.

Sickness yet prevailed. While at Alkali Springs on August 23, John Kerns wrote, "some of our train are severely afflicted with bloody diarrhea, the mountain fever and scurvy." He concluded, "begin to make us think we are treading the elephant's tail."[75]

About ten more miles over a hilly road brought travelers to Birch Creek, where they found the first good drinking water since leaving the Malheur, a distance of some 22 miles. On September 7, however, Martha Read wrote, we still "found ourselves most all sick from the effects of drinking sulphur water."[76]

From the Birch Creek camp, another rocky and rough three miles took them downhill to the Snake River at Farewell Bend. This would be the emigrants' last stay on the Snake. Here was ample grass and good water. The Read party, still suffering from the effects of drinking sulphur water, remained for six days. Martha wrote on September 13, "the Indians have visited us every day and brought us fish. They appear perfectly friendly."[77]

Finally, the emigrants would be leaving this great ribbon of water that they had followed for 330 miles. The hard journey had greatly weakened the emigrants and their livestock, and provisions were dwindling. Many persons were ill with diarrhea, scurvy, or mountain fever. While resting at Farewell Bend, Martha Read summarized, "There is an immense sight of sickness on the road." As if resigned to the inevitable, she noted that Lydia, her nine-year-old daughter, "is getting sick today with this mountain fever."[78]

Notes

1. John T. Kerns, "Journal of Crossing the Plains to Oregon in 1852," in *Transactions of the Forty-second Annual Reunion of the Oregon Pioneer Association* (Portland, Oregon, 1914), 175.

2. John G. Bond, *Geologic Map of Idaho*, scale 1:500,000, Idaho Bureau of Mines and Geology and U.S. Geological Survey, 1978; Bill Bonnichsen and Roy M. Breckenridge, *Cenozoic Geology of Idaho*, Idaho Bureau of Mines and Geology Bulletin 26 (1982).

3. Polly Coon, "Journal of a Journey over the Rocky Mountains," in *Covered Wagon Women: Diaries and Letters from the Western Trails*, 1852, vol. 5, edited and compiled by Kenneth L. Holmes and David C. Duniway (Glendale, California: Arthur H. Clark, 1986), 198.

4. Bond; Bonnichsen and Breckenridge.

5. John Tucker Scott, "Journal of a Trip to Oregon," in *Covered Wagon Women: Diaries and Letters from the Western Trails*, 1852, vol. 5, edited and compiled by Kenneth L. Holmes and David C. Duniway (Glendale, California: Arthur H. Clark, 1986), 108.

6. Enoch W. Conyers, "Diary of E.W. Conyers, a Pioneer of 1852," in *Transactions of the Thirty-third Annual Reunion of the Oregon Pioneer Association* (Portland, Oregon, 1905), 478–79.

7. Martha S. Read, "A History of Our Journey," in *Covered Wagon Women: Diaries and Letters from the Western Trails*, 1852, vol. 5, edited and compiled by Kenneth L. Holmes and David C. Duniway (Glendale, California: Arthur H. Clark, 1986), 237–40.

8. Peter D. Olich, "Treading the Elephant's Tail: Medical Problems on the Overland Trails," in *Overland Journal*, vol. 6, no. 1 (1988), 27; published by the Oregon-California Trails Association, Independence, Missouri.

9. Conyers, 471.

10. Abigail Jane Scott [Duniway], "Journal of a Trip to Oregon," in *Covered Wagon Women: Diaries and Letters from the Western Trails*, 1852, vol. 5, edited and compiled by Kenneth L. Holmes and David C. Duniway (Glendale, California: Arthur H. Clark, 1986), 95.

11. Conyers, 472.

12. Aubrey L. Haines, *Historic Sites along the Oregon Trail*, third edition (St. Louis, Missouri: Patrice Press, 1987), 303.

13. Abigail Scott, 96.

14. John McAllister, "Diary of Rev. John McAllister," in *Transactions of the Fiftieth Annual Reunion of the Oregon Pioneer Association* (Portland, Oregon, 1922), 496; see additional information under note 2 in chapter four.

15. Leslie M. Scott, *History of the Oregon Country by Harvey W. Scott*, compiler's appendix 3 (Cambridge: Riverside Press, 1924), 295.

16. John Tucker Scott, 97.

17. Kerns, 175.

18. John Spencer, "Daily Journal Kept by John Spencer, 1852 from Wellsville, Ohio to Portland, Oregon," typescript manuscript, Oregon Historical Society, Portland, Oregon, 18.

19. Kerns, 175; Merrill J. Mattes, *The Great Platte River Road: The Covered Wagon Mainline Via Fort Kearny to Fort Laramie*, Nebraska State Historical Society, vol. 25 (1969), 61.

20. Abigail Scott, 99.

21. Spencer, 19.

22. Haines, 323.

23. Conyers, 480.

24. Ibid.

25. Cecelia Adams, "Twin Sisters on the Oregon Trail: Cecelia Adams and Parthenia Blank," in *Covered Wagon Women: Diaries and Letters from the Western Trails*, 1852, vol. 5, edited and compiled by Kenneth L. Holmes and David C. Duniway (Glendale, California: Arthur H. Clark, 1986), 288.
26. Conyers, 480.
27. "Oregon Trail in Idaho and other Emigrant Trails," Idaho Travel Council and Idaho State Bureau of Land Management (brochure).
28. Kerns, 175.
29. Adams, 288.
30. Ibid., 289.
31. Abigail Scott, 105.
32. Coon, 198.
33. "Salmon Falls and Thousand Springs," Reference Series No. 184, Idaho Historical Society, Boise, Idaho (1987), 3.
34. Haines, 325.
35. This information is reported in "Salmon Falls and Thousand Springs," 3. However, none of the 1852 accounts that the author examined made reference to this crossing.
36. *A Guide to the Oregon Trail in Southwest Idaho*, Cultural Resources Information Series No. 2, Bureau of Land Management, Boise District, 3.
37. Adams, 290.
38. Coon, 199.
39. Read, 240.
40. Adams, 290.
41. Al R. Hawk, "Down the Snake River by Boat," in *Told by the Pioneers*, vol. 1, U.S. Public Works Administration, Washington Pioneer Project (1937), 163.
42. Ibid., 158.
43. Ibid., 163.
44. Ibid., 163–64.
45. Conyers, 481.
46. Kerns, 176.
47. James Akin Jr., *The Oregon Trail Diary of James Akin, Jr.: The Unabridged Diary with Introduction and Contemporary Comments by Bert Webber* (Medford, Oregon: Webb Research Group, Pacific Northwest Books, 1989), 47.
48. Conyers, 481.
49. Kerns, 176.
50. Abigail Scott, 106.
51. Conyers, 481.
52. Akin, 47.
53. Ibid., 48.
54. Ibid.
55. Kerns, 176.
56. Abigail Scott, 107.
57. Ibid.
58. Kerns, 177.
59. Bond; Bonnichsen and Breckenridge.
60. Kerns, 177.
61. John Tucker Scott, 108.
62. Ibid.
63. Haines, 335–36.
64. Kerns, 178.
65. Abigail Scott, 111–12.

66. Adams, 296.
67. Conyers, 485.
68. McAllister, 499.
69. Conyers, 485; Akin, 50; Read, 242.
70. Abigail Scott, 113.
71. Spencer, 24.
72. Kerns, 178.
73. Thomas White, "To Oregon in 1852, Letter of Dr. Thomas White," edited by Oscar O. Winther and Gayle Thornbrough (Indianapolis, Indiana: Indiana Historical Society, 1964), 18.
74. Kerns, 179.
75. Ibid.
76. Read, 243.
77. Ibid.
78. Ibid.

Chapter Eleven

Blue Mountains

Now we have reached the Blue Mountains [and] camped at the foot of them [where we] had plenty of good, clear, cold water [and] wood in boundanc.
—Mary Ann Boatman

AT LEAST 350 MILES of difficult terrain lay ahead before reaching the Willamette Valley; the foremost challenges being the Blue Mountains and Cascade Range. Knowing these obstacles must be conquered before the onset of winter, the weary Oregon-bound travelers trudged onward from Farewell Bend. Today, U.S. Route 30 closely follows where the emigrant trail led steeply out of the Snake River Valley for four miles to the Burnt River.

Many took a moment to reflect during the ascent from Farewell Bend. Origen Thomson's thoughts and actions probably were typical.

Turned around to take a last view of the Shoshonee [Snake] River. The scene . . . was very beautiful. The broad river lay spread out before, glittering under the rays of the arising sun like a river of moulten silver. . . . I took off my hat and made my best bow, and bade a long last farewell to its clear rippling waters.[1]

Many made the first of their several camps along the Burnt River at or near present-day Huntington, Oregon. Most who earlier had floated the river had deemed it wise to continue on land from Farewell Bend, but a few of the more adventurous and over optimistic continued downstream. Obviously, they were unaware of the treacherous and impassable rapids and falls that lay immediately ahead and which culminated in today's aptly named Hells Canyon.

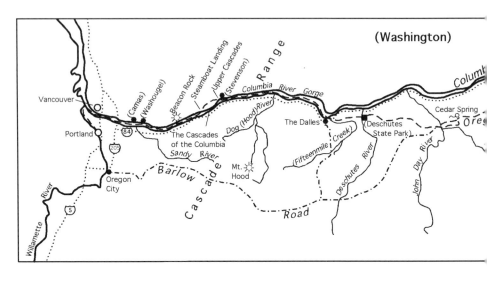

(Washington)

Vancouver

Portland

(Camas)
(Washougel)

Beacon Rock
Steamboat Landing
Upper Cascades
(Stevenson)

Columbia River Gorge

C a s c a d e   R a n g e

Columb

Cedar Spring

The Dalles

(Deschutes
State Park)

O r e

The Cascades
of the Columbia

Dog (Hood) River

Sandy River

(Fifteenmile Creek)

Deschutes River

John Day River

Mt.
Hood

Oregon
City

B a r l o w

Road

Willamette River

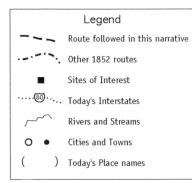

Legend

— — — Route followed in this narrative

—··—·· Other 1852 routes

■ Sites of Interest

····(80)···· Today's Interstates

⌒⌒ Rivers and Streams

O ● Cities and Towns

(   ) Today's Place names

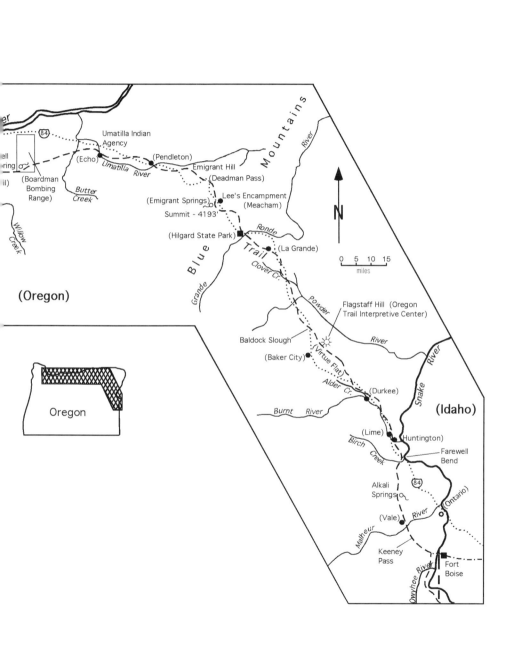

Enoch Conyers, departing Birch Creek on August 22, arrived at the Burnt River and camped, being among the first of his party to arrive. "We had not been in camp but a short time when here comes the boys [i.e., William and Payson, other members of his party], bringing with them Wilson Hess, a Quincy boy and a cripple." Enoch explained:

> Quite a number of emigrants took some discarded wagon beds at our last crossing on the Snake River, near Fort Boise, calked them with strips of rags, loaded their provisions and blankets and started down the river, as they said, for Oregon City. . . . Wilson Hess had cast his lot with these unfortunate emigrants.
>
> The river [w]as very swift and filled with large boulders and perpendicular cliffs of rocks (basalt formation) touring up 400 and 500 feet on either side, and exceedingly dangerous to navigate. One of the wagon beds struck a rock and capsized. They lost all of their provisions, bedding and clothing, the occupants barely escaped with their lives. They became frightened by their adventure down the Snake River in a wagon bed and concluded to desert their boat and take the emigrant road for the balance of the way. They packed their blankets and what provisions they had on their backs and traveled over the mountain about one mile to the emigrant road, where they left young Hess to shift for himself.[2]

Although the Conyers party fully intended to take care of the boy, they soon learned that his train was "but one day back." Thus the lad waited in camp while the Conyers train moved on.[3]

Mary Ann Boatman tells a similar of story of harboring two destitute rafters, but the precise location of the encounter is unknown. As Conyers related, however, some travelers did attempt to float downstream from Farewell Bend and the lucky ones who survived had to trek cross-country back to the emigrant trail. It is probable that the following incident occurred in the Huntington vicinity or along the lower Burnt River. Mary Ann's reference to the "Snake River Mountains" probably identifies the rugged Burnt River terrain. Furthermore, her mention of having "the privilege of resting under" the first trees in a thousand miles suggests they were in the mountainous Burnt River locality.

> **We are crawling [at a] snail pace making our way to the Snake River Mountains, after a long and hard pull for both man and teames. We are now making the ascent, at times, it seems as if it will be an impossibility to make the summit of the mountains on the account of the jaded condition of the teames. But after a long and hard drive**

the summit is reached. Water is hauld for cookin and dish washing. The cattle had to be driven some distant for water and grass. Wood was plentiful as we had been deprived of proper fuel so long. We wer[e] not satisfied with a ordinary camp fire as wood was so easy obtained. In a very short time smoke was curling skyward [and] flames leaping high in the air. All glad that one more hard climb had been accomplished in saft[e]y. The night was passed in quiet rest for those who had the opportunity of lying down to rest and slee[p] As for the men on guard, [it] was about the same old story, tired and no chance to rest, only on the hard, cold earth.

Morning came after the usual hours of night had passed. Oh what a lovely sight met our gaze. The sun was pushing up his golden rim in the far a way eastern horizon, threading all the mountain tops and trees with threads of gold. The sight was unexplainable to a tired lot of emigrants who had traveled a 1000 miles without having the privilege of resting under one of God's natural shade made for the benefit of man and beast. The green trees with their sweet odor of pine and the rich perfume of wild flowers wer[e] so refreshing to all. But little did we realize the sufering of two human beings only a short distance a way. Fires blazing high, all busy making re[a]dy for another days journey, after all had partaken of the ration allowance [and] camp utensil[s] safely stored a way in the[i]r usual place. As the men came with the teames . . . two men come up out of the woods. Bare headed and . . . what clothes that remained hanging on their frail bodies, torn in shreds. [Their] feet cut and bleeding [and] faces as pale as dead men. [They were] lank and starved all most to death. [They] had nothing to eat but wild berries and young twigs from the brush for 12 days. They wer[e] 2 of a party of 6 that started down Snake River in their wagon beds for boats. In going through a narrow canyon where the river made it[s] course over a steep falls, all of the party wer[e] lost but those 2. Every thing was gone, they wer[e] lucky, if luck one may term it, thrown close to the bank on the side of the river that the wagon road was. The bank was all most perpendicular with a few small shrubs growing on the side of the bank, [but] they managed, in some way, to grasp hold of the bushes and climb to the top of the bank. There they wer[e], miles from any one in a strang[e] mountain country. No food or clothes to speak of, no means of obtaining the staff of life, only guided by natural instinct which way to go. After 12 days wanderin without food, except wild berries and young sprouts, they had come within hearing of our men when they wer[e] driving the cattle to camp . . . Their attention [attracted], and thinking perhaps there was a little chance for life, hurried as fast as their languid condition would allow them. They arrived at our camp just as we wer[e] re[a]dy to start. Oh, what a sight met our gaze. Two emaciated human beings almost starved, feet lacerated and bleedin, clothes torn to shreds, pale and shrunken cheeks, eyes dull, lips and tongue parched for the want of water. They told their story. They had been 2 of the unfortunate who had listen to the tails of the traders and had lost all but their lives.

Companions an[d] boat, all were lost. They wer[e] soon feed and clothed as good as we could. . . . Our boys almost fit them out as our dear brother [who] had pass a way from earth and needed none of his earthly possession. They wer[e] given to them. [After] they were . . . clothed and feed, we move on [and] left them to their fate.

After reaching the Burnt River, the emigrant trail mostly continued along the canyon bottom, past peaks towering thousands of feet above the valley floor. Today, Interstate 84 approximates the route through this area.

The sedimentary and volcanic formations constituting the mountains in this part of Oregon were deposited in a marine environment during the Mesozoic Era, 100 to 200 million years ago. The formations since have been upturned, folded, and faulted, and in places were altered by heat and pressure into metamorphic rocks, which sometimes are highly mineralized.[4]

Unknown to the travelers of the 1850s, some of these formations contained valuable minerals, mainly gold. Hordes of wealth-seekers would seek their fortunes in the region within a decade. The emigrants were entering a locality that after the 1860s became the well-known Baker Mining District, one of the main gold producing areas of Oregon.[5]

Limestone quarries, particularly in the vicinity of today's Lime, Oregon, was another type of mining activity that developed along the Burnt River, beginning in the 1880s. Much of this limestone has been used in making cement. At times as much as 225,000 tons per year has been quarried. Large quantities of limestone also have been shipped for making fertilizer and refining sugar.[6]

Because the rapidly flowing Burnt River is continually carving its channel downward through the upturned rock formations, the canyon remains narrow, with little, or any, valley floor. The emigrants had limited space in which to negotiate their way. Parthenia Blank aptly described their situation on September 26.

Here the mountains are so high and so close that they leave no room for bluffs and when they close down upon us on one side of the river our only alternative is to flee to the other. Crossed the river 5 times in about 6 miles.[7]

The Conyers train, having nearly completed their trek up the Burnt River on August 24, crossed the stream "six times today, nine times in all."[8]

John Kerns on August 26, after a day's travel beyond today's Huntington, described the route as, "the roughest road we have encountered on the journey, being up and down the sidling mountains, into the brush and across the creek every 200 or 300 yards, and over stoney places enough to hide all dispairing sinners."[9]

In the Burnt River country, patience was running out, tempers frequently flared, and desperation set in for some. On August 23, Conyers recorded an incident illustrating both human cruelty and compassion. In the second day of travel along the Burnt River, the Conyers party came upon a man and wife with four small children stopped alongside the road in the shade of some bushes—curiously, no wagon or livestock were in sight. The husband was sick and lying on the ground. Upon inquiry, Conyers learned that a man who had agreed to drive them to Oregon had abandoned the family. The forlorn wife explained the situation.

> Everything went along all right until my husband took sick and unable to walk, and then everything went wrong. I tried to do the very best I could under these trying circumstances. I took the whip and drove our team and made my sick husband as comfortable as possible in the wagon, with our four little children, praying to God to give me strength that I might be able to hold out and save my sick husband and little ones alive to our journey's end. But the owner of the team . . . became very cross . . . saying "the cattle and wagon belongs to me, and if you let them young ones ride the cattle will very soon give out and die."

After the wife tried to reason with the owner, explaining to him that her husband was too sick to walk and the children could not be afoot all the time, he still refused to let the children ride in the wagon. She related, "he became so enraged that he took what few things we had and set them out by the roadside and left us here . . . with only two days' provisions."

During the course of the conversation, the woman showed her feet and those of her children. Conyers wrote:

> We were indeed surprised and horrified at the sight which met our eyes when that poor, grief stricken mother tenderly removed the rags

from those little feet and also those from her own. The sole of each little foot was covered with sores, and swollen to nearly twice their natural size. . . . Their shoes having given out, the mother had swathed their little feet in rags, to protect them . . . from the sharp rocks and burning sand.[10]

Conyers assured them, "we would not leave them here to suffer and die, but would . . . take them along with us, and would make them as comfortable as we possibly could."

The woman expressed gratitude and emotion: "We thank you gentlemen, with all our heart, and may God reward you for your kind offer in this hour of our grief and want."

As circumstances would have it, a neighbor and old friend of the family, a Reverend Yantis and his party, were but a day back. Upon receiving this news, the family decided to wait for the Yantis train. The Conyers party moved on. Enoch concluded, "if there is any meanness in a man, it makes no difference how well he has it covered, the plains is the place that will bring it out."[11]

Sickness continued to be prevalent. On August 22, John Kerns "Saw some very sick persons afflicted with mountain fever and flux." One man was about to die.[12]

The John Tucker Scott family was yet plagued with illness too. Although John was recovering from diarrhea, his four-year-old son Willie finally died on August 28 after being violently ill for days with "Cholera Infantum or Dropsy in the brain."[13] He was buried alongside the Burnt River in the vicinity of today's Weatherby Rest Area.

When camped on September 6, after one day's travel along the Burnt River, James Akin Jr. noted "considerable sickness in the company."[14] On September 14, Martha Reed recorded that her little "Lydia is quite sick yet."[15]

At today's Durkee, the emigrant road left the Burnt River and followed a northwest course up Alder Creek, also sometimes referred to as Birch Creek. After seven miles, the trail left Alder Creek to proceed more northerly for about fifteen miles over upland bluffs, ridges, and hollows to what is known today as Virtue Flat, a few miles east of present-day Baker City, Oregon. Travel over this road was considered reasonably good. On August 25, Conyers noted that the route was "very good, except the crossings, and, as usual, very dusty." Continuing the following day to the western edge of Virtue Flat, he commented, "good, hard [and] in some places . . . quite sidling."[16]

From Virtue Flat, the emigrant road made a gradual descent into the Powder River Valley, passing by Flagstaff Hill. From this vantage, emigrants were inspired by their views of the fertile Powder River Valley. Although traveling in cold and rainy weather, John Kerns recorded on August 30:

> This valley is the most handsome that we have seen since leaving the Bear River. The valley is several miles wide, covered with a heavy coat of grass, and the creek runs through its center, its banks lined with willow, cottonwood, etc. On the west is a high range of mountains, called the Blue mountains, which are covered with forests of pine, fir, etc., and the whole country abounds with game.[17]

On the same day, William Byers was equally impressed, "this is a handsome valley of considerable extent, producing a good crop of grass of excellent quality."[18]

An especially spectacular view was in store for those hardy emigrants who might have ventured up Flagstaff Hill. From the summit, they observed the trail stretching northwestward across the valley floor for nearly as far as the eye could see. Even today, the faint traces and locations of the old trail can be depicted for some distance in the valley. Also today, remnants of the trail are clearly visible across sagebrush-dotted Virtue Flat and down to the base of Flagstaff Hill. The lines of covered wagons slowly descending toward the valley must have been a striking sight. The U.S. Bureau of Land Management maintains an excellent Oregon Trail interpretive center on Flagstaff Hill for modern-day visitors.

Despite problems with illnesses, low provisions, and jaded oxen, travel conditions usually were fairly pleasant for the next thirty miles. Their first stop in the valley often was at Baldock Slough, sometimes referred to as Pool Creek because its water typically stood in ponds.[19] This stream and its tributaries had to be crossed several times before arriving at a fork of the Powder River. Though the valley had been lush with springtime growth, latecomers in 1852 found little grazing for livestock, particularly near the road.

While resting on September 26 at a branch of the Powder River, John Spencer observed, "a train overtook us. They had been for several days without any kind of bread stuff! . . . Many more are reported to be in the same condition."[20]

On September 17, Martha Reed recorded desperate conditions in the Baldock Slough area. "Saw 20 dead cattle to day. It looks like misery along here. The cattle are dying off and people are getting out of provision and a great many sick and some are dying."[21]

The Adams and Blank party arrived late in the season. While camped on the North Powder River on September 30, "Oregon traders" advised them that "we must hurry if we get over the Blue Mountains."[22]

For the next eight miles beyond the North Powder River, the emigrant trail followed much the same route as today's Interstate 84. Ascending bluffs out of the Powder River Valley, they followed Clover Creek for several miles. Then, as Enoch Conyers described, "three miles more over hills and hollows, and a very rough and rocky road. And dust! . . . This brought us to the summit of the mountain, overlooking the Grande Ronde Valley, one of the prettiest and most welcome sights seen on the whole route."[23]

The descent of more than 1,300 feet into the Grande Ronde Valley was a major challenge, some proclaiming it the worst so far. On October 2 Parthenia Blank noted, "Grande Ronde a beautiful level valley nearly round I would think some 15 miles in diameter—but O the getting down to it over a long steep and stony hill is equal to any getting down stairs I ever saw, and I have seen some on this road."[24]

On September 1, Abigail Scott recorded, "the longest and most difficult descent of any hill which we had yet encountered; . . . the dust [would] blow in clouds, hiding the wagons teams and roads entirely from our view, . . . The rocks so filled the road, that anyone who had not begun to 'see the elephant' would have been afraid to have attempted the descent."[25]

Today's travelers can view where the emigrants descended into the Grande Ronde Valley from the nearby Charles H. Reynolds Rest Area. An Oregon Highway Department kiosk provides interpretation about the trail in this locality.

Most early travelers made their first camp in the Grande Ronde Valley at the base of the hill, immediately east of the rest stop along Ladd Creek and at a nearby spring. After the long, grueling day's journey down the steep, dangerous hill into the valley, they welcomed this pleasant setting. After his August 28 descent, Conyers wrote, "we crossed a nice cool spring branch just at the foot of the mountain, and the entrance to the valley. Here we laid by and camped for the night."[26]

At this site on October 2, Parthenia Blank recorded that they "found another trading station from Oregon," where they could purchase such supplies as flour, salt and "first rate fat beef."[27]

⊂◌⌐⌐◌⊃

The final words in Mary Ann's narrative describe the descent into the Grande Ronde and their campsite near today's La Grande, Oregon.

> **We [finally began our] . . . descent of the Snake River mountains, a rough and uneven road requiring the greatest skill of driver to keep oxen and wagon from going hundreds of feet down the side of the mountain. On onward we go.**
>
> **Now we have reached the Blue Mountains [and] camped at the foot of them [where we] had plenty of good, clear, cold water [and] wood in boundance.**

Mary Ann's account inexplicably ends here and it remains unclear why she never finished the narrative. A fuller discussion of this topic is presented in the Introduction. Fortunately, Willis recorded much of their later experiences during the journey, both in his personal writings and in later-day newspaper interviews and accounts.

The Grande Ronde Valley was oasis-like. Clear, cool streams flowed here, tall grass abounded for livestock, and the native population was friendly and eager to trade. Arriving on September 1, John Kerns declared this "the best and most beautiful place we have seen on the whole road or, in fact, in our lives." He estimated that the valley "would give home to 1,500 or 2,000 settlers."[28]

On the same day, William Byers proclaimed, "verily this is the place to please the eye of the farmers, the soil is excellent, producing a wonderful crop of grass of different varieties."[29]

The following day, while camped in the La Grande vicinity, Abigail Scott described the valley as "near ten miles wide and covered with luxuriant look[ing] grass; high mountain are ranged all around it. . . . Grand Round river runs through the western part of the valley; it's banks are adorned with willow birch bitter cottonwood, & alder."[30]

Most 1852 travelers also were impressed with the native people in this beautiful valley. Though mostly not permanent residents here, the Nez Perce, Cayuse, and other Columbia Plateau tribes frequented the Grande Ronde in the warmer months of the year. Some had been moderately educated and introduced to Christianity and agriculture at missionary stations under Dr. Marcus Whitman in the Cayuse's Walla Walla country and Henry Spalding among the Nez Perce on the Clearwater River.

On September 1, John Kerns saw "quite a number of the Nez Perce tribe of Indians here, who appear to be more intelligent, clean and sociable than any Indian I ever saw." He added that their chief had been educated by Dr. Whitman and seems much of a gentleman." Kerns believed the horses were "as good as I ever saw in any country," and noted, the Indians "are eager to trade them for cattle."[31]

Byers made similar positive observations:

> They cultivate considerable land, producing grain and vegetables of various kinds. . . . Hundreds are now in this valley trading horses, buying cows, selling potatoes, berries etc., carrying on quite a brisk trade with the Emigrants. These Indians . . . seem anxious to learn more of the customs and manners of the whites. They are . . . becoming a decided advantage to Emigration.[32]

In summary, Abigail Scott said the native people were "very wealthy, they have numerous herds of horses and possess many of the luxuries of life in abundance."[33]

For generations, the Umatilla, Nez Perce, Walla Walla, Cayuse, and other tribes had conducted a brisk trade in the valley. During the emigrant period, bartering became even more extensive, with white entrepreneurs coming from the Willamette Valley with goods and supplies to set up shop in the Grande Ronde. Although prices were high and hard bargains were the norm among the Indians, emigrants, and white traders, business usually was fairly conducted. However, there was the occasionally less than scrupulous person who took advantage of the emigrants as well as the native people.

Willis Boatman, in an interview in later years, related such an incident.

> When we got to the Grand Ronde Valley, . . . we found a lot of settlers in the valley resting after their long trip and grazing their cattle. It was quite a sight, the huge camp of tents and covered wagons.
>
> One evening, just about sundown, we saw 12 or 15 Indians come riding up, looking pretty mean . . . [and] seemed quite excited, and did more talking among themselves than was usual, but when they rushed in among the cattle, picked out a fine ox and lassoed him, talking angrily all the while, we didn't know what to think.
>
> Of course the man that owned the ox was indignant, and while none of us could understand what the Indians said, this man kept telling them in loud, angry tones (as if by raising his voice he could make them understand). "Look here, you can't take off [with] my ox

like that. I tell you, I won't stand it. I just bought that ox from a trader a few days ago." . . . [Hearing the confusion] an old fellow [came up] who had been living [out] West and who told us a lot about conditions there and about the Indians, and what we might expect. "Friends" he drawled, "I speak Chinook. Maybe I can get at this."

Things looked pretty bad, and it begin to seem as if real trouble was brewing. You couldn't blame the settler for not just standing by and seeing a perfectly good ox he had just paid good money for taken from him under his very nose. But you didn't want any serious trouble started with the Indians either.

Presently the interpreter turned around and said, "Somebody's got to lose on this deal. This fellow says he bought the ox from a trader, too. Looks mighty like a slick deal to me. Probably some rascal has went and sold you and him the same animal. Maybe sold him to more. I don't know. But if I was you, now, if I were in your place, friend, I'd just let the Injun have it peaceful like and not no fuss, for, either way, whether it's you that gets the ox or the trader that cheated him, it's all the same to him. And he and his tribe'll take it out on white folks, maybe on this party, maybe the next one."

So, they explained the best they could to the Indians and they rode off and peace . . . settled down again over the valley, but I think the man who had been cheated felt it was at a pretty high price, for money as well as cattle was scarce.[34]

The steep rocky surfaces that the emigrants negotiated into the Grande Ronde Valley and which they next climbed when ascending into the Blue Mountains are composed of rugged, eroded basalt. These rock masses, part of the Columbia River Basalt Group, resulted from a series of nearly two hundred lava flows. During the Miocene Epoch, about 16 million years ago, repeated extrusions of liquid lava crept out of fissure vents or cracks in the earth's crust, inundated vast areas, and eventually cooled in layers.

The flows covered 80,000 square miles of western Idaho, eastern Oregon, and eastern Washington. The formations exposed in the Grande Ronde and Blue Mountains are some of the older and more extensive flows of the series. As a specific group, they are referred to as Grande Ronde Basalt. These flows have been gently folded, broken by faults, and eroded by streams, forming the rugged topography of the area.[35]

⊂⊙⊃

Upon leaving the Grande Ronde Valley, the climb into the Blue Mountains was a long, hard pull. Cecelia Adams recorded on October 3, "very steep in many places and continued to ascend for about 6 miles. It was a very hard drive."[36]

After crossing a few miles of relatively level upland, the trail made a steep descent again to the Grande Ronde River. Abigail Scott penned on September 3, "the descent of the mountain down to the river bottom was down the most dangerous looking place we had yet come down."[37]

Reaching the river, they were in the vicinity of today's Hilgard State Park. Many camped here for the night, whereas others either "nooned" or rested before ascending again into the Blue Mountains. In a short distance, the road led into the Pelican Creek Valley, where today approximately a mile or so of the trail is marked by the U.S. Forest Service. Recently, the Oregon-California Trails Association also has identified much of the trail through the Blue Mountains. Throughout the range, in fact, many segments are well preserved, traversing both federal and private land. A few miles north of Hilgard State Park, the U.S. Forest Service has constructed access from Interstate 84 to an excellent Oregon Trail interpretive park.

Continuing to negotiate through the irregular, rocky terrain and thick groves of pine, spruce, fir, and tamarack, early travelers pushed on to the summit of the Blue Mountains at an elevation of 4,193 feet. Because many emigrants were unaccustomed to being in mountainous, forested terrain, they were fascinated by how sound traveled in the high country air. Abigail Scott noted on September 3:

> In this place common conversations can be overheard at the distance of one hundred and fifty yards, and the noise of men speaking to cattle in a loud voice sounds loud enough for a savage war whoop . . . the noise of discharging a rifle is equal to the report of a canon and may be heard a half dozen times reverberating from mountain to mountain.[38]

The weakened oxen especially suffered in the rugged terrain. On October 5, Parthenia Blank wrote, "many cattle are failing and all are very poor and a good many get lost among the thick timber. A good many wagons are left, some broken and some good and sound because the cattle are not able to take them along."[39]

A recent view looking east along a segment of the Oregon Trail in the Blue Mountains. *Greg MacGregor*

From the summit, it was only a few miles to a relatively open upland area. Many camped here or a few miles further at today's Emigrant Springs State Park.[40]

Six miles through the timber beyond Emigrant Springs, following much the same route as U.S. Route 30, travelers came to what is known today as Deadman Pass. Here, trail ruts are well preserved on both sides of Interstate 84. On the north side of the freeway, multi-track swales may be seen heading westward uphill, but eventually becoming obscure in the vicinity of a radio tower. Swales again appear a short distance north of the tower leading down what is now known as Emigrant Hill. Here, wayfarers for the first time viewed the golden, grassy prairies of the spacious Umatilla Valley. Parthenia Blank claimed, the plains were "literally dotted with indian ponies—and cattle."[41]

Arriving here on September 8, Abigail Scott described the scene as one of "unparalleled beauty while for as far as the eye could penetrate [over] the plain the country was a rolling prairie, with no timber in sight except that which grows along the Umatilla."

When skies were clear, the far off Cascade Range came into view for the first time from this vantage point. Mount Hood loomed high, serving as a beacon guiding them to the journey's end. Abigail Scott stated, "mount Hood reared its snow crowned summit in awful granduer high above the other mountains . . . appearing as a stationary white cloud."[42]

Notes

1. Origen Thomson, *Crossing the Plains* (Fairfield, Washington: Ye Galleon Press, 1983), 61.
2. Enoch W. Conyers, "Diary of E.W. Conyers, a Pioneer of 1852," in *Transactions of the Thirty-third Annual Reunion of the Oregon Pioneer Association* (Portland, Oregon, 1905), 487.
3. Ibid., 488.
4. George W. Walker and Norman S. MacCleod, *Geologic Map of Oregon*, scale 1:500,000, 2 sheets, U.S. Geological Survey.
5. Howard C. Brooks and Len Ramp, *Gold and Silver in Oregon,* State of Oregon Department of Geology and Mineral Industries Bulletin 61 (1968), 58–59.
6. Howard C. Brooks, *Limestone Deposits in Oregon*, State of Oregon Department of Geology and Mineral Industries Special Paper 19 (1989), 36–37.
7. Cecelia Adams, "Twin Sisters on the Oregon Trail: Cecelia Adams and Parthenia Blank," in *Covered Wagon Women: Diaries and Letters from the Western Trails*, 1852, vol. 5, edited and compiled by Kenneth L. Holmes and David C. Duniway (Glendale, California: Arthur H. Clark, 1986), 298.
8. Conyers, 488–89.
9. John T. Kerns, "Journal of Crossing the Plains to Oregon in 1852," in *Transactions of the Forty-second Annual Reunion of the Oregon Pioneer Association* (Portland, Oregon, 1914), 179.
10. Conyers, 488–89.
11. Ibid., 490.
12. Kerns, 179.
13. John Tucker Scott, "Journal of a Trip to Oregon," in *Covered Wagon Women: Diaries and Letters from the Western Trails*, 1852, vol. 5, edited and compiled by Kenneth L. Holmes and David C. Duniway (Glendale, California: Arthur H. Clark, 1986), 115–17.
14. James Akin Jr., *The Oregon Trail Diary of James Akin Jr. in 1852: The Unabridged Diary with Introduction and Contemporary Comments by Bert Webber* (Medford, Oregon: Webb Research Group, Pacific Northwest Books, 1989), 51.
15. Martha S. Read, "A History of Our Journey," in *Covered Wagon Women: Diaries and Letters for the Western Trails,* 1852, vol. 5, edited and compiled by Kenneth L. Holmes and David C. Duniway (Glendale, California: Arthur H. Clark, 1986), 238.
16. Conyers, 491.
17. Kerns, 180.
18. William N. Byers, "The Odyssey of William N. Byers," edited by Merrill J. Mattes, in *Overland Journal*, vol. 2, no. 1 (1983), 17; published by the Oregon-California Trails Association, Independence, Missouri.
19. John McAllister, "Diary of Rev. John McAllister," in *Transactions of the Fiftieth Reunion of the Oregon Pioneer Association*, (Portland, Oregon, 1922), 501; see additional information under note 2 in chapter four.

20. John Spencer, "Daily Journal Kept by John Spencer, 1852 from Wellsville, Ohio to Portland, Oregon," typescript manuscript, Oregon Historical Society, Portland, Oregon, 22.
21. Read, 244.
22. Adams, 300.
23. Conyers, 492.
24. Adams, 301.
25. Abigail Jane Scott [Duniway], "Journal of a Trip to Oregon," in *Covered Wagon Women: Diaries and Letters from the Western Trails*, 1852, vol. 5, edited and compiled by Kenneth L. Holmes and David C. Duniway (Glendale, California: Arthur H. Clark, 1986), 120.
26. Conyers, 492.
27. Adams, 301.
28. Kerns, 181.
29. Byers, 18.
30. Abigail Scott, 120.
31. Kerns, 181.
32. Byers, 18.
33. Abigail Scott, 121.
34. Mabel Cleland, "On the Pioneer Tacoma Trail," in *Tacoma News Tribune* (Tacoma, Washington), June 20 and 21, 1922
35. John E. Allen, *The Magnificent Gateway: A Layman's Guide to the Geology of the Columbia River Gorge* (Forest Grove, Oregon: Timber Press, 1979), 34–39; Keith L. Stoffel, *Geology of the Grande Ronde Lignite Fields, Asotin County, Washington,* Washington Report of Investigation No. 27, Washington Division of Geology and Earth Resources (1984), 6–10.
36. Adams, 302.
37. Abigail Scott, 121.
38. Ibid., 122.
39. Adams, 303.
40. Aubrey L. Haines, *Historic Sites along the Oregon Trail,* third edition (St. Louis, Missouri: Patrice Press, 1987), 361–63.
41. Adams, 304.
42. Abigail Scott, 124.

A modern-day view of the descent into the Umatilla Valley. Abigail Scott described the scene as one of "unparalleled beauty while for as far as the eye could penetrate . . . the country was rolling prairie." *Greg MacGregor*

Chapter Twelve

At Last The Dalles

[At the Dalles] my brother was taken down with the Mountain or nervous fever. Mrs. Boatman was still sick with the scurvy and I was taken with a kind of flux there. Not one of us was able to help the other. —Willis Boatman

W ITH THE BLUE MOUNTAINS behind them and the last major obstacle in sight on the far horizon (the Cascades), the emigrants were encouraged as they gazed down on the beautiful landscape before them. The friendliness and assistance of the native people in the Grande Ronde would be equaled in the Umatilla Valley. Although provisions were dangerously low for many emigrants, the journey's end and relief now seemed to be within their grasp.

The long and generally gradual descent into the Umatilla Valley approached an Indian village near the Umatilla River. On September 24, John McAllister noted there were "many indian wigwarms" here.[1]

Having arrived here earlier, John Kerns observed on September 5, the "Cayuse tribe . . . resemble the Nez Perce, are wealthy and to some extent civilized. The chiefs speak the English language well and are very free and friendly with the whites."[2]

William Byers arriving the same day recorded, "the valley is the residence of the principal Chiefs of the Cayuse nation. They are very wealthy, owning large herds of Cattle, Horses, sheep, etc. They also have a number of cultivated fields in the valley." Byers also observed, "this is a beautiful valley, good soil, many springs and rivulets."[3]

Today, Pendleton, Oregon, is situated in this valley, and a large portion of the nearby area is encompassed by the Umatilla Indian Reservation, home of the confederated Cayuse, Walla Walla and Umatilla tribes.

From the Pendleton vicinity, early travelers continued along the Umatilla River for two miles before ascending to a gently rolling, bunch-grass-covered upland, which is blanketed today by grain crops. Following nearly due west for some twelve miles, emigrants once again came to the Umatilla.

According to John Kerns, who camped in this vicinity on September 7, there were "plenty of Indians along here of the Walla Walla tribe." His evaluation of their trustworthiness was somewhat less than stellar, stating they "would steal swill from the hogs if they had a favorable lay."[4]

Five more miles northwest along the stream brought travelers to the Umatilla Indian Agency, located on the west bank of the river crossing at today's Echo, Oregon. Established just the year before for the Umatilla, Cayuse, and Walla Walla tribes, the presence of the agency was a surprise to emigrants and boosted their morale in a unique way. As Conyers recorded on September 4,

> we saw the first frame house since leaving the Missouri River. This house is about eighteen or twenty feet square, and one story high. The sight of this house, although standing all alone out here in the wilderness, proved to be a great stimulus to the poor emigrants, worn out by their long trip across the continent, who received new encouragement, believing their long and tiresome journey was nearing its end.[5]

Many journalists took note of the agency. Kerns on September 8 said, "it was a building about 40 by 20 feet of frame and nicely painted"[6]; Origen Thomson on September 3 described it as, "frame, one and a-half stories high, a porch on the west side, a good well, and an old-fashioned windless graces the porch"[7]; and John McAllister on September 27 noted that emigrants here could trade weak and lame cattle or horses for those in better condition. Supplies, such as flour, beef, sugar, coffee, and tea, also were available for purchase.[8] However, some found prices too high and sought alternatives.

When John Spencer arrived on October 8, he refused paying "25 cents per lb for rib or lower end of limb." When the young man at the agency offered to shoot some prairie chickens for him, John concluded, "if he could get them so easy I might perhaps get a mess. While teams went on I staid back and shot 3 myself."[9]

In 1855, the agency was burned by the Cayuse at the beginning of the Yakama War (1855–58), and shortly thereafter, the Oregon militia established Fort Henrietta at the site.[10]

The route forked at the agency. The right-hand road continued down the east side of the Umatilla to the Columbia River, then west along the Columbia's south bank to The Dalles. The left-hand road was the main route. It immediately crossed the Umatilla and continued westward over dry uplands to near the mouth of the Deschutes River, before descending to the Columbia and The Dalles. By 1852, most travelers followed this road.

Eight miles along this route over a very sandy road brought the emigrants to Butter Creek, also sometimes referred to as Alder Creek. Many camped here, as it was about twenty miles to the next available water at Well Spring. Today, most of the area between the Umatilla and Butter Creek is cultivated, and only short segments of the trail are still visible.

Emigrants regarded the road continuing from Butter Creek to Well Spring as good, but somewhat sandy.[11] It passed through low hills and broad valleys, described by John Kerns as "a dry prairie stretch of twenty miles."[12] Although much of this land now is privately owned, the last six miles of road to Well Spring and for several miles beyond crosses within the U.S. government's Boardman Bombing Range. Here the trail is quite visible, and in recent years has been marked by OCTA. It may be hiked with permission from the proper authorities.

Looking west along the Oregon Trail on the Boardman Bombing Range, some four miles east of Well Spring, Oregon. *W. W. Rau*

Unfortunately, after a long, dry day, Well Spring had little to offer weary travelers. John Spencer arriving on October 12 declared it "a horrible place—little water and much mud."[13] John Kerns had no better opinion of the spring on September 10: "think it is a pretty sick one myself, at least, we had to carry out about two wagon loads of mud before we could get water enough for cooking purposes."[14]

Besides the questionable quality of the spring, the campground usually was crowded, putting further strain on the limited water supply. Abigail Scott arriving at sundown on September 10 noted, "there were about thirty wagons here before us and the cattle had to be watered out of buckets; a slow process when so many were wanting water."[15]

Now late in the season, much-needed relief began arriving from the Willamette settlements. In 1852, travelers who had made quick time to Portland, Oregon City, and other communities brought news that many emigrants were yet on the trail and conditions were grim. The particularly large emigration of 1852 had resulted in a shortage of grazing for later travelers. Cattle were dying or weak and ill, causing many emigrants to abandon their wagons because they no longer had the livestock to pull them. Provisions were dangerously low and of poor quality, of course, and sickness prevailed. Even though they had met traders with supplies along the route, many emigrants could not afford the inflated prices.

While camped on the John Day River on September 9, Conyers predicted, "any of the emigrants will without doubt suffer for want of food if help does not reach them in time."[16]

The news alarmed the settlements, which organized efforts to assist the destitute travelers. The *Oregonian* and other newspapers publicized the need and encouraged contributions, resulting in gifts of supplies, particularly flour, and cash from businesses, churches, and individuals. Generous and compassionate John McLoughlin, the retired Chief Factor of the HBC's Fort Vancouver, donated a thousand pounds of flour.

Other kind-hearted individuals and commercial firms distributed supplies. A Columbia River steamboat company provided transport to the Cascades and The Dalles free of charge. From there, individuals hauled supplies by wagons as far as the Blue Mountains. Prominent among these caring individuals was the merchant Lot Whitcomb who, drawing upon his personal funds, proceeded as far as the Blue Mountains, bringing assistance and supplies to those desperately in need.[17]

According to Cecelia Adams, while camped at Well Spring on October 15, "here we met Lot Whitcomb direct from Oregon. . . . He had provisions but not to sell but gives to all he finds in want and are not able to buy."[18]

Family members and friends who had settled earlier in Oregon also rendered assistance to late travelers. Learning of the need, many loaded up wagons with produce and supplies and drove out to meet their friends and relatives.

On September 14, having just crossed the John Day River, the John Tucker Scott family was elated by the arrival of relatives with provisions. Abigail wrote,

> to our inexpressible joy, met Mr. Lawson Scott, a cousin of father's and our cousin Foster Johnson. . . . They were just from the Garden of the *World* and we were all much rejoiced to meet each other, in this wild and romantic spot our hearts were filled with gratitude to know that these estimable young men would leave their pleasant homes and undergo the toil and privations of this laborious and toilsome journey and for pure friendship without expectation of pecuniary fee or reward.[19]

Martha Read was among other 1852 travelers who expressed gratitude for the relief effort. Shortly after her arrival in the Willamette Valley, Martha wrote in a letter to Loinda Sheldon of Norwich, New York, "a great many would have suffer for want of provisions if the people of Oregon had not gone out with provisions to meet the emigrants. Those that were not able to buy, they gave it to them."[20]

From Well Spring, another day's drive of twelve miles over rolling terrain brought emigrants to Willow Creek. By September, the stream had stopped flowing, but sufficient water was found standing in pools. A trading post operated here in 1852, but the high prices prohibited purchases except for those with sufficient means or a dire need for supplies.

Arriving on September 12, John Kerns grumbled, "there is a trader station here to cheat the emigrants. He asked 50 cents per pound for flour but all he got off us will not make him very aristocratic."[21]

The road continued almost due west for about twenty-five miles through barren, rolling terrain to the John Day River. On October 19, Parthenia Blank described the country as "about as barren and desolate as any we have passed over."[22]

At Cedar Spring, five or six miles east of the John Day River, travelers had a choice of two routes. One continued westward along a ridge for about five miles and then descended to the river in another mile. The other road turned south for two miles to Rock Creek, and then westward along it for five miles to the John Day River. Having used the latter route on September 14, Abigail Scott described it as "through a deep rocky kanyon; we crossed the stream several times."[23] On the same day, John Kerns traveling on the other route, described it as "about due west, and . . . led us up and down several large hills. . . . we had to come down a very long, steep hill."[24]

Another trading post operated at the John Day River in 1852, but supplies were limited and, of course, prices high. John Spencer passed this way on October 18, recording, "flour 50 cents per pound." He added, "the Indians brought in some miserable meat. . . . It look like some meat made from some worn out brute left to die. They must have a dollar for a little bit of it. I bought none."[25]

The John Day crossing was variously reported from twenty yards wide and knee deep by Kerns on September 14, to seventy yards wide and two or three feet deep by McAllister on October 3.[26] After crossing the river, emigrants confronted a long, steep climb out of the valley. Many declared it the worst hill yet. After crossing the river on October 20, Parthenia Blank penned, "pass[ed] up a very rocky and sandy hill as bad as any we have had all things considered."[27]

The road divided at the top. To the left, a route led to the Cascades and over the range via the Barlow Road. The road to the right continued to the Columbia River and The Dalles. A need for supplies and rest prompted most of the later 1852 travelers to proceed to The Dalles, including the John Tucker Scott family, the Adams and Blank party, the John Spencer family, John McAllister, John Kerns and party, and the Boatman and Scott group. The Enoch Conyers train, meanwhile, chose to proceed directly toward the Barlow route over the Cascades past Mt. Hood.

From the John Day crossing, the right-hand road continued about twenty-five miles over rolling, grass-covered hills to the Columbia. Finally, grazing for cattle again was plentiful, as noted by John Spencer on October 18: "there is remarkably fine grass between John Day River and The Columbia."[28] John Tucker Scott, too, observed on September 15, "the grass is good over this part of our road."[29]

The route following down to and along the Columbia River wound through outcrops of Columbia River basalt. Today, the emigrant road is quite visible here in places, and a segment of the descent has been marked by the OCTA. Parthenia Blank observed on October 22, "had a very long but not steep hill to descend."[30] At the foot of the hill, they found another trading station selling flour, pork, sugar, and tobacco.

Three more miles along the Columbia brought travelers to near the mouth of the Deschutes River. Today, Oregon's Deschutes State Park is located here and, due to a hydroelectric dam, the Deschutes flows placidly at its mouth. In 1852, however, it cascaded over basalt into the Columbia River. Arriving on October 22, Parthenia Blank described the stream as "dashing down over rocks—as rapid as water can come on a plane inclined one foot in 20."[31] On September 20, Abigail Scott too noted, "this stream is about one hundred and fifty yards wide, and courses its rapid way through rocky Kanyons forming numerous cascades until it reaches the Columbia."[32]

The Deschutes crossing was formidable. Travelers chose either to ford at its mouth or ferry a short distance upstream in the vicinity of today's state park. Arriving here on October 6, McAllister described the Deschutes as,

> 130 yrds wide 10 to 12 feet deep at the ferry very rapid current large rocks on the bottom There is a ford below 1/4 or 1/2 mile at the mouth where water is divided by 2 Islands. some danger attends the crossage here having many large rocks and at the same time a very rapid current.[33]

John Kerns wrote on September 17, "ferried our wagons over Deschutes River, paying $2.50 and forded our stock."[34] Ferry fees must have varied from time to time, because Parthenia Blank reported on October 22:

> Here is a ferry of $2.00 for those who have money and a ford for those who have not. The latter is the most numerous class. . . . There are . . . 2 houses at the Deschutes River. and some tents belonging to the Walla Walla indians who do some ferrying and act as guides to those who ford[35]

According to Abigail Scott on September 16, Indians charged four dollars "to pilot the wagons across the river and also . . . take the females over in a canoe."[36]

After crossing the Deschutes, emigrants faced another steep ascent to the upland. Today, this route up the hill can easily be seen from the state park vicinity. Abigail Scott related, it was "a long, steep and rocky hill." From the top, she observed "the Columbia river adorned on each bank with lofty bluffs of basaltic rock."[37]

Five more miles over barren, irregular terrain brought the emigrants to Fifteenmile Creek, which they referred to variously as Raven, Olney, or Fivemile Creek. Here was the home of Nathan Olney and his wife Annette Hallicola, a member of the Wasco tribe.[38] Nathan was well known among the native people and conducted trade with them, as well as with emigrants. From Olney's place, it was only about six miles down to the Columbia and The Dalles. John McAllister, passing this way on October 7, described the road as,

> a little sidling after crossing strike a branch which follows up to a small spring then turn to the right wind gradually up a hollow to the top of bluff descend in a hollow pass a nice stream 10 or 12 feet wide [Fifteenmile Creek]. . . . You [then] follow down this creek on side of bluff nearly to where you descend to the Columbia River.[39]

At The Dalles, the Columbia River flowed rapidly through a narrow passageway with high, vertical basalt walls. Kerns arriving here on September 18, penned the following: "the whole Columbia river runs through a channel of some twenty or thirty yards in width for about one-fourth of a mile. . . . The banks are solid rock of the basaltic species."[40] John C. Fremont wrote that the passageway measured at the narrowest 58 yards and the walls averaged 25 feet in height above the water.[41]

Today, The Dalles Dam stands here and much of the original scene is inundated. A barren, rocky bench extends along the river's east side from The Dalles Dam Visitor's Center to several miles downstream. Here, emigrants parked their wagons and set up camp while waiting for passage down the river.

Alvah Davis arriving on October 5 saw "over 100 wagons with families and many left to be forwarded at this place." Twenty-seven-year-old Alvah Isaiah Davis, a single man, had left Lockport, Illinois, on April 17, 1852. Although he started out with a small party heading for California, somewhere along the way he changed his mind and joined an Oregon-bound train. Near the Malheur River, he became part of a party of fourteen that continued on with packs and three horses.[42]

Kerns described The Dalles community as consisting of "a store, the Government barracks [Camp Drum] and a Catholic mission, besides some few dwelling houses below the narrows."[43]

In 1852, transportation facilities for hauling wagons, livestock, and people downstream were limited, particularly during the peak time of the emigrants' arrival. Therefore, travelers often laid over for a few days at The Dalles, providing much needed rest and recuperation for the many suffering from fatigue and illness—particularly those severely sick enough to be lingering near death.

The Boatman party was typical in this regard, as is evident in Willis Boatman's poignant and gripping description of the latter part of the journey from the Blue Mountains to The Dalles.

> We were getting pretty near the Blue Mountains, where one of Mr. Scott's men who had been complaining for some time of the scurvy, got so bad that he had to be hauled. About this time Mrs. Boatman commenced to get ill with the scurvy. We expected at this time to cross the Cascade Mountains with our teams. We concluded to go by The Dalles and get some more provisions as we had not enough to last us into the settlement on the west of the Cascade mountains. On arrival at The Dalles the last of September, Mr Scott's man was so low that we could not move him. So we lay there about two weeks waiting for him to get better or die. Finally he died and we buried him at The Dalles. Before he died my brother was taken down with the Mountain or nervous fever. Mrs Boatman was still sick with the scurvy and I was taken with a kind of flux there. Not one of us was able to help the other. My wife lay for three days with a broken tooth in her mouth and could not open her mouth wide enough to get it out,—her mouth was so sore and swollen from the effects of the scurvy. At last I got so bad that I did not expect to ever recover. I called my wife to the bed and told her that I never expected to be up again and that I wanted her and John, if they lived, to sell the wagon and remaining team and try to get back to the States to her people. We all lingered along for a few days and my wife commenced to get a little better. My brother still got worse and before we got able to travel it had commenced clouding up and the old settlers at The Dalles told us that it was not safe to start across the mountains as it was then snowing there and we would likely be snowed under. There were several parties there in the same fix that we were in and so we began to look around to see if we could find any conveyance by

water. Finally we found a man who had a small boat (old bateau), so
we hired him to take us down to the cascade falls on the Columbia
river, and we got all our stuff aboard.[44]

Notes

1. John McAllister, "The Diary of Rev. John McAllister," in *Transactions of the Fiftieth Annual Reunion of the Oregon Pioneer Association* (Portland, Oregon, 1922), 502; see additional information under note 2 in chapter four.
2. John T. Kerns, "Journal of Crossing the Plains to Oregon in 1852," in *Transactions of the Forty-second Annual Reunion of the Oregon Pioneer Association* (Portland, Oregon, 1913), 183.
3. William N. Byers, "The Odyssey of William N. Byers," edited by Merrill J. Mattes, in *Overland Journal,* vol. 2, no. 1 (1983), 19–20; published by the Oregon-California Trails Association, Independence, Missouri.
4. Kerns, 183.
5. Enoch W. Conyers, "Diary of E.W. Conyers, a Pioneer of 1852," in *Transactions of the Thirty-third Annual Reunion of the Oregon Pioneer Association* (Portland, Oregon, 1905), 496.
6. Kerns, 183.
7. Origen Thomson, *Crossing the Plains* (Fairfield, Washington: Ye Galleon Press, 1983), 66.
8. McAllister, 503.
9. John Spencer, "Daily Journal Kept by John Spencer, 1852 from Wellsville, Ohio to Portland, Oregon," typescript manuscript, Oregon Historical Society, Portland, Oregon, 31–32.
10. Aubrey L. Haines, *Historic Sites along the Oregon Trail,* third edition (St. Louis, Missouri: Patrice Press, 1987), 368; Diane Berry, "The Umatilla Agency, 1851–55," in *Pioneer Trails,* vol. 12, no. 4 (1988), 1–3; published by the Umatilla County Historical Society, Pendleton, Oregon.
11. Conyers, 497.
12. Kerns, 184.
13. Spencer, 24.
14. Kerns, 184.
15. Abigail Jane Scott [Duniway], "Journal of a Trip to Oregon," in *Covered Wagon Women: Diaries and Letters from the Western Trails*, 1852, vol. 5, edited and compiled by Kenneth L. Holmes and David C. Duniway (Glendale, California: Arthur H. Clark, 1986), 126.
16. Conyers, 498.
17. John D. Unruh Jr., *The Plains Across: The Overland Emigrants and the Trans-Mississippi West, 1840–60,* paperback edition (Urbana, Chicago, and London: University of Illinois Press, 1982), 307–8; Leslie M. Scott, *History of the Oregon Country by Harvey W. Scott,* compiler's appendix 3 (Cambridge: Riverside Press), 226–28.
18. Adams, 306.
19. Abigail Scott, 127.
20. Martha S. Read, "A History of Our Journey," in *Covered Wagon Women: Diaries and Letters from the Western Trails*, 1852, vol. 5, edited and compiled by Kenneth L. Holmes and David C. Duniway (Glendale, California: Arthur H. Clark, 1986), 248.
21. Kerns, 185.

22. Adams, 308.
23. Abigail Scott, 127.
24. Kerns, 185.
25. Spencer, 25–26.
26. Kerns, 185; McAllister, 504.
27. Adams, 308.
28. Spencer, 26.
29. John Tucker Scott, "Journal of a Trip to Oregon," in *Covered Wagon Women: Diaries and Letters from the Western Trails*, 1852, vol. 5, edited and compiled by Kenneth L. Holmes and David C. Duniway (Glendale, California: Arthur H. Clark, 1986), 128.
30. Adams, 308.
31. Ibid., 309.
32. Abigail Scott, 129.
33. McAllister, 505.
34. Kerns, 180.
35. Adams, 309.
36. Abigail Scott, 129.
37. Ibid.
38. Adams, 309; Haines, 386–87.
39. McAllister, 505.
40. Kerns, 187.
41. Haines, 383.
42. Alvah Isaiah Davis, "Diary of Mr. Davis, 1852," in *Transactions of the Thirty-seventh Annual Reunion of the Oregon Pioneer Association* (Portland, Oregon, 1909), 355, 365, 378–79.
43. Kerns, 187; Haines, 384.
44. Willis Boatman, "Story of My Life," hand-written manuscript in possession of the writer (family document no. 2). A version is printed in *Told by the Pioneers,* vol. 1 (U.S. Public Works Administration, Washington Pioneer Project, 1937), 184–90.

C.E. Watkins photograph of the Bradford store, community, and tramway at the Upper Cascades of the Columbia in 1867. In the autumn of 1852, Willis buried his brother in a graveyard situated in the woods at right. Lumber for the coffin was obtained from the sawmill at lower right. Fort Lugenbeel, standing on the bluff, was built during the Yakama War of the late 1850s. *Oregon Historical Society, OrHi 21111*

Chapter Thirteen

Final Effort

[W]hen I got down to the Cascades, there I found the folks camped. My brother was not expected to live. I went to him and found him in a dying condition.
—Willis Boatman

WHEN LEAVING THE DALLES and continuing downstream for about fifty miles, emigrants next ventured through the Columbia River Gorge, one of the most scenic and geologically fascinating sections of the entire Oregon Trail. Geologist John E. Allen appropriately refers to it as "The Magnificent Gateway."[1] For thousands of years, the gorge had served Native Americans as a passageway through the Cascade Range, linking the trade routes of the coastal and interior tribes. The Lewis and Clark Expedition, the first Americans to venture overland to the Northwest Coast, passed through here in 1805–6, and soon were followed by American and Canadian fur traders after 1811, and by thousands of American emigrants beginning in the 1840s. Today, this passageway is an important commercial water route and also is traversed by two major railways and several highways.

This gap through the formidable Cascade Range is the result of a series of amazing and dynamic geological processes. Beginning around 17 million years ago and continuing for about 7 million years, lava flows of the Columbia River Basalt Group poured westward to the sea through the broad, ancestral Columbia River Valley. This was long before the Cascade Range was uplifted to its present height. Flows spread as far south as today's Salem, Oregon, along the coast to Newport, and north as far as Grays Harbor. Most of these basalt layers are part of the same ones that the emigrants first encountered in the Grande Ronde. Over time, the flows repeatedly displaced the river north and west around their edge.[2]

Beginning 10 million years ago, the future Cascade Range began to arch upward. During this period, the Columbia River shifted its course gradually northwest, finally coming to rest near its present location about 5 million years ago. As the Cascade Range rose, the river continually cut deeper and deeper into the basalt, forming a deep V-shaped canyon.[3]

The river, which drains more than a quarter million square miles of the Northwest, soon was affected by yet another series of spectacular geologic events, this time during the Ice Age. In the past 2 million years, vast continental ice sheets advancing from Canada have entered the northern United States and retreated four times. Worldwide, so much water was tied up in the earth's mantle of glaciers that sea level at times dropped 300 feet lower than today. Thus, streams leading to the sea, including the Columbia, cut their channels ever deeper.[4]

Advancing and retreating glaciers have removed much of the proof for events occurring in the first part of the Ice Age. However, for the late Pleistocene between 15,000 and 12,800 years ago, the evidence is apparent that at least forty cataclysmic floods poured across eastern Washington and through the Columbia River Gorge to the sea.[5] The root cause of these floods was a tongue of the Continental Ice Sheet that repeatedly blocked a major Columbia tributary, the Clark Fork River, near today's Idaho-Montana border. Repeatedly, this advance formed an ice dam 2,500 feet high and impounded water in vast Lake Missoula, which over time could accumulate as much as 500 cubic miles of water.

Many experts suspect that when the lake water became deep enough, the ice dam actually began to float, causing sudden and massive failure. A huge surge of water and ice swept southwest over the Columbia Plateau at thirty to fifty miles per hour, bringing with it great amounts of rock and sediments, and stripping bare the thick, wind-deposited loess soils in its path. Today, these broad scoured-out areas are the scablands of eastern Washington.[6]

The Columbia River provided the outlet to the sea for the incredible oft-repeated floods. The Columbia Gorge's present appearance is largely the result of the impact of these massive volumes of water, silt, mud, sand, rocks, and boulder-studded icebergs pouring through the passageway. Sometimes, the floods backed into the Willamette Valley, redepositing much of the rich silt and sand that had been removed from east of the Cascades.

Melting masses of ice and rock also left scattered boulders throughout the valley.[7] Interestingly, the fertile Willamette soils that the emigrants came to claim and cultivate were transported from eastern Washington just 13,000 or 15,000 years before.

Between 500 and 700 years ago, a great landslide forming the Cascade Rapids was the final key geologic event shaping the Columbia River Gorge. Millions of tons of rock and soil, and carrying an entire forest with it, slid southward off 3,400-foot, basalt-capped Table Mountain and dammed the Columbia.[8] Today, a yet apparent, large, nearly vertical scarp on the mountain's south side, together with a broad swath of hummocky topography below, leaves little doubt as to what took place here. Eventually, the Columbia cut a boulder-strewn channel across the top of the slide, some one and a half miles south of the river's original channel.[9]

Since the Cascade Rapids were unnavigable, early travelers had to portage, mainly along a four-mile route on the north side. Furthermore, the debris-clogged rapids yet impounded the river nearly to The Dalles. As the emigrants soon discovered, this was a body of water with virtually no current. Curiously, the original flooding had inundated low-lying forests along the river and the tree stumps still were visible in the water centuries later. Captain Meriwether Lewis noted in his journal on April 14, 1806, "we find the trunks of many large pine trees s[t]anding erect as they grew at present [standing in] 30 feet [of] water."[10]

Today the Cascade Rapids, as well as the drowned forests, are deeply submerged beneath the reservoir behind Bonneville Dam.

For the voyage from The Dalles to the Upper Cascades, a distance of about forty miles, emigrants boarded almost anything that would float. Many, like the Akins, built rafts.[11] The Adam-Blank party employed "an open kiel [keel] boat rowed by three men."[12] Alvah Davis hired an Indian with a canoe, and John Spencer engaged a person to take his family and equipment by flatboat to the Upper Cascades, while he drove the cattle downstream on the pack trail.[13] Other types of craft, such as the "old bateau" as mentioned by Willis Boatman, also were employed.

It would seem that river travel should have been reasonably easy compared to the trials of the road. Nevertheless, emigrants did encounter difficulties, with a major problem being the wind. In the Columbia River Gorge, the frequent, strong upstream breezes created problems for the hand- or sail-powered craft used by the emigrants. In addition to adverse winds, the river virtually was a lake down to the Cascade Rapids. Essentially, no natural current assisted in moving vessels downstream.

These difficulties appear frequently in the emigrants' accounts, and Willis's story exemplifies the problems.

I hired a man to help drive my cattle down the river by the trail. Myself and wife and brother got aboard the boat, then everything being ready, we pushed out from the shore and started down the river. But had only gotten a few miles til the wind commenced to blow a perfect gale and blew us up against a rocky bluff where the rocks were probably thirty or forty feet high and almost perpendicular. Fortunately we all had our tent poles on board, so the men all gathered a pole apiece and stood on the edge of the boat next to the rocks, the women all getting on the opposite side to trim the craft so that when she came up to the rocks we were all ready with our pole to keep her from hitting the rocks. We had to stand there about four hours and hold her off those rocks before the wind lulled enough so that we could drop down to a place where we could land and get ashore. We finally landed and lay there the rest of that day and night. About ten o'clock the next day it calmed down and we again loaded up and started out.

That evening we pass the boys with the cattle. They called aboard and told me that my man had left and that I would have to come and tend to my cattle myself or they would have to leave them. That was bad news for me, for I was so weak I could hardly walk. So I went ashore and started on with the cattle getting along better than I expected. We drove on down to where we had to ferry our cattle across the Columbia river, about five miles above the Cascade falls.

The boat landed about one hundred yards from the bank of the river and we had to drive our cattle over a rocky flat. Some of the rocks two feet high in the trail we had to drive over, and water some times was two feet deep. I mention this to show the disposition that some acquire in crossing the plains.

When I got to the ferry there was one man ahead of me, but his cattle had got away and when the boat came I drove my cattle thru this narrow and rugged trail which was hard work to do. Before I got my cattle aboard this man came and demanded his turn and wanted me to drive my cattle out so he could get in with his. I told him that it would be almost impossible for me to get my cattle back. He swore that he would thrash h— out of me if I didn't drive them out and let him in. I was sitting on a big rock when he was talking, hardly able to stand. I raised up and told him to get at it as soon as he felt like it;

that I would not try to get them back nor he would not either. I finally told him that if he could get his around mine he could do so. He did this. I got across and when I got down to the cascades, there I found the folks camped.[14]

The Adams-Blank party in their "kiel" boat was fortunate, as Parthenia Blank indicated on October 24: "had a very favorable run for the weather was calm." Although frequently in hard rain, they managed to get within six miles of the Cascades on the first day. The following day, they reached the rapids, which Parthenia described as, "consisting of an emmense pile of loose rock across the stream over which water runs with great rapidity for 6 miles."[15]

The Akins on their raft were not as lucky. They had started on October 12, but for three days battled upstream winds. Having floated just seventeen miles, all of the party except two men left the raft and employed an Indian with a canoe to take them to the Cascades, arriving about 2:00 P.M. on October 15.[16]

The downstream trail was used primarily for moving livestock to the Cascade Rapids. It was a difficult route demanding nearly all the strength and stamina that the tired emigrants could muster. Along much of the way, mountains extended to the water's edge, rarely allowing passage at bank level. It was necessary to constantly ascend and descend steep ridges, side canyons, and tributary streams. The coming of the rainy season by September added to the misery. This, along with the wind and the mud generated by thousands of cattle hooves, generally made travel unpleasant.

The pack trail's first part to Hood River, then called Dog River, went almost entirely up and down rugged ridges. On reaching "Dog River" on October 12, John McAllister said the cattle trail, in addition to ascending and descending several mountains, had a surface of "loose gravel which slips under foot making it almost unsurmountable for weak stock." The following day in a vicinity McAllister referred to as the "Upper Ferry," he recorded, "here the mountains joins the river & is most awful place I suppose that ever stock were driven over the surface being huge rocks which lays loose & mavible [movable]. . . . many cattle and horses killed here."[17] The "Upper Ferry" probably was located near today's Wyeth, Oregon, some seven or eight miles upstream from the Cascades.

John Spencer reaching this ferry on October 31, also referred to the "unmercifully bad road." Although losing no cattle, he "saw numbers which had tumbled over and perrished. . . . It was a horrible place." In addition to the bad road, "the rain increased so as to pour down." That evening after finding a tolerable place to camp, Spencer's party was "wet to the skin and cold we hunted up stuff for fire got supper laid down tired limbs and weary frame in wet clothes, and wraped ourselves in wet covering."[18]

The "Lower Ferry," according to McAllister who crossed there on October 15, was "4 miles by land through the timber and about 2 1/2 miles by water" from the Cascades.[19] This ferry operated just upstream from present-day Stevenson, Washington.

For the river travelers, even though winds frequently hampered their craft's progress, the trip usually was quicker than taking the pack trail. Families often waited at the Cascades a few days for men to bring the livestock along the trail. By late fall, camping in the open usually was miserable. The cold, rain, and mud, compounded by prevailing illness and exhaustion and the inadequate means to care for the sick, caused much suffering. John Spencer, arriving at the Cascades with his cattle on the evening of November 5, wrote the following gloomy report.

> All stuff . . . had been lying *in* the wet . . . for near two weeks. . . . all was wet in the tent. . . . All were sick. I was fatigued almost to death. . . . Wet clothes, *wet beds,* rain, mud, cold, bad wood, and poor fire, with little to eat, and to crowded all sick myself and family, all work hard up on me.[20]

Because Willis says he crossed the river about five miles above the Cascades, and John McAllister states that the "Lower Ferry" was about four miles upstream from the rapids, it is likely that Willis took this ferry. Upon arriving at the Cascades, Willis learned that his brother's condition had worsened. After loading the cattle aboard the ferry,

> I got across and when I got down to the cascades, there I found the folks camped. My brother was not expected to live. I went to him and found him in a dying condition. He lived until next morning when about two a. m. on the sixteenth day of October he died. This was another hard duty to perform but we had to make the best of it. So Mr Scott and myself went down to an old mill and got some lumber and made a box. We buried him at the grave yard at the Cascade Falls on the Columbia.[21]

In later years, Willis recalled,

> digging that grave and laying him away so near the end of the long trail, pretty nearly took all the strength we had. But we couldn't give

up. It was strange how lonely we were, never out of sight of hundreds of other emigrant wagons all the way across, and yet we ourselves, just absolutely alone in our two wagons, and now, my wife and I had no one but each other.[22]

The graveyard where Willis buried his brother is located on a wooded knoll overlooking the Columbia. The trace of the old wagon trail that led up the ravine from the head of the rapids lies just below this site.[23]

By 1852, a small community had developed here on the Columbia's north bank, a mile or so west of present-day Stevenson, Washington. It primarily served the needs of travelers and commerce at the upper end of the Cascades. At this point, all travel continued by portage for four miles around the rapids, either on a recently constructed tramway or, more commonly in 1852, by wagon road.

Origen Thomson described the community as consisting "of three houses, in which are two stores and one dwelling; one of the houses is two stories high—in the upper story is a boarding house, and below a store."[24]

The brothers Daniel and Putman Bradford owned the general store,[25] and operated the sawmill where Willis obtained lumber for his brother's coffin. The mill stood a short distance down the wagon road from the graveyard.[26]

Loading their wagons, the Boatmans and Scotts traveled about "six" miles on the trail around the Cascades to a "steamboat landing at the lower end of the falls." On September 22, Origen Thomson declared this "a very bad road; hilly, rocky and stumpy—In fact the worst I have met with." Along the way, "we passed a pile of human bones. . . . scattered all around—skulls, backbones, thigh-bones and pelvis in high profusion." He believed these were the remains of Indians who had died in "the contagious fever of 1839."[27]

The Adams-Blank party, arriving in the Cascades rain on October 25, made use of the recently constructed tramway. Their belongings were conveyed on it while they walked to the lower Cascades. Parthenia described the tramway.

> a railroad 3 miles long made of scantling [timber frame] and plank without iron. On this runs a small car propelled by a mule attached to by a long rope for an engine and a pair of thrills [shafts on each side of the mule] between which the engineer stations himself and walks and guides the car. on this the charge is 75 cts. per cwt. but takes no passengers. At the end of the railroad the goods have to be let down

perpendicularly some 150 feet [others estimated 50 feet] to the river from whence they are taken on a boat to the steam boat landing about 3 miles more.[28]

They completed the remaining sixty-five miles to Portland in relative comfort aboard the steamer *Multnomah*.[29] John Spencer and family likewise made use of the tramway and completed their journey by steamer.

When the Boatmans reached the steamboat landing by way of the trail, probably on October 16 or 17, they understandably were in poor spirits, and nearly out of food. Willis recalled:

> Our supplies were about gone . . . and our appetites were not good after the fever. It was hard to eat the little stale and mouldy food we had left. We were in this plight, hardly able to move, wondering what to do, how best to get down the Columbia to Portland, when a kind-hearted settler, a James Stevens, came up to meet the train with a whole scow load of fresh vegetables. I arranged with him, after the treasures he had brought us was divided up among us all, to take my wife and household goods back with him.[30]
>
> We again unloaded our stuff, took our wagons apart, loaded them on the boat and started again by water to Portland. I with some others started on the trail with the remains of our teams.[31]

Thus, Mary Ann proceeded by water down the Columbia to the Willamette's mouth and then upstream eight or ten miles to the thriving frontier community of Portland. Meanwhile, Willis drove the livestock along the Columbia's north bank, following a course similar to today's State Route 14. He soon passed directly by massive Beacon Rock. On October 21, John McAllister described the landmark as "about 1000 ft nearly all the way perpendicular is probably ½ mile in circumference has timber growing on top."[32]

From Beacon Rock, the trail ascended and descended in mountainous terrain until the valley finally widened just a few miles east of today's Washougal. McAllister noted that a ferry crossed the Columbia here at the "mouth of the Sandy River on the other side of here." He further reported, the "ferry of the Columbia . . . is just above [an] Island."[33]

Willis apparently crossed the cattle here. Although the course of the pack route from here is not fully known, it led overland from the mouth of Oregon's Sandy River west to Portland, a distance of at least thirteen miles.

The scow hauling Mary Ann and their possessions landed on the east side of the Willamette, presently East Portland, on October 22, 1852. Willis recalled:

> I'll never forget the sorry picture my young wife made sitting on the banks of the river, keeping guard over her pitiful household goods crying, when I drove up.[34]

After camping on the riverbank that night, Willis went into Portland the next day to find a house.

> I looked all over the place (and by the way, that did not take long for there were not more than twenty houses in the place), but I could find nothing but an old shed which had an old dirt fireplace in it and one side out to the commons. I secured it and moved over that night. We carried what little stuff we had on our backs, made our beds down on the dirt floor without sweeping. This was the first roof that we had been under for seven long months.[35]

During the previous long months, Willis and Mary Ann had focused on surviving the seemingly never-ending journey. Now, with the journey completed, they realized their struggle was far from over. Willis's summary of their thoughts and emotions that night likely exemplifies those of many others reaching the end of The Oregon Trail.

> I presume you think we had a good night's sleep, but far from it! We got to our journeys end but we then just begin to realize our situation. Here we were three thousand miles from our homes and relatives, without money and without home, among strangers and in a strange land. So you may imagine that there was not much sleep that night. There were more tears shed than sleeping done that night.[36]

Notes

1. John E. Allen, *The Magnificent Gateway: A Layman's Guide to the Geology of the Columbia River Gorge* (Forest Grove, Oregon: Timber Press, 1979).
2. Ibid., 18, 36, 47.
3. Ibid., 41.
4. John E. Allen, Marjorie Burns, and Sam C. Sargent, *Cataclysms on the Columbia: A Layman's Guide to the Features Produced by the Catastrophic Bretz Floods in the Pacific Northwest* (Portland, Oregon: Timber Press, 1986), 79, 177.
5. Ibid., 103–4.
6. Ibid.
7. Ibid., 104

8. Rebecca T. Smith, "The Geology of the Columbia River Gorge," in *Overland Journal,* vol. 10, no. 1 (1992), 9; published by the Oregon-California Trails Association, Independence, Missouri.

9. Ibid., 10.

10. Meriwether Lewis, *Original Journals of the Lewis and Clark Expedition, 1804–1806,* vol. 4, edited by Reuben Gold Thwaites (New York: Antiquarian Press, 1959), 279.

11. James Akin Jr., *The Oregon Trail Diary of James Akin Jr. in 1852: The Unabridged Diary with Introduction and Contemporary Comments by Bert Webber* (Medford, Oregon: Webb Research Group, Pacific Northwest Books, 1989), 55.

12. Cecelia Adams, "Twin Sisters on the Oregon Trail: Cecelia Adams and Parthenia Blank," in *Covered Wagon Women: Diaries and Letters from the Western Trails,* 1852, vol. 5, edited and compiled by Kenneth L. Holmes and David C. Duniway (Glendale, California: Arthur H. Clark, 1986), 310.

13. Alvah Isaiah Davis, "Diary of Mr. Davis, 1852," in *Transactions of the Thirty-seventh Annual Reunion of the Oregon Pioneer Association* (Portland, Oregon, 1909), 379; John Spencer, "Daily Journal Kept by John Spencer, 1852 from Wellsville, Ohio to Portland, Oregon," typescript manuscript, Oregon Historical Society, Portland, Oregon, 27.

14. Willis Boatman, "Story of My Life," hand-written manuscript in possession of the writer (family document no. 2). A version is printed in *Told by the Pioneers,* vol. 1, U.S. Public Works Administration, Washington Pioneer Project, 1937, 184–90.

15. Adams, 310.

16. Akin, 56.

17. John McAllister, "The Diary of Rev. John McAllister," in *Transactions of the Fiftieth Annual Reunion of the Oregon Pioneer Association* (Portland, Oregon, 1922), 502; see additional information under note 2 in chapter four.

18. Spencer, 27.

19. McAllister, 507.

20. Spencer, 29.

21. Boatman.

22. Mabel Cleland, "On the Pioneer Tacoma Trail," *Tacoma News Tribune* (Tacoma, Washington), June 23, 1922.

23. Clifford Crawford, personal communication, 1989. The author had the opportunity to spend a day in the area with Clifford Crawford, a historian for the Skamania County Historical Society in Stevenson, Washington. We visited the graveyard and found it totally overgrown with brush and timber. According to Crawford, until a few years before two graves still remained intact; however, by the time of my visit, there was very little left to identify these burials.

24. Origen Thomson, *Crossing the Plains* (Fairfield, Washington: Ye Galleon Press, 1983), 72.

25. Crawford.

26. Ibid.

27. Thomson, 72.

28. Adams, 311.

29. The 108-foot side-wheeler *Multnomah* was capable of a speed of fourteen miles per hour and served on the Columbia between the Cascades, Fort Vancouver, and Portland from the early 1850s to 1864. G. Thomas Edwards, "The Oregon Trail in the Columbia Gorge, 1843–1855: The Final Ordeal," in *Oregon Historical Quarterly*, vol. 97, no. 2 (1996), 170.

30. Cleland.

31. Boatman.
32. McAllister, 507.
33. Ibid.
34. Cleland.
35. Boatman.
36. Ibid.

View of Front and Stark streets in the thriving community of Portland, Oregon Territory, in 1852. The mast of the brig *Henry* is visible in the background; the vessel was docked on the nearby Willamette River. Portland was the goal for the Boatmans and other exhausted emigrants coming down the Columbia River from The Dalles. *Oregon Historical Society, OrHi 13137*

Chapter Fourteen

Pioneering

When I concluded to take a trip to Puget Sound, I told J.M. Hawk, a friend that I had traveled with on the plains. . . . He then proposed going with me.
—Willis Boatman

ALTHOUGH THE BOATMANS were in Oregon, many more miles had to be traveled before they were settled in this new land. They managed through the severe winter of 1852–53 in the little, dirt-floored shack in Portland. Willis relates some of their experiences.[1]

I drove my cattle down on the Columbia bottom with five oxen and one cow. Our finances were getting very low and my wife was still sick. I was not able to do anything yet and everything to buy at exorbitant prices and a hard matter to get at any price. We had to pay as high as eight dollars per bushel for potatoes with the eyes taken out to be used for seed next year, and twenty dollars per hundred for graham flour, and everything else in proportion. I was still gaining strength but not able to do a day's work, and finally I got a job cutting a few cords of wood at six bits a cord. About the time I got that done I was taken down with the chills and fever. I shook for about six weeks which reduced me so that I was not able to do anything for some time. During that time my wife was taken sick. We had to call in a doctor and there was a doctor bill of fifteen dollars to pay. Finally she was able to get up and do her work [and] the chills began to leave me and I was getting a little stouter.

In December it commenced snowing and it continued to fall till it was about two feet deep. It covered up all the grass where my cattle were, so deep that they were about to starve to death. I went to a rancher who had plenty of hay and wanted to buy some. He would not sell a pound. I then wanted him to feed them. He said "no" but

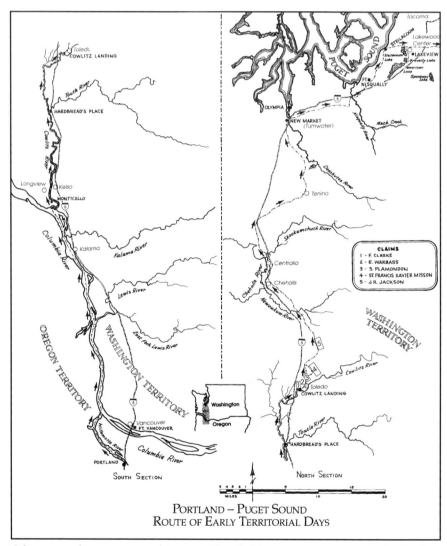

PORTLAND – PUGET SOUND
ROUTE OF EARLY TERRITORIAL DAYS

Other scattered contemporary claims, not identified here, also were located in the Cowlitz-Columbia corridor, the Centralia-Chehalis area, and at other locations in the southern Puget Sound lowland.

that he would buy them and would give me fifty dollars per yoke for them and forty dollars for the cow. I looked around and could not find a pound of hay for love nor money, so I sold them. The next spring those same cattle were sold - one yoke for three hundred dollars and the other for two hundred and fifty dollars per yoke and brought over to Puget Sound.[2]

On December 31, 1852, Mary Ann gave birth to their first child. The pregnancy that she never mentioned undoubtedly was the cause of much of her illness, at least during the first part of the journey. They now were the proud parents of a healthy baby boy, George Washington Boatman.

By February 1853, Willis regained much of his strength and began giving thought to where his family might make a home. Although their original plan was to settle in the Willamette Valley, they became discouraged because much of the valley already had been claimed. About this time, Willis heard that work was available in timber camps on Puget Sound. He decided to go north in search of employment.

At the time, settlers north of the Columbia River were becoming increasingly determined that a separate territory should be created in their region. Since roads and waterways were virtually undeveloped there, undue hardships were placed on those attending the territorial legislature or doing business south of the river. Furthermore, being remote from the social and economic centers along the Willamette, northern settlers felt they were not given due consideration in political matters while business development was hampered by an unsupportive territorial government.

After two conventions considering separation from Oregon Territory—one held in August 1851 at Cowlitz Landing and another in October 1852 at Monticello near today's Longview—forty-four delegates signed a document urging a territorial division. Petitions were sent to the Oregon territorial legislature and the U.S. Congress. On March 2, 1853, the U.S. Senate passed a bill designating the separation, and a few days later President Millard Fillmore signed the act into law, forming Washington Territory.

By this time, many Oregon Trail emigrants arriving from the east were aware of the largely unclaimed country north of the Columbia and considered it as a place to settle. A few Americans had trickled northward earlier, but not until the 1850s did a growing number give serious attention to making it their home.

Until the late 1840s, the Hudson's Bay Company had conducted a thriving trade with the Indians in this region and had developed a colonial plantation system, the Puget's Sound Agricultural Company, near present-day Toledo on the Cowlitz River, at Fort Nisqually on southern Puget Sound, and in the San Juan Islands. Furthermore, HBC employees had taken up claims along the Cowlitz corridor between the Columbia River and Puget Sound. It was into this frontier country that Willis was about to venture.

When I concluded to take a trip to Puget Sound, I told J.M. Hawk, a friend that I had traveled with on the plains, what I had decided to do. He then proposed going with me. [John M. Hawk settled in the Olympia, Washington area on what is known today as Hawk's Prairie.] We bought some lumber and built a skiff in which to travel by water as far as we could. The rest of the way we planned to travel on foot. Hopefully we would have our boat for the return trip. When the boat was completed and we were ready to go, two other fellows wanted to go. We charged them ten dollars apiece to take them as far as we could up the Cowlitz River.

On the morning of the fifteenth of February [1853] we set sail for the Sound. We went down the Willamette [and Columbia] to the mouth of the Cowlitz River and went up that river about six miles, until the current got so strong that we had to leave our boat. From there we took a trail on foot. It was a hard and rough trail and in places the snow was two and a half feet deep.

The route to Puget Sound was not an easy one. Long used by Indians, it proceeded by water up the Cowlitz River almost to present-day Toledo, Washington. The route then continued overland through today's Chehalis, Centralia, and Tenino localities, and on to Puget Sound. For years, Hudson's Bay traders had utilized this corridor between Fort Vancouver and Fort Nisqually on Puget Sound.

The earliest American settlers further developed the route. In 1845, the Michael T. Simmons party cut the first crude wagon road from Cowlitz Landing to southernmost Puget Sound. Here, they established the first American community on the Sound, known then as New Market and today as Tumwater. Others, such as John R. Jackson in 1844, settled in the eligible prairies and timber groves along the way. Jackson's cabin yet stands today a few miles north of Toledo. It is a Washington State Parks Historical Site and is listed on the National Register of Historic Places. Judge Jackson's hospitality made it a favorite stopover place. By 1853, the influx north-ward over this route was noticeably increasing.

> We carried nothing with us except our small packs in our blankets.
> Every man carried his own blankets because lodges were scarce and
> costly. Of course we could stop at almost any settler's place along the
> way, but if we did we rolled up in our blankets and slept on the floor.
> For supper we had salmon and hard-bread, and for breakfast hard-
> bread and salmon! The cost was about a dollar or a dollar and a
> quarter a meal.
>
> Finally we reached a place called Clark's Landing. [Here] . . .
> there was an old fellow who made a business of taking in strangers.
> He and his son had taken an old deserted farm house and made it
> into a sort of inn. He literally fed his guests nothing but hard-bread,
> and so they dubbed him "Old Hard-bread." I thought the name
> very appropriate.

Old Hardbread's place was located at the junction of the Cowlitz and Toutle rivers. Ezra Meeker identified the man as "Gardner, the old wid-ower that kept Bachelor's hall at the mouth of the Toutle River."[3]

> We partook of his hospitality and enjoyed it very much. We were
> tired and hungry. So we spread our blankets and were fast asleep. . . .
> The next day we got to the old Cowlitz Landing.

Cowlitz Landing was situated about 1¼ miles downstream from Toledo. By 1853, it was a thriving community at the junction of Cowlitz navigation and the northern road. The community had developed mainly through the efforts of E.D. Warbass and Fred A. Clarke, who had adjoin-ing donation land claims in the locality. Originally, Cowlitz Landing was developed on Clarke's land and consisted of a blockhouse, general store, and the Clarke hotel, where the 1851 convention calling for a territorial separation was held. A few homes and farms grouped around the commer-cial center.

Warbass also established an inn (the Cowlitz Hotel), a saw and grist mill, and a store at adjacent Warbassport. In a few years, however, the two places were considered one, with the name Cowlitz Landing prevailing. Today no vestige of the town remains. Over the years, the Cowlitz River has repeatedly changed its course eroding away the site.

> It took us over a week to walk to Olympia. We walked two or three
> miles through deep mud in a swamp opposite where Chehalis is
> now. There was a sawmill at Tumwater [New Market], and Olympia

had a few houses, really just cabins, but a real boarding house with plenty of good food.

We only stopped over night in Olympia. In the morning we met three other fellows who wanted to go to Steilacoom, so the five of us hired a boat, sort of a yawl, to take us as far as Fort Nisqually. From there we walked the eight or nine miles to Steilacoom. Here we began looking for work and soon met Lafayette Balch who informed us that he needed some men to go across to Henderson's Bay to work in a timber camp. We made arrangements to go to work the next day at seventy five dollars per month and board.

Steilacoom was founded by Captain Lafayette Balch in 1851. He had brought two ships loaded with merchandise to Puget Sound and established his town some ten miles north of Olympia. By donating money for civic needs, such as establishing a Masonic lodge, courthouse, school, and the first American church in the southern Puget Sound area, he encouraged pioneers to settle nearby. Balch died suddenly in San Francisco on November 25, 1862, ending his twelve-year enterprising career in the Pacific Northwest.

Steilacoom during the early years had high hopes of being a hub of the Puget Sound country, and by 1855 it was a thriving community. However, Seattle and Tacoma eventually overshadowed the small port city. Today, Steilacoom remains a quaint community, whose residents take great pride in the town's pioneer heritage.

I had been there a month when I was told they needed a woman cook, and if I would bring my wife over, they would pay her fifty dollars a month to cook for the camp. So, I went back.

When Willis arrived in Portland and told Mary Ann about the job offer, she reportedly replied,

Yes I'll cook. I'll work at anything that will earn money enough to take us home, away from this awful lonely country!

Willis continues:

Henry Winsor . . . had a large bateau that he ran from Portland to the Cowlitz Landing. So, I shipped my wagon on a sailing vessel from Portland to Steilacoom and took passage with captain Winsor for Cowlitz Landing.

Henry Winsor also crossed the plains in 1852, but with a horse team. By spring 1853, he started a canoe and bateau transport business on the

Columbia and Cowlitz rivers. The next year, he conducted the first regular government mail service by mule between the Columbia River and Olympia.

> Several families had decided to go. The boat was just large enough for passengers.
>
> When we came to the Cowlitz it took passengers as well as crew to get the boat upstream because the current was so terrific. We worked her almost foot by foot, fastening the rope to big trees ahead and every able man doing his share at pulling. Those of us not busy at the rope, poled.
>
> When we finally got to Cowlitz Landing, I went to my wife and found her feeling pretty miserable.. . . Oh Willis, I can't even see the baby! I can't see anything! Am I going blind? I mustn't go blind!

Mary Ann thought she had caught a cold and, being extremely weak, she temporarily lost her eyesight. Even though Mary Ann was very ill, the next day they started on foot for Olympia. Soon, two more of the party became sick, at which time it was concluded that measles had struck their party. Eventually they came upon a man with a wagon but no team. Inasmuch as their party had two oxen and no wagon, they combined their resources and manage to get the sickly group safely to Olympia.

> We got through to Olympia safe enough where we rested over night. The next day we hired an Indian to take us in his canoe over to Henderson's Bay.
>
> We had our jobs alright, but it wasn't long before we saw that our $125 a month was too slow. We wanted to go home quick. We worked [at the timber camp] only about three months and then went back to Steilacoom.[There we] built a house and started a boarding house.
>
> All the time our minds were set on going home [to Illinois]. Day after day we looked for mail that we might learn what had happened since we left. . . . weeks passed and no news came. We had left home in March, 1852. . . . it was July [1853] before we got a letter, and when that letter came it brought the news of the death of my wife's mother. It was then that we gave up the hope of going home. We decided we might as well stay.

After about eight months, the Boatmans sold the boarding house and on January 11, 1854, filed a donation land claim in the Puyallup Valley, approximately twenty miles northeast of Steilacoom and about ten miles up the valley from today's Tacoma. The route from Steilacoom to the Puyallup Valley was by canoe on the Sound to Commencement Bay, and

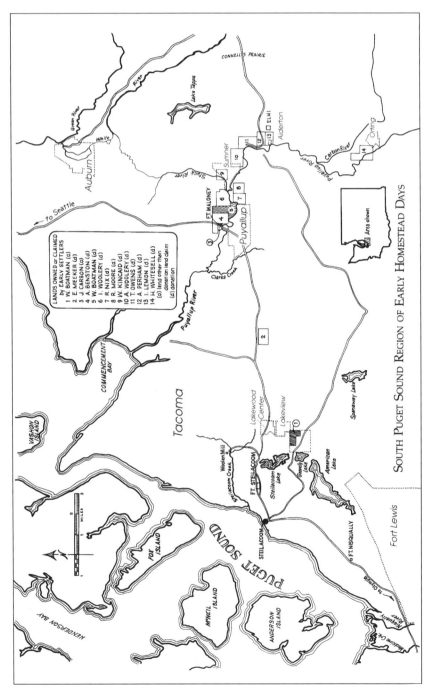

**LANDS OWNED or CLAIMED
by EARLY SETTLERS**
1 W. BOATMAN (o)
2 E. MEEKER (d)
3 J. CARSON (o)
4 A. BENSTON (d)
5 W. BOATMAN (d)
6 I. WOOLERY (d)
7 R. NIX (d)
8 R. MOORE (d)
9 W. KINCAID (d)
10 A. WOOLERY (d)
11 OWENS (d)
12 A. PERHAM (d)
13 I. LEMON (d)
14 H. WHITESELL (d)
(o) land other than
    donation land claim
(d) donation

SOUTH PUGET SOUND REGION OF EARLY HOMESTEAD DAYS

Claims of the Boatmans and their Puyallup Valley neighbors.

then up the Puyallup River, portaging a number of times because of log jams.

> In a few days I started back [to the Puyallup valley] in company with John Carson to build a house on my claim. I exchanged work with Mr. Carson. He was a fine carpenter and we built my house first. . . . I found a big cedar fallen on my place with the best lumber in it I ever saw. . . . we could have built a half a dozen more [houses] like it and had wood left over. . . . [It] was the first house weather boarded with shakes in the valley. . . . I could hardly wait to bring Mary Ann to see her nice home.
>
> In a few days we moved down to our new home. Mr. Carson and family moved down at the same time and stayed with us in our house 'till he got his house built. Then they moved into their house.

The Boatmans and Carsons, the first white families in the Puyallup Valley, soon were followed by other Oregon Trail pioneers. Included were several families of the first train to cross Naches Pass in the Cascade Range in 1853. In the spring of 1854, Willis cleared land and planted a small garden. By summer,

> we began to be very happy there . . . everything promised well. That summer the second baby came.

John William Boatman was the first white child born in the valley. The Boatmans had finally reached their trail's end and everything went well that year. The following spring, Willis planted even more crops and was surprised how well they produced.

> As the summer advanced our little crops matured and when harvest came, we were surprised at the large yield that we had on our little patches of ground. We got all our stuff harvested and most of it thrashed and put away in good shape.

Finally the Boatmans began to feel settled and life was enjoyable.

> Notwithstanding all the hardships and privations of life, I was becoming satisfied and content.

But serenity was not to prevail, for awhile at least.

The pressures on Native Americans caused by the growing influx of whites throughout Washington Territory resulted in a portion of the region's tribes taking up arms in the fall of 1855. West of the Cascades, trouble began with the massacre of several families by tribesmen mainly from east of the mountains near today's Auburn, just a few miles from the Puyallup Valley settlement. Only due to the diligence and faithfulness of a local Indian that the Boatmans had befriended, were they and other settlers saved from the same fate. Salitat, one October morning about daybreak, came to the Boatman cabin:

> We were wakened by an Indian's voice, low but insistent, at the door: "Hello! Hello! Boatman, hello! Boatman, Boatman!" I hurried to the door and found "old Salitat" looking grave and terrified. "My people on warpath," he whispered. "If they know I tell they kill me. Take your klootchman and mokst tenas [Chinook jargon for wife and two children] to the Fort. My people kill and burn."

Frightened, the settlers lost no time taking the old Indian's advice, making a hasty retreat to Fort Steilacoom. A Boatman daughter summed up the situation many years later—a story probably related to her by her parents.

They hastily hid those possessions they could not take with them and with that degree of resignation that only a pioneer can boast of, left for Fort Steilacoom over a newly made road through the thick timber and across the prairies for sixteen miles.[4]

Arriving the next day, they found the primitive fort in a state of pandemonium, with settlers coming in from all directions. Years later, Ezra Meeker described the scene: "A sorry mess this, of women and children crying, some brute of men cursing and swearing, oxen and cows bellowing, sheep bleating, dog howling, children lost from parents, wives from husbands, on order, in a word, the utmost disorder."[5]

Although called Fort Steilacoom, it simply was a U.S. Army encampment of log cabins and a few "light boarded houses." Fortunately, many of the troops already were in the field, leaving some housing available for the hoards of settlers. Lieutenant John Nugen wrote his superior in the new capitol of Olympia, "I have nearly all the women and children in the county at the post, and will of course protect them."[6]

During the conflict, all of the homes of Puyallup Valley settlers were ransacked and burned except the Boatman cabin. The conflict lasted until the following spring with the retreat of the Indians eastward over the Cascades. Willis did not take up arms as many settlers did, but instead, assisted the military as a carpenter in building blockhouses throughout western Washington.

Mary Ann and Willis Boatman stand by their original pioneer home in 1904. It was the only house in the Puyallup Valley not destroyed during the Indian-white conflict of 1855–56. *W.W. Rau family collection*

The Boatmans, however, remained in the Steilacoom area for another fifteen years after the conflict. Willis built a new home on 160 acres claimed by preemption and purchased from the U.S. government for a nominal fee. Here, he raised sheep and developed a large orchard. During these years, Willis also maintained his Puyallup Valley claim—clearing land, planting in the spring, and harvesting in the fall.

Early on, Willis became involved in community affairs. He was instrumental in planning and constructing some of the first roads in the territory. His name is frequently listed with those who served on grand and petit juries, and in 1889 he had the distinction of serving on the last Territorial grand jury.

Early in the 1870s, the Boatmans sold their property near Steilacoom and returned to their Puyallup Valley land. There, they built their final home and became one of the major hop ranchers in the valley. Hops were first introduced by another 1852 emigrant, Ezra Meeker. This enterprising and later renowned pioneer settled on the south side of the Puyallup River

Willis and Mary Ann Boatman's final home in the Puyallup Valley. Along with a son and daughters, Mary Ann stands on the balcony at far right and Willis is below on the left. *W.W. Rau family collection*

immediately across from the Boatmans. He platted his land, creating the town of Puyallup. Along with Willis and many other settlers, Meeker prospered for a number of years by growing hops. Meeker was largely responsible for promoting, finding markets, and distributing the crops worldwide.

During the latter nineteenth century, Willis became involved in banking and, for a number of years, was president of one of the first banks formed in Puyallup. The Boatmans had seven children—four boys and three girls. The boys were George Washington, John William, Charles Henry,[7] and Ernest Alonzo. The girls were Caddie, Lettie Bell, and Lucy May. Mary Ann and Willis continued to reside at the "Old Homestead," as it was known and, with the aid of their sons, operated the ranch for many more years.

The year 1911 was one of happiness and sorrow for the Boatman clan. Willis and Mary Ann commemorated their sixtieth wedding anniversary on October 14. Through many hardships, they had carved out a life in the wilderness, finally achieving a comfortable prosperity from their own land and property, a dream they had held from the beginning. The wedding anniversary was celebrated by a family gathering at the homestead. However, only nine days after this festive occasion on October 23, 1911, Mary Ann died of a chronic heart ailment.

She had been a typical pioneer wife, always standing beside her husband, supporting him in all of his endeavors. And, as a mother of seven children, she properly raised a family, initially under adverse conditions. She obviously was a lover of nature and the ordinary beauties of life. As a young woman traveling across the plains, Mary Ann vividly demonstrated this appreciation in descriptions of wild flowers, picturesque sunrises, and glowing sunsets. The youngest daughter, Lucy, remembered her mother:

> The custom of these early pioneers was "open house" to all who happened to pass their way, food and shelter for man and beast was given freely. Mother was a great lover of flowers all her life, and always had a beautiful flower garden. There was always an organ in the house ever since I can remember; the children would gather around and play and sing church songs, especially on Sunday.[8]

Mary Ann Boatman, at the age of seventy-eight, had come to the end of a fulfilling life—a faithful wife and outstanding homemaker. She rests today in the Powers Woodlawn Abbey Mausoleum in the Sumner, Washington, cemetery.

Willis, then eighty-five and still in fine health, remained on the homestead for another ten years. During that time, family members took turns living with and caring for him. By that time, his land largely was leased out for farming. Finally, in about 1921, he left the old homestead to move in with his daughter Caddie Frie in Sumner. There, Willis became known as "the old snowy headed man in the window," as his favorite chair was by a front window and he waved to all passing by. Willis Boatman died peacefully in his sleep on New Year's night, 1926, at the age of 99 years and 3 months. A eulogy to the old pioneer in a local newspaper summarized his character.

> Those who knew Mr. Boatman best tell of his patient, kindly traits of character, a lover of little children, temperate in all things. Very unusual was the health which he enjoyed during the last years of his life. He retained his mental power, kept abreast of the times, and was always interested in events of state, national and world importance, as well as the happenings of the community in which he had lived for nearly half of his life.[9]

Willis Boatman in the last year of his life. *W.W. Rau family collection*

Willis had fulfilled his dreams. The hardships endured together had rewarded Willis and Mary Ann with success and happiness. Willis rests next to Mary Ann in the Sumner cemetery, just a short walk down the road from the old homestead.

Notes

1. This chapter has been condensed from the author's *Pioneering the Washington Territory* published under the sponsorship of the Historic Fort Steilacoom Association, Steilacoom, Washington, in 1993. The reader is referred to this publication for additional details about the pioneering lives of Willis and Mary Ann Boatman.
2. Quoted material is largely from the hand-written manuscript, "Story of My Life" by Willis Boatman (family document no. 2). A version is printed in *Told by the Pioneers*, U.S. Public Works Administration, Washington Pioneer Project, vol. 1, 1937, 184–90.
3. Ezra Meeker, *Pioneer Reminiscences of Puget Sound* (Seattle, Washington: Lowman and Hanford, 1905), 554.
4. Hand-written account believed to have been authored by Caddie Boatman, daughter of Willis and Mary Ann Boatman, in the possession of the author (family document no. 5).
5. Meeker, 306.
6. W.P. Bonney, *History of Pierce County, Washington*, vol. 1 (Chicago, Illinois: Pioneer Historical Publishing, 1927), 181.
7. Charles Henry Boatman is the author's grandfather.
8. Lucy Boatman Benson, "Biography by Lucy (Boatman) Benson," typed manuscript in possession of the author, no date (family document no. 6).
9. "Oldest Pioneer Passes," *Sumner News Index* (Sumner, Washington), January 8, 1926.

Bibliography

FAMILY DOCUMENTS

Boatman, Mary Ann. Hand-written unpublished manuscript in possession of the author describing the Boatmans' journey on the Oregon Trail, 1852; includes her family biography. (Family Document No. 1)

Boatman, Willis. "Story of my Life." Hand-written manuscript in possession of the author. A version is printed in *Told by the Pioneers*, Vol. 1, U.S Public Works Administration, Washington Pioneer Project, 1937. (Family Document No. 2)

_____. Hand-written family biography in possession of the author. (Family Document No. 3)

Description of Louis B. Richardson, in possession of the author, source unknown. (Family Document No. 4)

Boatman, Caddie. Hand-written manuscript describing the retreat of Puyallup Valley pioneers to Fort Steilacoom during the Indian unrest of 1854–55, in the possession of the author. (Family Document No. 5)

Benson, Lucy (Boatman). "Biography by Lucy (Boatman) Benson." Typed manuscript in possession of the author. (Family Document No. 6)

OTHER UNPUBLISHED SOURCES

Dustin, Dorothy, and Charles Martin. Trail guide, Loup River to Wood River, 1944.

Jensen, Ross Lynn. "The Greenwood-Sublette Cutoff of the Oregon Trail." University of Utah, Department of History, M.A. Thesis, 1975.

Mousseau, Magloire Alexis. Statements made to Eli S. Ricker in an interview October 30, 1906. Tablet 28, 16–17, Ricker Tablets, MS 8, Eli Seavey Ricker Collection, Nebraska State Historical Society, Lincoln, Nebraska.

Spencer, John. "Daily Journal Kept by John Spencer, 1852 from Wellsville, Ohio to Portland, Oregon." Typescript manuscript, Oregon Historical Society, Portland, Oregon.

NEWSPAPERS

Cleland, Mabel. "On the Pioneer Tacoma Trail." *Tacoma News Tribune* (Tacoma, Washington), June 20, 21, and 23, 1922.

Colburn, Catherine Scott. "The Long Wearisome Journey." *Morning Oregonian* (Portland, Oregon), June 17, 1890.

"Oldest Pioneer Passes." *Sumner News Index* (Sumner, Washington*)*, January 8, 1926.

BOOKS, ARTICLES, BROCHURES

Adams, Cecelia. "Twin Sisters on the Oregon Trail: Cecelia Adams and Parthenia Blank." *Covered Wagon Women: Diaries and Letters from the Western Trails*, 1852, Vol. 5. Edited and compiled by Kenneth L. Holmes and David C. Duniway. Glendale, California: Arthur H. Clark, 1986.

Akin, James, Jr. *The Oregon Trail Diary of James Akin Jr. in 1852: The Unabridged Diary with Introduction and Contemporary Comments by Bert Webber*. Medford, Oregon: Webb Research Group, Pacific Northwest Books, 1989.

Bagley, Will (Editor). "The Pioneer Camp of the Saints: The 1846 and 1847 Mormon Trail Journals of Thomas Bullock." *Kingdom in the West: The Mormon American Frontier*, Vol. 1. Spokane, Washington: Arthur H. Clark, 1997.

Berry, Diane. "The Umatilla Agency, 1851–55." *Pioneer Trails*, Vol. 12, No. 4, 1988. [Published by the Umatilla County Historical Society, Pendleton, Oregon]

Bonney, W.P. *History of Pierce County, Washington,* Vol. 1. Chicago, Illinois: Pioneer Historical Publishing, 1927.

Brown, Mike W. "'Cutoffs' and Parting of the Ways." *Headed West: Historic Trails in Southwest Wyoming*. Edited by Mike W. Brown and Beverly Gorny. Salt Lake City, Utah: Artistic Printing, 1992. [Published for the Oregon-California Trails Association Tenth Annual Convention, Rock Springs, Wyoming]

Brown, Randy. "Childs' Cutoff." *Overland Journal*, Vol. 5, No. 2, 1987. [Published by the Oregon-California Trails Association, Independence, Missouri]

Byers, William N. "The Odyssey of William N. Byers." Edited by Merrill J. Mattes. *Overland Journal*, Vol. 1, No. 1, 2, 1983; Vol. 2. No. 1, 2, 1984. [Published by the Oregon-California Trails Association, Independence, Missouri]

Carnes, Bill. "Fort Hall: Origins of an Oregon Trail Outpost." *News from the Plains*, Vol. 11, No. 3, 1997. [Newsletter of the Oregon-California Trails Association, Independence, Missouri]

Conyers, Enoch W. "The Diary of E.W. Conyers, a Pioneer of 1852." *Transactions of the Thirty-third Annual Reunion of the Oregon Pioneer Association.* Portland, Oregon, 1905.

Cooke, Lucy Rutledge. "The Letters of Lucy R. Cooke." *Covered Wagon Women: Diaries and Letters from the Western Trails,* 1852, Vol. 4. Edited and compiled by Kenneth L. Holmes. Glendale, California: Arthur H. Clark, 1985.

Coon, Polly. "Journal of a Journey over the Rocky Mountains." *Covered Wagon Women: Diaries and Letters from the Western Trails,* 1852, Vol. 5. Edited and compiled by Kenneth L. Holmes and David C. Duniway. Glendale, California: Arthur H. Clark, 1986.

Cummings, Mariett Foster. "A Trip across the Continent." *Covered Wagon Women: Diaries and Letters from the Western Trails,* 1852, Vol. 4. Edited and compiled by Kenneth L. Holmes. Glendale, California: Arthur H. Clark, 1985.

Davis, Alvah Isaiah. "Diary of Mr. Davis, 1852." *Transactions of the Thirty-seventh Annual Reunion of the Oregon Pioneer Association.* Portland, Oregon, 1909.

Dillon, Richard H. "The Ordeal of Olive Oatman." *American History*, September 1995.

"Documents and Letters." *Annals of Wyoming*, Vol. 15, No. 3, 1943.

Duffin, Reg P. "The Miller-Tate Murder and John F. Miller Grave." *Overland Journal*, Vol. 5, No. 4, 1987. [Published by the Oregon-California Trails Association, Independence, Missouri]

Edwards, G. Thomas. "The Oregon Trail in the Columbia Gorge, 1843–1855: The Final Ordeal." *Oregon Historical Quarterly*, Vol. 97, No. 2, 1996.

Ellis, Martha H. "Martha H. Ellis." *A Small World of Our Own.* By R.A. Bennett. Walla Walla: Washington: Pioneer Press Books, 1985.

Franzwa, Gregory M. *Maps of the Oregon Trail.* Gerald, Missouri: Patrice Press, 1982.

_____. *The Oregon Trail Revisited.* Third Edition. Gerald, Missouri: Patrice Press, 1983.

A Guide to the Oregon Trail in Southwest Idaho. Cultural Resources Information Series No. 2, Boise District, Bureau of Land Management.

Haines, Aubrey L. *Historic Sites along the Oregon Trail.* Third Edition. St. Louis, Missouri: Patrice Press, 1987.

Hawk, Al R. "Down the Snake River by Boat." *Told by the Pioneers*, Vol. 1. U.S. Public Works Administration, Washington Pioneer Project, 1937.

Kellogg, Jane D. "Memories of Jane D. Kellogg." *Transactions of the Forty-first Annual Reunion of the Oregon Pioneer Association.* Portland, Oregon, 1913.

Kerns, John T. "Journal of Crossing the Plains to Oregon in 1852." *Transaction of the Forty-second Annual Reunion of the Oregon Pioneer Association.* Portland, Oregon, 1914.

Kimball, Stanley B. (Editor). *The Latter-Day Saints' Emigrants' Guide: Being a Table of Distance, Showing all the Springs, Creeks, Rivers, Hills, Mountains, Camping Places, and all other Notable Places, from Council Bluffs to the Valley of the Great Salt Lake, by W. Clayton.* St. Louis, Missouri: Patrice Press, 1983.

Laveille, E., S.J. *The Life of Father De Smet, S.J., 1801–1873.* Reprint Edition. Chicago, Illinois: Loyola University Press, 1981.

Lewis, Meriwether. *Original Journals of the Lewis and Clark Expedition, 1804–1806,* Vol. 4, Edited by Reuben Gold Thwaites. New York: Antiquarian Press, 1959.

Link, Paul K., and E. Chilton Phoenix. *Rocks, Rails and Trails.* Pocatello, Idaho: Idaho State University Press, 1994.

Mattes, Merrill J. *The Great Platte River Road: The Covered Wagon Mainline Via Fort Kearny to Fort Laramie.* Nebraska State Historical Society, Vol. 25, 1969.

_____. "The Northern Route of the Non-Mormons: Rediscovery of Nebraska's Forgotten Historic Trail." *Overland Journal,* Vol. 8, No. 2, 1990. [Published by the Oregon-California Trails Association, Independence, Missouri]

_____. *Platte River Road Narratives.* Urbana and Chicago, Illinois: University of Illinois Press, 1988.

McAllister, John. "The Diary of Rev. John McAllister." *Transactions of the Fiftieth Annual Reunion of the Oregon Pioneer Association.* Portland, Oregon, 1922.

McAuley, Eliza Ann. "Iowa to the Land of Gold." *Covered Wagon Women: Diaries and Letters from the Western Trails*, 1852, Vol. 4. Edited and compiled by Kenneth L. Holmes. Glendale, California: Arthur H. Clark, 1985.

McKinstry, Bruce. *The California Gold Rush Overland Diary of Bryon N. McKinstry, 1850–1852.* Glendale, California: Arthur H. Clark, 1975.

Meeker, Ezra. *Personal Experiences on the Oregon Trail: The Tragedy of Leschi*. Fifth Reprint. Seattle, Washington: Meeker, 1912.

_____. *Pioneer Reminiscences of Puget Sound*. Seattle, Washington: Lowman and Hanford, 1905.

Milikien, Herbert C. "Dead of the Bloody Flux, Cholera Stalks the Emigrant Trail." *Overland Journal*, Vol. 14, No. 3, 1996. [Published by the Oregon-California Trails Association, Independence, Missouri]

Olich, Peter D. "Treading the Elephant's Tail: Medical Problems on the Overland Trails." *Overland Journal*, Vol. 6, No. 1, 1988. [Published by the Oregon-California Trails Association, Independence, Missouri]

"Oregon Trail in Idaho and other Emigrant Trails." Idaho Travel Council and Idaho State Bureau of Land Management [brochure].

Paden, Irene D. *The Wake of the Prairie Schooner*. Reprint Edition. Gerald, Missouri: Patrice Press, 1985.

Parkman, Francis, Jr. *The Oregon Trail*. Edited with an introduction by Bernard Rosenthal. Oxford, New York: Oxford University Press, 1996.

Pratt, Sarah. "The Daily Notes of Sarah Pratt, 1852." *Covered Wagon Women: Diaries and Letters from the Western Trails,* 1852, Vol. 5. Edited by Kenneth L. Holmes and David C. Duniway. Glendale, California: Arthur H. Clark, 1986.

Rau, Weldon W. *Pioneering the Washington Territory*. Steilacoom, Washington: Historic Fort Steilacoom Association, 1993.

Read, Martha S. "A History of Our Journey." *Covered Wagon Women: Diaries and Letters from the Western Trails*, 1852, Vol. 5. Edited and compiled by Kenneth L. Holmes and David C. Duniway. Glendale, California: Arthur H. Clark, 1986.

Richey, Caleb, and Alice Richey. "A Letter to Lafayette Richey and Hanna Richey, Salem, Iowa." *The Oregon Trail Diary of James Akin, Jr.: The Unabridged Diary with Introduction and Contemporary Comments by Bert Webber*, Appendix D. Medford, Oregon: Webb Research Group, Pacific Northwest Books, 1989.

"Salmon Falls and Thousand Springs." Idaho Historical Society Reference Series No. 184, 1987.

Sawyer, Francis. "Kentucky to California by Carriage and a Feather Bed." *Covered Wagon Women: Diaries and Letters from the Western Trails*, 1852, Vol. 4. Edited and compiled by Kenneth L. Holmes. Glendale, California: Arthur H. Clark, 1985.

Schlissel, Lillian. *Women's Diaries of the Westward Journey.* New York: Schocken Books, 1982.

Scott, Abigail Jane, [Duniway]; Margaret Ann Scott; and John Tucker Scott. "Journal of a Trip to Oregon." *Covered Wagon Women: Diaries and Letters from the Western Trails*, 1852, Vol. 5. Edited and compiled by Kenneth L. Holmes and David C. Duniway. Glendale, California: Arthur H. Clark, 1986.

Scott, Leslie M. *History of the Oregon Country by Harvey W. Scott.* Compiler's Appendix 3. Cambridge: Riverside Press, 1924.

"Scotts Bluff National Monument, Nebraska." National Park Service, U.S. Department of Interior, 1988 [brochure].

Shorey, M.E. (Bonney). "A Pioneer Story." *History of Pierce County,* Vol. 2. By W.P. Bonney. Chicago, Illinois: Pioneer Historical Publishing, 1927.

Stansbury, Howard. "Exploration of the Valley of the Great Salt Lake." *Exploring the American West.* Reprinted 1988. Washington D.C.: Smithsonian Institution Press, 1988.

Stevens, Charles. "Letters of Charles Stevens." Edited by Ruth Rockwood. *Oregon Historical Quarterly*, Vol. 37, No. 2, 1936.

Stratton, Royal B. *Captivity of the Oatman Girls.* Third Edition. Lincoln, Nebraska: University of Nebraska Press, 1983 [paperback].

Thomson, Origen. *Crossing the Plains.* Fairfield, Washington: Ye Galleon Press. 1983.

Unruh, John D., Jr. *The Plains Across: The Overland Emigrants and the Trans-Mississippi West, 1840–60.* Urbana, Chicago, and London: University of Illinois Press, 1982 [paperback].

Washington Centennial Farms: Yesterday and Today. Olympia, Washington: Washington State Department of Agriculture, 1989.

Way, Frederick, Jr. (Compiler). *Way's Packet Directory, 1848–1994: Passenger Steamboats of the Mississippi River System since the Advent of Photography in Mid-Continent America.* Athens, Ohio: Ohio University Press.

White, Thomas. "To Oregon in 1852, Letter of Dr. Thomas White." Edited by Oscar O. Winther and Gayle Thornbrough. Indianapolis, Indiana: Indiana Historical Society, 1964.

GEOLOGICAL SOURCES

Allen, John E. *The Magnificent Gateway: A Layman's Guide to the Geology of the Columbia River Gorge*. Forest Grove, Oregon: Timber Press, 1979.

_____, Marjorie Burns, and Sam C. Sargent. *Cataclysms on the Columbia: A Layman's Guide to the Features Produced by the Catastrophic Bretz Floods in the Pacific Northwest*. Portland, Oregon: Timber Press, 1986.

Bond, John G. *Geologic Map of Idaho* [scale 1:500,000]. Idaho Bureau of Mines and Geology and U.S. Geological Survey, 1978.

Bonnichsen, Bill, and Roy M. Breckenridge. *Cenozoic Geology of Idaho*. Idaho Bureau of Mines and Geology Bulletin 26, 1982.

Brooks, Howard C. *Limestone Deposits in Oregon*. State of Oregon Department of Geology and Mineral Industries Special Paper 19, 1989.

_____, and Len Ramp. *Gold and Silver in Oregon*. State of Oregon Department of Geology and Mineral Industries Bulletin 61, 1968.

Conner, Carol Waite. *The Lance Formation: Petrography and Stratigraphy, Powder River Basin and Nearby Basins, Wyoming and Montana*. U.S. Geological Survey Bulletin 1917-I, 1992.

Love, J.D., and A.C. Christiansen. *Geologic Map of Wyoming* [scale 1:500,000, 3 sheets]. U.S. Geological Survey and Geological Survey of Wyoming, 1985.

Smith, Rebecca T. "The Geology of the Columbia River Gorge." *Overland Journal*, Vol. 10, No. 1, 1992. [Published by the Oregon-California Trails Association, Independence, Missouri]

Stoffel, Keith L. *Geology of the Grande Ronde Lignite Fields, Asotin County, Washington*. Washington Report of Investigation No. 27, Washington Division of Geology and Earth Resources, 1984.

Walker, George W., and Norman S. MacLeod. *Geologic Map of Oregon* [scale 1:500,000, 2 sheets]. U.S. Geological Survey.

Index

XYZ

About the Author

W ELDON WILLIS RAU is a great grandson of the principal figures in this narrative, Willis and Mary Ann Boatman. Rau graduated from the University of Puget Sound with a B.S. degree and later earned both an M.S. and Ph.D. from the University of Iowa. As a research geologist he has had careers with both the U.S. Geological Survey and the State of Washington. His geologic investigations focused largely on western Washington and Oregon, the results of which have been published in government documents, scientific journals, and several books.

With an interest in the Old West and piqued by his pioneer heritage, since retirement Rau has researched and written about Northwest history. His efforts have resulted in the book, *Pioneering the Washington Territory*, and several periodical articles. *Surviving the Oregon Trail, 1852* is the latest and most comprehensive of his historical endeavors. It represents the culmination of fifteen years of field investigation and library studies. Weldon and his wife Jane reside in Olympia, Washington.